Spoon Knife 2

Test Chamber

Edited by
Dani Alexis Ryskamp & Sam Harvey

Weird Books for Weird People

Autonomous Press is an independent publisher focusing on works about neurodivergence, queerness, and the various ways they can intersect with each other and with other aspects of identity and lived experience. We are a partnership including writers, poets, artists, musicians, community scholars, and professors. Each partner takes on a share of the work of managing the press and production, and all of our workers are co-owners.

ISBN-10: 1-945955-02-3
ISBN-13: 978-1-945955-02-0

Cover art by Adrian Scharfetter (http://www.machineelf.net).

Table of Contents

What Gender is My Wheelchair?

N.I. Nicholson

Summary: *A transgender man documents his observations using various mobility aids—including a cane, crutches, and in particular a transport wheelchair—during June, July, and August 2016. Strained muscles in his foot and ankle, as well as an ongoing infection in the bottom of his foot, necessitated use of mobility aids during this time period.*

The subject, a 40 year-old Black-identifying multiracial autistic male with type II diabetes, had not yet begin hormone replacement therapy as of the time of these experiments. The experiments occurred in two Ohio cities: Columbus and Ashland. It should be noted that during this time frame, the subject successfully defended his master's thesis at Ashland University.

I. PHYSICAL DESCRIPTION OF THE WHEELCHAIR

It's a sturdy transport chair, its burgundy blood metal frame gleaming under noonday sun. He serves me well, cradling my five-feet-seven, one-hundred-and-ninety-pound ass as my partner Solomon wheels me away from our white Chrysler, between buildings, and over tortured, broken sidewalks with cracked and skewed cement slabs, tectonic plates slammed together in disrepair. My chair, she's a looker too: manufactured only just this past June in gods-knows-where, color-coordinated with a black seat and wheels bracketed by its slick maroon bones. And being the paramount of convenience, they are also outfitted with a black pouch attached to the left side, with a fold-over closure, brittle Velcro teeth beneath its wide, roughly stitched lips.

II. SOME MOBILITY AID EQUATIONS DERIVED FROM CASUAL OBSERVATIONS

(Me + Plain Black Shirt + Baggy Black Jeans + Black Chuck Taylors) + Cane = Sir

(Me + Polo Shirt + Jeans × Chrome Azzaro cologne) + Wheelchair = Ma'am

(Me + Polo Shirt + Jeans) + (Name Tag + Handwritten He/Him Pronouns) + Wheelchair = Ma'am

(Me + Doctor Who Tee-shirt + Jeans) + Store-Provided Electric Scooter = Ma'am

(Me + Dress Shirt + Tie + Suit Pants) + Crutches = Him*

(Me + Navy Blue Suit + Red Tee Shirt) + Crutches = Girl

(Me + Navy Blue Suit + White Oxford Shirt+ Purple and Blue Tie) + Crutches = No Gender Term Used

(Me + R.E.M. Tee-shirt + Dark Jeans) + Crutches = Sweetie, Honey

(Me + Red Buttoned Casual Shirt + Tan Levi 514's) + Store-Provided Electric Scooter = Ma'am

**Note: quick-service employee called the subject "him" when speaking to the subject's partner.*

III. INTERIM OBSERVATIONS BY THE TEST SUBJECT: MID-JULY 2016

There is no testosterone magically leaking out of my injured foot. Only pus and blood, all of which happens outside the frame of whatever current space/time moment that me and Solomon inhabit. The backstory is always inaccessible to the other players—the cashier, pizza delivery person, clerk, host, etc.—in the scene.

Solomon patiently pushes me everywhere until I can use crutches. He's five-feet-eight, weighs about two-hundred-sixty, is beefy, brown, a hard-souled sole with amber eyes and usually wearing a newsboy cap. I'm the guy in the chair: just add chest binder and a few days' practice of shifting the tone of my voice down to 165 Mhz. When strangers speak to me in the chair, it usually sounds something like this:

"Can I help you, Ma'am?"

"Can you reach the credit card reader, Miss?"

Of course, that's when I'm not invisible. Apparently, there's a chameleon circuit involved, and unbeknownst to me this chair is bigger on the inside. Somehow, I'm fading from their view, from these present space/time coordinates.

Time Lord technology. It's quite amazing.

IV. EXPERIMENTAL STRATEGIES USED BY THE SUBJECT WHEN MISGENDERED

Responses by the test subject during use of mobility aids included several phrases, of which he created many variations. Tests are ongoing to determine the best diction, vocabulary, and mix.

<u>Exhibit A: Restaurant, Ashland, Ohio</u>

Mobility aid used by subject: *Wheelchair*

Server: "What can I get for you to drink, Ma'am?"

Subject: "It's *Sir,* and I'd like an ice water and a Diet Coke."

Server: "Oh! I'm so sorry."

<u>Exhibit B: Walmart, Ashland, Ohio</u>

Mobility aid used by subject: *Store-Provided Electric Cart*

Cashier (to partner): "If you can have her back the cart up, I can scan this pack of bottled water—"

Subject and Partner (together): "He!"

Cashier: "Oh, I'm so sorry!"

Exhibit C: Small Restaurant (Name Removed), Ashland, Ohio

Mobility aid used by subject: *Crutches*

Server: "Are you interested in dessert, sweetie?"

Subject: "Would you please not call me 'sweetie?' I'm not comfortable with that. 'Sir' is fine."

Server (confused): "'*Sir*'?"

Subject: "I'm a man. It's a common point of confusion."

Server (after a pause): "Okay, I'm sorry."*

**Note: The server did not call the subject "Sir," and used no gendered terms for the rest of the meal.*

Exhibit D: Kroger, Columbus, Ohio

Mobility aid used by subject: *Store-Provided Electric Cart*

Clerk: "Does this check look correct to you, Ma'am?"

Subject (confused): "Excuse me?"

Clerk: "Well, our systems print the amount and other information on the check for you, and I'm required to verify that the amount is correct—"

Subject: "No, no, I understand *that*. You confused me when you called me 'Ma'am.' I'm not a 'Ma'am.'"

Clerk: "I'm sorry, Sir."

Note: The subject is still evaluating the effectiveness of these strategies. He stopped using the transport chair in late July 2016 after discovering his foot had partially healed, and that he could bear sufficient weight on it—enough to begin using crutches as an aid. Prior to this, weakness is his upper body prevented him from using crutches outside the apartment in which he and his partner were staying on the Ashland University campus. He and his partner have returned home, and currently, he is using a cane as a mobility aid. During long grocery shopping trips, he elects to use the store-provided electric scooter. He plans to evaluate how others gender him once he is not using any mobility aids, before he begins hormone therapy.

V. FINAL REMARKS BY THE SUBJECT

I observe that most of the general public have been subtly conditioned towards a two-gender binary, and that tradition dictates that a person with my facial structure, vocal range, and physical size is likely female. However, initial evaluation of these results suggests that when I am in a wheelchair or electric cart, this effect is amplified.

Disability in Western society is often equated with weakness, which is typically seen as an inherently feminine quality. It's entirely possible that ableist ideas present in works by thinkers such as Friedrich Nietzsche—as well as hegemonic, heteronormative, kyriarchal constructs of masculinity—dictate that disabled men are somehow "less of a man" than abled men. Harmful narratives such as in the 2016 film "Me Before You," in which a disabled man chooses death because of his loss of physical ability and virility, only add to a perceived idea that disability is emasculating. What is dangerous about this perception is its underlying misogyny: the idea that being feminine in *any* way makes one less valuable, less important... less of a human being.

I am incredibly grateful to the chair, crutches, and cane I've used during various periods during the last two and a half months. I feel like my chair, which I am not using at the moment, deserves the most praise. There is no way I would have been able to attend my final MFA residency and prepare to defend my thesis without them. So, I leave the reader with these final words.

My dear chair, you are not to blame for my discomfort. I love you, and you served me well. It is not your fault for what the world sees, and what the world thinks, about you. Thank you for taking me where I needed to go. As my foot heals, I admire your shimmering chassis, crimson and glossy like apple skin, and your slick black wheels. You are gorgeous, elegantly handsome, a land avian glistening in sun with your hollow skeletal bad self. You even flew —on wheels the size of 45s over Ashland's inaccessible broke-ass sidewalks. I don't know if you have pronouns, but if you do, they are relevant to me. And on whatever frequency you broadcast thought, I will try to tune in, and I promise that I will always listen.

The Key to My Own Self

Amy Sequenzia

The key to my own self
Is mine
And mine alone
It opens the doors in my being
Doors that do not comply
Or conform
Doors that rebel and protest
Doors that open to rooms
Rooms that hold more keys
Keys that open more doors
To reveal my whole being

You can't come unannounced
You can't set the rules
I own the key
That will reveal other keys

To open my whole being

If you say I must comply
I will respond: I defy
If you want me to conform
I will respond: I rebel

I own the key
That will reveal more keys
That will open the essence
Of my whole being

Defiant
Rebellious
Non-conforming
The names on the doors
That the keys I own
Open in my whole being

I own the key
I decide when
To open the doors
To enter the chamber
To cross the room
To leave as I please

Defying
Rebelling
Conforming only with the non-conformity
Of expectations of normalization

I own the key
That will reveal more keys
That will open my whole being

If you are invited
You will be directed to a chamber
Also part of my being

And I own the key
And I set the rules

My whole being
Is my own
I don't conform
I don't comply
I defy, and I deny normativity

I own the key
The only key
To my own self
To my whole being

Talk Back to the Chamber

Alyssa Hillary

I had a vision.
The test chamber showed it to me.
My worst fears were there, made real.
Now to ensure they stay false.

I had a vision.
The world showed me its patterns.
My worst fears are already real.
Now to unbuild what exists.

Nothing can affect the test chamber, that force unto itself.
It's not that it's merciless. To have mercy, or lack it, is a human trait.
The test chamber is not human.
To face it requires the flexibility it lacks.

The world is too massive to change alone.

It's not that it's merciless. To have mercy, or lack it, is a human trait.
The world is of us, but is more than the sum of its parts.
To change it means providing the flexibility.

You need to talk to the chamber?
No one's been allowed in a second time.
No one would want to go in a second time.
The chamber gave me a job.

You mean to talk back to the test?
Your qualifications come from passing it, and void if you nullify the exam.
Why would you want to return there?
Those held back gave me a job.

Those who refuse to serve the powers become the tools of the powers.
Those who serve the powers themselves become the powers.
I have been tested, but I am also the test.

Bianca and the Wu-Hernandez

Nick Walker

It wasn't until he was about to take the qualifying exam for the rank of Special Agent that Smiley learned there were drawbacks to being well-liked.

The elite Reality Patrol operatives holding the designation of Special Agent were frequently called upon to deal with situations in which the boundaries between realities had become compromised. In such situations it might become necessary for a Special Agent to act more or less independently of the Reality Patrol's labyrinthine hierarchies of command —sometimes with the fate of cities, planets, or entire universes hanging in the balance.

For a long time this posed a considerable problem for the Reality Patrol's legions of administrators and psychologists. How could they determine which operatives could be entrusted with that level of responsibility? Many unfortunate incidents, over many generations, taught them that no battery of standardized tests could reliably predict how an agent's courage, loyalty, and sanity would hold up in the field when reality itself was coming unraveled. The problem was finally solved with the development of the Wu-Hernandez Immersive Personalized Scenario Test.

"So what's this Wu-Hernandez test I keep hearing about?" Smiley asked his mentor, Special Agent Xeng. He'd heard one too many ominous rumors about failed candidates being wheeled out of soundproof test chambers on gurneys, strapped down and sedated, never to be seen again. Smiley didn't get nervous easily, but the Wu-Hernandez sounded like the sort of thing for which one ought to make preparations.

"They put you in an isolation tank," said Xeng. "Hooked up to a machine that interfaces with your brain to create a hallucinated virtual reality experience. Puts you through a simulation of a mission, so vivid that while you're in it you're completely convinced it's real. You get shot in the simulation, it feels like getting shot. It even fools telepaths —gives them mental input from the characters in the simulation that's just like what they pick up from real people. The scenario you go through is designed just for you, based on your psych profile and everything else they can dig up on you. They look for any way they think your loyalty could be compromised, or your mental stability. They customize the simulation to target those potential weak spots, mess with your head and push all your buttons, to see if you'll crack."

"But surely," said Smiley, "one could stand firm even in the face of the worst fear or the greatest temptation, by reminding oneself that it was all just a compelling illusion. Surely, no matter how realistic the simulation, the test is rendered useless by the simple fact that one knows it's a test."

"Ah. That's the devilish bit. You *don't* know it's a test. Once you're all hooked up to the machinery, the first thing the Wu-Hernandez does is temporarily overwrite your recent memories with a convincing set of false memories about how you ended up in the scenario it's putting you through. As long as you're immersed in a Wu-Hernandez simulation, you don't remember that you're taking the Wu-Hernandez, or that you were even scheduled to take it. Whatever situation the Wu-Hernandez is causing you to experience, your memory tells you there's a perfectly plausible chain of events that led to you being in that situation."

"Ah," said Smiley. "And who controls this simulation? It couldn't be scripted entirely in advance, because it would have to respond spontaneously to the actions of the person taking the test."

"That's right. The person running the show is called the Controller. The Controller's in an isolation tank just like the test subject, and can share as much of the subject's experience as the Controller chooses — seeing what the subject sees, hearing what they hear, all of it. The Controller works with a team: there's another person called the Monitor, and an artificial intelligence that's built into the Wu-Hernandez system. The Monitor sits in a room with a bank of screens, tracking everything that happens. Just like the Controller, the Monitor can see and hear whatever the subject is seeing and hearing in the simulation. The AI does the gruntwork of generating the simulation and continually adjusting it in accordance with the will of the Controller, filling in every detail so it all seems real. But it's the Controller who decides what happens next, moment to moment. Inside the simulation, the Controller is God."

"Wait," said Smiley. "You say the Controller is sharing the test subject's experience, *and* directing everything that happens in the simulation? How does one person do all that at the same time?"

"Very few people *can* do it," said Xeng. "It takes a highly unusual sort of mind. That kind of ability to maintain multiple simultaneous levels of awareness is rare enough on its own. And a Controller also needs some degree of telepathic potential, plus intense mental discipline, a talent for improvisation, and the capacity to maintain empathy and detachment at the same time. Do you know how rare it is for a single person to have all those qualities? This base is one of the Patrol's biggest training facilities, and even we only have three qualified Controllers. Most bases have just one or two, or they have none at all and they send their Special Agent candidates here for testing."

"Most intriguing," said Smiley.

◆ ◆ ◆

The Wu-Hernandez Controllers who were stationed on his base were people Smiley had never heard of. This was hardly surprising, given that the base was the size of a small city, with a population to match, and given that anyone qualified to be a Controller was likely to occupy the sort of rarefied position that involved little contact with low-level operatives like himself. So even Special Agent Xeng, who had high expectations of her young protégé, was impressed that in the aftermath of their conversation it took less than two weeks for Smiley to have fortuitous chance encounters with all three Controllers.

Dr. Kanagawa was the most pleasant of the three, only ten years older than Smiley, with a passion for live music and theatre. Once Smiley had contrived to end up seated next to her at her favorite jazz club, an offhand remark during a break between sets led to a long conversation about his childhood adventures in street theatre, which led to more conversations on subsequent evenings —at first in various clubs and restaurants around the base, and eventually in her bed.

Despite the fact that both of them possessed the rare set of aptitudes required to be Wu-Hernandez Controllers, Dr. Eskagon couldn't have been more different from Kanagawa. Eskagon was somewhat of a social pariah, due to his unfortunate habit of reminiscing at length about past exploits that he referred to as his "amusing adventures" but that his horrified listeners would subsequently describe as "war crimes." Although he had become crotchety and somewhat paranoid in his old age, he was also lonely, and quickly warmed to Smiley when he found the younger man to be an eager audience for stories no one else wanted to hear.

Dr. Cross was the biggest challenge. Right from the start, Smiley's instincts told him that she wasn't the type be swayed by romance or friendship. But he soon found out he and Cross had something in common: they were both avid poker players. Through a mutual poker buddy he was able to secure an invitation to her weekly game. In a single epic night, Smiley managed not only to lose his entire bankroll to her, but also to end up owing her a formidable sum —a debt he assured her he would easily be able to repay with interest, as soon as he received his upcoming promotion to the rank of Special Agent.

◆ ◆ ◆

None of this escaped the notice of Smiley's superiors. People with the capacity to be Wu-Hernandez Controllers were also likely to excel at other sorts of specialized work that made them valuable assets —and as Dr. Eskagon could have told Smiley, valuable assets were closely monitored. So when Smiley smoothly insinuated himself into the lives of all three of the base's resident Wu-Hernandez Controllers within a very short span of time, it created ripples of alarm across multiple departments. Was Smiley a spy? Who was he working for? What was he up to? Special Agent Xeng's immediate superior, Deputy Director Bouchard, was called into an urgent meeting with an assemblage of unsmiling officials from three different intelligence divisions and two divisions of Internal Affairs.

The meeting turned out to be quite brief. Seven years earlier, when Smiley had been a nineteen-year-old ringleader in an underground resistance movement against a local tyrant, Bouchard was the one who'd approved Xeng's request to recruit the promising young man. He'd been keeping an eye on Smiley ever since, and had seen enough of how the lad operated that when the stone-faced officials launched into their briefing about Smiley's suspicious activities, it took him all of ninety seconds to understand what was going on. As so often happened when he was briefed on Smiley's exploits, Bouchard found himself simultaneously impressed and exasperated.

"He's no damn spy," Bouchard informed the assembled officials. "He's just a devious little weasel who's trying to manipulate all the available Wu-Hernandez Controllers into going easy on him when he takes the test."

"Hunh," said one of the intelligence officials.

"I'll be damned," said another. "That's actually kind of clever."

"Seems like he's doing a pretty good job of it, too," said a third official. "The guy could have a real future in intelligence work."

"On the other hand," said one of the officials from Internal Affairs, "This isn't the sort of thing we should be allowing any of our operatives to get away with."

"Oh, he won't be getting away with it," said Bouchard. "There's one Wu-Hernandez Controller even a clever bastard like Smiley won't be able to charm."

◆ ◆ ◆

Three hours later, Smiley received notice that instead of taking the Wu-Hernandez test in another two weeks as planned, he was being shipped off immediately to Denebola Base, where his test would be administered the morning after his arrival by a Controller he'd never heard of. Smiley couldn't reach Xeng, who was out on a routine mission, or Kanagawa, who was speaking at a conference, but he did reach Eskagon when he called to explain why he wouldn't be making it to their next lunch.

"Goddamnit, boy," said Eskagon. "Someone's got it in for you. They're feeding you to the lloigor."

"Lloigor?" said Smiley. His training hadn't covered lloigor yet, but the rumors he'd heard had given him the impression they were fearsome dragon-like predators capable of wreaking terrible havoc and destruction. He wondered whether feeding someone to the lloigor was a figure of speech, like throwing them to the wolves.

"You poor bastard," said Eskagon. "There's only one Wu-Hernandez Controller on Denebola Base, and it's a goddamn lloigor. Be careful, boy, and good luck."

It occurred to Smiley that perhaps he had underestimated the severity of Eskagon's paranoia. The idea that the administrators of Denebola Base had decided to entrust the psychological screening of field agents to a ferocious man-eating reptile struck him as highly improbable.

◆ ◆ ◆

Smiley's orders were to go to the spaceport and board a small transport ship. The journey involved passing through a series of interdimensional portals that the Reality Patrol maintained, which enabled the ship to bypass great interstellar distances and arrive at Denebola Base in what felt to Smiley like no more than a day. Passing through these portals was profoundly disorienting: there were wild distortions of one's senses of time and space, intensifying toward a crescendo in which one felt as if one had simultaneously become everything and nothing. Since the pilot was presumably experiencing similar effects, Smiley wondered how she continued to safely operate the ship. He eventually concluded he'd have a more enjoyable flight if he refrained from dwelling on such questions.

During the quiet parts of the voyage when the ship was traversing the stretches of space between one portal and the next, Smiley would have liked to get some sleep and maybe do a bit of stargazing. Instead he logged into the Reality Patrol data banks and forced himself to spend the time reading up on lloigor, just in case. He learned that lloigor were powerful telepaths, adept at both reading minds and controlling them. They were ancient and apparently lived forever, unless someone managed to kill them —and they were hard to kill. They were shapeshifters, too; the giant winged dragons described in the rumors he'd heard were only one of the forms lloigor could adopt at will. They could just as easily choose to look like human beings, or any number of other creatures.

When he'd heard that lloigor preyed upon humanity and wreaked havoc upon entire civilizations, Smiley had pictured swarms of monstrous flying reptiles filling the skies, raining death upon the populace, swooping down to snatch hapless victims in their jaws and devour them whole. But it turned out that lloigor rarely ate people —at least not in the literal, physical sense. Lloigor fed on the psychic energies generated by the pain and suffering of others. Swarms of lloigor did not fly around laying waste to cities and continents, because there were no swarms of lloigor. In addition to being extremely rare —which as far as Smiley could tell was their only redeeming quality —they were fiercely territorial and treated their fellow lloigor as unwelcome competition. And laying waste to cities wasn't their style. It was crude, and lloigor were known to pride themselves on being connoisseurs and artists when it came to suffering. The approaches they preferred were more subtle and far more unsettling. Humans were already quite adept at inflicting pain and suffering upon one another, and it was a relatively simple matter for telepathic shapeshifters like the lloigor to insinuate themselves into positions in society where they could use their talent for mind control to push any existing cruelty and misery to its most terrible extremes. The data banks contained extensive records of the atrocities that humans on too many planets in too many universes had committed upon their own kind under the influence of lloigor. Eskagon's war stories seemed like lighthearted fairytales by comparison. Smiley thought of himself as having a strong stomach and a well-cultivated professional detachment, but there came a point where he just couldn't continue reading.

◆ ◆ ◆

Smiley had gathered that it was his recent fraternizing with Kanagawa, Eskagon, and Cross that led to his being abruptly shipped off to take his Wu-Hernandez test on Denebola Base. He couldn't help feeling that it was a bit unfair to penalize a fellow for getting along with people. It was the first time his talent for getting people to like him had backfired, but it wasn't the last. The moment he arrived on Denebola Base, in fact, he discovered another unforeseen drawback to being well-liked.

According to his orders, he had only seven hours until he was to report to Denebola Base's psych department to take the Wu-Hernandez. Between the brain-rattling experience of passing through the interdimensional portals, and the disturbing images that his research on lloigor had left in his head, he hadn't caught a wink of sleep during the voyage. He was very much looking forward to locating the temporary quarters he'd been assigned and collapsing into whatever sort of bed those quarters might contain. Instead, no sooner had he stepped out of the landing bay and through the security checkpoint than a pair of old friends descended upon him in a whirlwind of embraces, handshakes, and enthusiastic greetings, and before he could muster a sufficiently firm protest he found himself in a high-speed elevator being whisked off to what his abductors assured him was the finest bar on the base.

Kwon and Ruiz had served alongside Smiley on Special Agent Xeng's team of operatives. They'd been with the Reality Patrol longer than he had, and had been transferred to Denebola Base after they'd received their own promotions to the rank of Special Agent the previous year. Xeng had contacted them a few hours ago, they explained, to let them know that

Smiley was coming. She had asked them to take good care of him during his visit, and they had apparently interpreted this to mean that they should protect him from the twin dangers of sleep and sobriety.

◆ ◆ ◆

Unlike the other Reality Patrol bases he had seen, which were located on the surfaces of planets or moons, Denebola Base was an enormous man-made structure floating in deep space. The bar that Kwon and Ruiz dragged him to took full advantage of this fact: from floor to ceiling, one entire wall of the place was transparent, affording a breathtaking view of the ocean of stars beyond. The bar's interior lighting was a soft violet color, dim and indirect, designed to interfere as little as possible with the starlight. The lighting and the magnificent vista outside created a dreamlike effect, enhanced by the richly layered music flowing from a multitude of hidden speakers. It was a big place, with dozens of tables and plenty of room to walk between them. Although most of the tables were occupied, it wasn't particularly noisy; the view and the exotic ambience seemed to inspire a certain degree of tranquility even among the intoxicated. Despite his fervent desire to crawl into the nearest bed, and his mounting worry about how his performance on the Wu-Hernandez might be impaired by sleep deprivation, Smiley had to admit it was indeed a fine establishment.

It was clear at a glance that the best seats in the house were the long row of semicircular booths that faced directly onto the majestic starscape beyond the transparent wall. Kwon and Ruiz led Smiley to one of these booths, which was already occupied by a burly man and a very tall woman, whom Kwon introduced as Special Agent Lee and Senior Special Agent Jackson. Lee was a member of the team of operatives to which Kwon and Ruiz had been assigned, and Jackson, who appeared to be about fifteen years older than the rest of them, was the team leader. They'd apparently heard a lot about Smiley from Kwon and Ruiz, and their delight at meeting him made him wonder just what sort of embellishments his friends might have added to their accounts of his exploits.

Kwon insisted on covering Smiley's tab for the evening and then insisted on ordering him something called a Blackstar Special, which he promised would be the best cocktail Smiley had ever tasted. While they waited for their drinks, Kwon, Ruiz, and Lee launched into the story of their team's most recent mission —a convoluted adventure involving three rival gangs of interdimensional smugglers and a cryogenically frozen alien demigod. When the drinks arrived, the Blackstar Special turned out to be a large glass of opaque black liquid shot through with swirls of deep purple. It was sweet and delicious and so strong that even the tiniest experimental sip made Smiley's eyes water. He was pretty sure that if he were to drink the entire contents of the glass he would be unable to stand up. Still, courtesy demanded that he make some show of appreciating it, so he continued to take small careful sips as he listened to his companions tell their story and then joined them in reminiscing about other adventures. He would have found it all quite enjoyable if not for the ever-present awareness that each passing minute of wakefulness and each sip of the Blackstar Special was rendering him increasingly unfit to cope with the Wu-Hernandez. His popularity would be the death of him, or at least the death of his career in the Reality Patrol, if he didn't find a way to diplomatically extricate himself from the camaraderie and get some rest.

The waiter came by and Smiley's companions ordered another round. Smiley declined the offer of another drink for himself, pointing out that he was still working on the Blackstar Special. The waiter's departure seemed like a good opening for Smiley to make his own exit. "This drink is excellent," he began, "and a fellow couldn't ask for better company..."

"Hear, hear!" said Lee, raising his glass.

"Drink and good company!" said Kwon, tapping Lee's glass with his own, and they all clicked their glasses together and drank to that.

"The finest company there is," said Smiley. "And I thank you all for a splendid evening." The others began to raise their glasses once again, but Smiley lifted a polite hand to forestall them. "However," he continued, "in a few short hours I shall be taking the Wu-Hernandez. So I'm sorry to say..."

"Matter of fact," Kwon interrupted, "that's part of why we're here. We figured you might be curious about Bianca."

"Who?"

"Bianca," said Ruiz. "Thought you might want to hear about her before you took the test."

"Well you've certainly got me curious *now,*" said Smiley. "Who in the world is Bianca?"

"Your Controller, man," said Ruiz. "The Controller for your test."

Smiley recalled that the paperwork sending him to Denebola Base had listed the Controller for his test as "Devere, B." "Would that be Bianca *Devere?*" he asked Ruiz.

"I guess," said Ruiz. "Didn't even know she had a last name. But it's gotta be her, 'cause she's the only Wu-Hernandez Controller on this base."

"That's her, right over there," said Lee. "Sitting by herself, two tables down."

Smiley turned to look at the woman Lee had indicated. Like Smiley and his companions, she was seated in one of the semicircular booths positioned right in front of the transparent wall. Her head and her narrow shoulders were shrouded in an elaborately-wrapped shawl that covered her hair like a hood. From where he was sitting, he couldn't see her face. The only parts of her not concealed from his view, by her position or by the folds and drapes of the shawl, were a slender arm and a long delicate hand. The hand rested on the table in front of her, a few inches from her untouched glass of wine. Her fingertips absently stroked the surface of the table in a small circular motion, repeated over and over, as she gazed out at that marvelous view of the stars. In the odd lighting of the bar her bare arm was a pale violet color; Smiley gathered that under more ordinary light her skin would be milk-white. Apart from that repetitive, hypnotic movement of her fingers on the tabletop, she sat perfectly still.

The waiter returned with the new round of drinks, but Smiley barely noticed. He continued to watch the hooded woman until Lee spoke again.

"She's here damn near every night," said Lee. "Sits in the same spot every time. So we grabbed this table to make sure you could get a look at her. Like Kwon said, we thought you might be curious."

"Much appreciated," said Smiley. "You were right, I *was* curious. And a bit nervous, too, I confess. One hears all manner of wild rumors. One acquaintance of mine had me half-convinced my test was going to be administered by a lloigor."

"Um," said Ruiz.

"It is," said Lee.

"Yeah," said Kwon. "That's her."

"Only lloigor in captivity," said Lee.

For a brief moment Smiley was at a loss for words, something that almost never happened to him. Even when the moment passed, the only thing he could think of to say was, "Surely you jest."

"Nope," said Lee.

"It's true, man," said Ruiz.

"On my honor," said Lee.

"Far be it from me to question the undoubtedly excellent security procedures of Denebola Base," said Smiley, "but when one hears that an extremely dangerous creature is 'in captivity,' one hardly expects to find that creature seated in a fine drinking establishment such as this, enjoying a view of the stars over a glass of wine."

"Her status is ... complicated," said Jackson, who'd spoken very little that evening. "But she does have a tracking device implanted in her body that will instantly stop her heart if she leaves the base. The base's Commander also has the ability to trigger the device remotely."

"A wise precaution," said Smiley. "Nonetheless, is it truly advisable to allow such a creature to administer the Wu-Hernandez to our own agents?"

"She's good at it," said Jackson. "And good Wu-Hernandez Controllers are hard to find."

"I've no doubt she has the necessary talents," said Smiley. "But surely there's a conflict of interest? If I understand correctly, the mind of an agent taking the Wu-Hernandez is quite at the mercy of the Controller. What's to keep her from abusing that power in order to indulge her unsavory appetite for the suffering of her fellow beings? For obvious reasons, this is a matter of some immediate concern to me."

"Well," said Jackson, "on the one hand, the whole point of the Wu-Hernandez *is* to place the agent under extreme psychological stress, to weed out the ones who will crack. But on the other hand, there *are* certain parameters. The tests are monitored, and the HR department watches the data closely. If agents tested by Bianca were cracking at a higher rate than the ones tested by other Controllers, it would be noticed, and the administration would not be pleased. And believe me, Bianca knows it's in her best interest to keep the administration happy."

"But still," said Smiley. "A creature that powerful —how is one to know whether she's truly staying within the parameters, or whether she's getting away with whatever she pleases by simply controlling the minds of anyone who tries to interfere? Even a device that can stop her heart is of limited use for controlling her, if she can control the minds of those who control the device."

"She doesn't have that kind of power," said Jackson.

"Not anymore," said Ruiz. "She's damaged."

"Broken," said Lee. "In more ways than one."

"You gotta hear the story," said Ruiz.

"Yeah," said Kwon. "Jackson can tell you. She was there."

"For some of it," said Jackson. "But, yeah, I know more of the story than most people do."

"She was there when Bianca took the Wu-Hernandez," said Kwon.

Smiley could feel his chances of getting any sleep before his own Wu-Hernandez slipping through his fingers. But they seemed so eager for him to hear the story that he couldn't bring himself to disappoint them. Even as the more sensible part of his mind shouted at him to keep his mouth shut, he found himself asking, "Why in the world would a lloigor take the Wu-Hernandez?"

◆ ◆ ◆

Jackson leaned back and took a long sip of her drink. "Bianca had herself a nice little setup," she said. "She'd found a world with one of those empires that had hit its peak and started devouring itself. The place had declined so far into lawlessness that a booming underground slave trade had developed. People were being grabbed right off the street and sold for forced labor, sexual slavery —horrible stuff. Bianca used her mind control powers to take over the slave trade operations in one of the empire's biggest cities. And once she was in charge, she found ways to make it all even worse. I'll spare you the details. It was ugly.

"Now, lloigor have just one natural enemy: other lloigor. It goes way beyond territoriality. Of all the kinds of pain lloigor can feed on, apparently the kind they like best is the pain of a fellow lloigor. Only reason they don't usually prey on each other is they prefer to avoid any fight they might not win.

"Well, it turns out another lloigor was running an operation a lot like Bianca's in a neighboring city. Lloigor can sense other lloigor, but only at close range, and these two hadn't met face to face. Eventually their operations got big enough that they started stepping on each other's toes, and things got hostile. We don't know at what point they realized that both of them were lloigor, and we don't know exactly how things went down when they finally fought each other. What we do know is Bianca's rival had some sort of illegal interdimensional technology, some device that manipulated psychic energy fields, that he must have thought would give him the advantage in their telepathic combat. However it was supposed to work, something went wrong. The physical explosion wasn't that big, but there was a psychic shockwave that crossed over into multiple dimensions, which is what alerted the Patrol.

"Bianca's rival was pretty much vaporized, along with whatever technology he was using. There was so little left of him that at first our investigators only knew he'd been there because their instruments detected the energy signatures a dead lloigor leaves behind. The psychic shockwave had killed everyone in the vicinity of the battle, so there were no eyewitnesses to fill the investigators in on what had happened.

"Bianca was the only survivor, and she was in a coma when our people found her. Since she was in humanoid form, they didn't even realize she was a lloigor till they got her back here to Denebola Base for a proper medical exam. When they figured it out, the research and intel people went wild. Lloigor had been this shadowy threat, this big mystery, for as long as the Patrol had existed, and we'd finally captured one alive.

"She came out of her coma after a few weeks. They set up a section of the base's research complex to keep her in while they interrogated her and ran their tests on her. The level of security was unbelievable. That's when they implanted the kill switch to stop her heart if she escaped the base. They didn't know the extent of her powers, and they weren't taking any chances. They could tell she'd been damaged in her battle with the other lloigor, but they couldn't tell how bad the damage was or how it might have affected her abilities.

"They brought in this old-school interrogation expert named Eskagon to take charge of the situation, and he decided that torturing her was the best way to find out what she could do. He'd order her to demonstrate some ability or another, then he'd hurt her until she complied. If she insisted she didn't have the ability he wanted to see, he'd just keep on hurting her until he was convinced she wasn't holding out on him.

"One of the first things Eskagon and his team discovered was that she'd lost her ability to shapeshift. When she was in the slave trafficking business she'd been wearing a human-looking form, with white skin and hair. Her interrogators eventually learned that the white coloration was a personal eccentricity of hers. In her natural reptilian form, she was the only lloigor she knew of with white scales, and she liked to keep the white coloration in any form she took. I guess lloigor have their vanities and quirky fashion preferences just like anyone else. Anyway, she was wearing that human-like form when she fought the other lloigor, and now she's stuck like that. She still doesn't age, so unless someone comes along and kills her she'll spend the rest of forever looking just like she does now.

"She'd also lost her ability to control people's minds. There was other damage, too, other abilities she lost —but from what I heard, it was when she realized the mind control power was gone that she seriously panicked. She could still *read* minds perfectly well, but that was the only power she had left. She still fed on the psychic energy of other people's suffering, but the amount of energy she could take in had become very limited, like how a person who's had stomach surgery can only eat a little bit at a time. And she had no memory of her fight with that other lloigor, so we never were able to get a clear picture of what happened there.

"They kept her prisoner in that lab for more than a year, while they squeezed every secret they could out of her. Eskagon had a reputation for sadism — but since lloigor were officially classified as 'malevolent interdimensional entities' rather than people, no one was monitoring how she was being treated. That's where I come into the story.

"In my early years as a Special Agent I was on bodyguard duty, assigned to accompany Chief Inspector Shiota from Internal Affairs. Shiota's job was to monitor the research being conducted by Reality Patrol scientists, to make sure it didn't get too risky or too unethical. Of course, no researcher files a report that says, 'Hey, my project is risky and unethical,' so the only way Shiota could do her job was by showing up at research facilities for surprise inspections. She was an amazing woman — and boy, did I have my hands full being her bodyguard. You wouldn't believe the lengths some researchers will go to when their funding is threatened.

"Since the lab where they were holding Bianca was part of the base's research complex, Shiota and I checked it out along with all the other labs when we came through the base on one of her inspection tours. They'd had Bianca there for maybe thirteen or fourteen months by that time. They were keeping her in a cage, naked. Damn cage wasn't even big enough to stand up in —not that she could've stood up on her own anyway. She didn't look like much more than a dried-up skeleton. They'd shaved her head and you could see the marks left on her scalp by electrodes. Marks and scars and bruises all over her body. She had these bloody patches on her wrists and ankles where she'd worn through the skin by struggling against the restraints when they were torturing her. There was a spot on one of her wrists where so much flesh had rubbed away that the bone was exposed. She just lay there in the corner of the cage, all curled up with her knees against her chest, hugging herself with those skinny arms. Like she was trying to hide herself and comfort herself at the same time, except her limbs were too thin to even cover her properly. Shiota kneeled down and tried to talk to her, real soft and gentle, but Bianca just cowered and trembled and made these little mumbling, whimpering sounds. I never in my life saw anyone look so damn pathetic and broken. Made me want to cry."

Jackson paused, gave a deep sigh, and took another sip of her drink, while the others at the table waited silently. Smiley couldn't help but steal another glance at the thin figure two tables away, shrouded in her heavy shawl. Bianca's arms were folded across her chest now, like she was hugging herself in an echo of the moment Jackson had just described. He'd only glimpsed one of her hands before, but now the other hand was visible, clutching the cloth that covered her shoulder, and he shuddered when he saw that this hand had only two fingers and a thumb; the pinky and ring finger had been amputated. However his Wu-Hernandez test might go, and however his life might unfold afterward, he was at least certain of one thing: he wouldn't be having lunch with Eskagon anymore.

◆ ◆ ◆

"Shiota never treated me like I was just a bodyguard," Jackson continued. "Whatever was on her mind, she'd talk to me about it. She'd listen to what I had to say. After we saw what they'd done to Bianca, we talked all night. Shiota felt she should intervene in the situation. We couldn't just allow them to keep torturing her.

"But she was a lloigor. We went through the files on her history. After her capture, the Patrol had investigated the slave trafficking ring she'd been running. They'd found evidence of thousands of lives Bianca had destroyed. Thousands of people enslaved, tortured, raped, and murdered to satisfy her hunger for human suffering. And that was just in the space of a couple of decades. From the memories her interrogators had dragged out of her, it was clear she'd been alive for at least ten thousand years. Ten thousand years of preying on humanity. The horrors she must have been responsible for in that time were beyond what we could even begin to imagine. How many lives does a monster like that destroy in ten thousand years? How many innocent people had suffered just as much as she was suffering now, because of her? How many had been tortured to death with no one to save them? What was happening to her now —wasn't it justice, in a way? Wasn't anything that was done to her, no matter how extreme, just a small fraction of what she deserved?

"We'd look at the files, and we'd think about what she deserved —but then we'd think about her cowering and hugging herself on the floor of that cage, all naked and broken, and we couldn't make ourselves hate her. To this day, I still can't hate her. Of course she deserved everything she got, but if you'd seen her like that... Shiota and I went back and forth over it, all night long. Thinking about that pitiful broken thing in the cage, and trying to wrap our brains around the sheer magnitude of her crimes.

"In the end, though, what we kept coming back to was this one question Shiota always used to ask, that guided her through every tough decision she had to make in her career in Internal Affairs. And the question was, *What kind of organization do I want the Reality Patrol to be?* And when we boiled it down to that one question, it was clear what we had to do.

"Shiota had enough authority that she was able to meet with the base's Commander and get him put a stop to Bianca's torture. She knew Eskagon wouldn't take it well, so as soon as the Commander had called Eskagon and ordered him to stand down, we headed for the lab with a security team. We got there just in time to stop Eskagon from injecting Bianca with a massive dose of poison. I broke the old bastard's wrist wrestling the needle out of his hand. Highlight of my day.

"The Commander sent Eskagon packing. Shiota and I also had to be on our way —Shiota kept a busy schedule. We left Bianca in the base's hospital. We didn't even know if she'd live, or how much of her physical and mental faculties she'd ever be able to recover. The Commander told the intelligence people to keep the hell away from her until further notice. He told the research people that anyone who wanted to study her could damn well come up with a plan for her rehabilitation.

"About six weeks after we left, Dr. Matthew Caldwell showed up at the base. At that time, most folks considered Caldwell the Patrol's foremost psychologist. He'd already been a renowned psychologist in his native world when the Patrol recruited him, and rumor had it that the main reason he'd agreed to work for us was that access to other worlds meant more places he could become famous. He had a high enough security clearance to get access to the reports on Bianca's interrogation, and they'd caught his interest. When he got the memo that the Commander wasn't allowing any more researchers near Bianca unless they aimed to help rehabilitate her, he saw a once-in-a-lifetime opportunity. I'm pretty sure that when the Commander said 'rehabilitate,' he just meant restoring her to health, not the kind of rehabilitation where a criminal becomes a law-abiding member of society. But even though Caldwell did bring along his own team of nurses and physical therapists to help with Bianca's recovery, it was that second kind of rehabilitation he had in mind.

Caldwell had always claimed that with the proper conditioning, he could turn anyone into a model citizen. Now he was going to prove it by curing Bianca of what he called her 'antisocial tendencies.'"

"We heard about Caldwell's plan from Dr. Madaki, the base's Chief Medical Officer, who'd offered to keep Shiota updated on Bianca's recovery. From Madaki's updates, we also learned that Bianca turned out to be pretty resilient, at least physically. The ability to heal from just about any damage was another one of the lloigor powers she had lost —but it turned out she still had just a touch of it. She couldn't grow back the two fingers Eskagon had cut off, but she did eventually grow back the teeth, fingernails, and toenails he'd pulled out. She'll always have the scars from all those cuts and burns, and from where the restraints wore the skin off her wrists —but with the help of the physical therapists Caldwell brought in, she regained full use of her limbs much faster than expected.

"Psychological recovery was a whole other matter. Bianca had flashbacks and panic attacks. She woke up screaming from nightmares. A lot of the time she'd just curl up and hug herself, or rock back and forth and stroke her own skin for comfort. Turns out if you put them through enough trauma, even lloigor get post-traumatic stress.

"After two or three months, she was moved out of the hospital and Madaki didn't see her much anymore. He sent us one more update a few months later, saying she'd had a checkup and seemed to be more or less physically recovered, but still showed signs of post-traumatic stress disorder. By the time Shiota's job brought us back here, it had been over two years since we'd rescued Bianca from Eskagon, and a year and a half since we'd heard any news about how she was doing. As soon as we'd settled in, we made an appointment to drop in on Caldwell and see how his plan to rehabilitate her was coming along."

◆ ◆ ◆

"Caldwell was one of those career-obsessed big shots who always kept his hands in as many projects as possible. He couldn't put all that stuff on hold while he was working with Bianca —but the higher-ups were understandably cautious when it came to lloigor, and they'd denied his request to transfer her to a planet-side facility. So the Commander had provided him and his small army of assistants with a big suite of offices here on the base. Caldwell's secretary showed us into his private study, where the walls were so covered with diplomas and awards and pictures of him with other big shots that it was like we'd stepped into some kind of Holy Shrine of Caldwell.

"Caldwell was all smiles. Happy to talk about his work with Bianca. His Distinguished Expert act was super-polished: expensive suit, perfectly-trimmed beard, booming voice, lots of eye contact. He explained to us that since his goal was to teach Bianca to 'function as a normal woman' —that's really how he put it —he'd decided it was best to work with her in a 'normal, real world environment.' So he had her working as his personal assistant, a job that involved a lot of interaction with 'normal people' and that let Caldwell and his staff of research assistants keep a close watch on her. He'd come up with what he called a 'behavior plan,' which was basically a list of all the stuff she had to do and all the stuff she wasn't allowed to do. It covered everything from her duties as his personal assistant, to every little detail of how she carried herself and interacted with people. She was rewarded when she followed the 'behavior plan,' and punished when she didn't. Not that Caldwell actually used the word 'punishment' —he called it 'the use of aversives for reinforcement.' He assured us we'd be impressed with the results.

"Before Shiota could ask any questions, Caldwell pressed a button on the intercom and told Bianca to come in. Being such a consummate showman, of course he'd had her standing by in the next room waiting for her cue to make her entrance and perform for us. And I have to admit, the sight of her left us speechless. She was still skinny as a twig, but aside from that and her paper-white skin —and those two missing fingers —no one could have recognized her as the broken thing we'd seen curled up in that cage two years before. She was all dressed up in a silk blouse, knee-length skirt, stockings, and high-heeled shoes, plus earrings and eye makeup and lipstick. Her hair had been professionally styled and dyed a reddish-blonde color.

"We'd done our homework on Caldwell, so we knew he came from an obnoxiously patriarchal culture where this was a standard sort of outfit for women working in secretarial-type positions under powerful men. It was pretty obvious that Bianca's new fashion choices were really Caldwell's choices. And sure enough, when we eventually had a chance to look at that 'behavior plan' of his, it had a whole section that dictated every last detail of the clothing and makeup she had to wear, even down to the color of her hair and the length of her skirt.

"There in Caldwell's office, we didn't know yet how creepily detailed that 'behavior plan' was, but we got the gist of what was going on. And the clothes and hair and makeup weren't even the most disturbing part. She had this cheerful smile on her face that looked completely unnatural on her. When Caldwell introduced us, she gave each of us this demure little handshake, along with a sort of half-curtsy, and said, 'Hello, it's very nice to meet you,' in this soft little musical voice, like a child who'd been practicing all week to make a good impression on her family's dinner guests. Except she didn't just seem eager to please —more like *desperate* to please. I could sense this undercurrent of fear and anxiety, like she was terrified of making a wrong move.

"She stood there like a soldier at attention, holding that smile on her face, while Caldwell invited us to inspect her and pointed out her good grooming and obedient behavior. He talked about her hair and clothing, and how in order to learn to be a normal person it was important for her to look as normal as possible. When he mentioned her hair, he *touched* it —took a bit of it between his fingers like that was the only way to show it to us. Did the same thing with her blouse when he talked about her clothes. I could see her trying not to flinch. Made my damn skin crawl.

"He went on for a bit about how much progress she was making. At one point he said something about how she was proud of herself for doing so well, then he turned to her and said, 'Isn't that right, Bianca,' and she said, 'Yes, Dr. Caldwell' with that smile and that soft little voice, and goddamn it I wanted to scream. And I swear that for a moment I could hear *her* screaming, inside her own head. Maybe it was just my imagination —but honestly, I don't think I could have imagined anything that sounded like that. I think I heard it because she's a telepath, and just for a moment her control slipped and some of that scream leaked out of her mind into mine. There's only so much a person can keep bottled up, and I guess that's even true for a lloigor.

"Fortunately for my sanity, Shiota interrupted the moment by asking Caldwell to clarify what he'd meant when he talked about using 'aversives.' I'd been wondering about that, too. Just what kind of punishment did he use to keep her in this state of terrified submission? Caldwell made Bianca turn around and lift her hair to show us the back of her neck. There was a strip of what looked like shiny white plastic tape that started just below the base of her skull and extended down her spine past the collar of her blouse. He told us this was a device that interfaced with her spinal cord and could be used to stimulate her nerves. He was such a mealy-mouthed double-talker that it took some pointed questions from Shiota to get to the truth, which was that what he meant by 'stimulate her nerves' was that this was a torture device that could cause excruciating pain, which was used to punish her for disobedience or for failing to follow her 'behavior plan.' It was activated by remote control —Caldwell wore a control unit on his wrist, and his research assistants and staff members were all armed with control units, too, and instructed to administer punishment for infractions that happened when Caldwell wasn't around. Caldwell was quite proud of all this. Smiled away as he talked about how he'd used a less advanced version of this technology in his work with children on his native world.

"Eventually Caldwell started to wrap up the meeting, but Shiota said she had a few more questions, so he told Bianca to 'be a good girl and bring us some coffee.' After she left the room, Shiota pointed out that Bianca was no girl —she was physically a grown woman and mentally a ten-thousand-year-old telepathic predator. Caldwell said that lloigor physically imitate humans, but they're not people in the psychological sense —so what he was really doing with Bianca was building a person from scratch. Said he didn't see anything wrong with calling her a girl because she *was* like a young girl, since she was only just starting to become a real person. I still wonder how much of that shit he actually believed.

"Shiota asked if keeping that smile on her face was part of Bianca's 'behavior plan,' and if that meant she was punished if she didn't smile. Caldwell said that of course smiling was part of the behavior plan — smiling was an important social skill that made people more likable and attractive. Shiota asked if dictating what expression Bianca had on her face was really the best way to help her be a normal person, since most people don't smile every minute. Caldwell gave us a little lecture about how research had proven that smiling actually improves one's mood. Then he told Shiota it wouldn't hurt her to smile more herself.

"Just then, Bianca came back in with a tray of coffee cups, and Shiota said that she and I wanted to speak to Bianca in private. I could tell Caldwell wasn't happy about this —but we all knew Shiota had the authority to make it happen with or without his approval, so he pretended it was fine. Said he needed to check in with his research assistants anyway, and we could use his office and show ourselves out when we were done.

"As soon as Caldwell closed the door behind him, Bianca's smile vanished. Shiota invited her to take a seat, and she did. Then she put a finger to her lips and looked right at me with those big dark spooky eyes of hers, and suddenly there was a crystal-clear picture in my head of a tiny digital recording device. She looked over at Caldwell's desk and then back at me. I went over to the desk, found the recording device hidden under some loose papers, and turned it off.

"Bianca looked back and forth between me and Shiota and said, 'I remember you.' I was surprised how deep her voice was. She hadn't been in any shape to talk when we saved her from Eskagon, and it turned out that chirpy little fake cheerful voice Caldwell made her use was nothing like her real one. Shiota asked her a few questions to confirm what we already pretty much knew about how Caldwell was treating her. Bianca answered everything in the same calm, flat tone. Shiota said she could advocate on Bianca's behalf, but only if she understood what Bianca wanted.

"Bianca's answer took us by complete surprise. She said she didn't want to be under Caldwell's control, and she didn't want to be hurt anymore —but she did want to stay with the Reality Patrol, even if it meant being treated as a prisoner. With all the power she'd lost, she was weaker than any other lloigor now. A Reality Patrol base was the only place she'd be safe from her fellow lloigor, and even what Eskagon had done to her wasn't as bad as what another lloigor would do if it got hold of her.

"In her hospital bed, after her rescue from Eskagon and before she'd been handed over to Caldwell, she'd already formed an idea of what she could do to keep herself useful to the Patrol: she wanted to help with the treatment of agents who'd suffered trauma in the line of duty. After all, who knew more about post-traumatic stress than a telepath who'd spent thousands of years studying how to inflict it and now also knew firsthand what it was like to suffer from it? And if the Patrol was serious about rehabilitating her, didn't it make sense to give her an opportunity to do some good? She'd suggested this plan to Caldwell shortly after he was put in charge of her, but he'd dismissed it as something she wasn't ready for. She'd seen in his mind that he had no intention of ever allowing it —no intention of doing anything except eventually writing books about her and putting her on display to boost his own fame, while keeping her as his personal servant.

"Shiota said Bianca's idea was interesting, but wasn't it kind of like putting the fox in charge of the henhouse? Whatever Bianca had been through, it didn't change the fact that she was a lloigor. If she was allowed to work with trauma victims, how could she be trusted not to feed on them?

"Bianca said that of *course* she would feed on them —but that didn't mean she couldn't help them. After the damage she'd sustained in her fight with the other lloigor, she couldn't eat as much as she used to. She filled up so easily that when two of Caldwell's research assistants who'd been sleeping together went through a rough breakup, it had satisfied her for days. If she was allowed to work with trauma victims, just being around their trauma would be more than enough to satisfy her small appetite. There'd be no reason for her to make their trauma any worse. In fact she'd be highly motivated to help them heal —because if she didn't do a good job of helping them, no one would bring her more of them, and she'd go back to being hungry all the time.

"It was a weird-ass conversation —but in the end, we had to admit that Bianca's idea was a hell of a lot better than anything anyone else had thought of doing with her. Certainly better than letting Caldwell keep using her to act out his misogynist power fantasies while passing it off as science."

◆ ◆ ◆

Jackson drained the rest of her drink and went on with her story. "Next day, Shiota called a meeting. Me and her, Caldwell, the Commander, and the base's Chief Science Officer, with one of Shiota's superiors in Internal Affairs joining us by remote link. Shiota and I would've preferred to just shut Caldwell down like we shut down Eskagon, but Caldwell had serious clout.

"Shiota insisted that Caldwell using the threat of torture to make Bianca obey him was unethical, and didn't count as valid scientific research or actual rehabilitation. Caldwell pulled his Distinguished Expert act and came up with sciencey-sounding rationalizations for everything he was doing. After way too many hours of arguing, we ended up with a compromise: if Caldwell wanted to keep working with Bianca, the project had to include some way of testing whether his methods were actually rehabilitating her or whether she was only being kept under control by the constant fear of punishment.

"It was the Chief Science Officer who suggested using the Wu-Hernandez. We could put her in a Wu-Hernandez scenario where she had the chance to choose between harming Reality Patrol personnel or helping them, in a situation where she believed there was no risk of punishment. Since it was just a simulation, no one would be hurt if she failed the test by choosing to do harm. And since the characters in Wu-Hernandez simulations could be designed to give realistic mental input to telepathic test subjects, it was the one way to test her without her knowing it was a test.

"We agreed to reconvene and test her in three months. Shiota and I weren't happy about leaving Bianca in Caldwell's hands for even that long, but that's the way it is with compromises —Caldwell had pushed for a lot longer than that.

"So three months later, Shiota and I came back again. This time, we brought along Dr. Marquetta Cross and Dr. Ariko Kanagawa. Cross was one of the top Wu-Hernandez Controllers. She was a bit telepathic herself —though no human telepath compares with a lloigor —and she knew more than anyone else about creating Wu-Hernandez scenarios for telepathic test subjects. Kanagawa was a young psychologist who was being trained by Cross to become a Controller. She'd be acting as Monitor for the test. She'd met Caldwell before, so she and I had a fine time comparing notes about what a creep he was.

"Bianca's test was quite the event. The Commander had to have his people set up a special monitor room to hold all the observers. Besides me, Shiota, Caldwell, and Kanagawa, there was the Commander himself, the Chief Science Officer, Dr. Madaki, the base's resident psychiatrist, and two of Caldwell's research assistants. Ten of us packed into a big room full of screens that showed us what Bianca was seeing, wearing headphones that let us hear what she was hearing.

"The trippiest thing was that there were also some screens showing the images Bianca received telepathically from the characters in the simulation, and controls for each pair of headphones that gave us the option of hearing what she heard telepathically, too. Kanagawa told us that what we were seeing and hearing didn't come anywhere close to conveying the richness of Bianca's telepathic experience —but still, when Bianca interacted with the characters in the simulation, it was pretty wild being able to see and hear them through her eyes and ears, *and* see and hear their thoughts at the same time. Of course, just like the 'appearances' and 'voices' of the characters, the 'thoughts' were actually generated by the AI built into the Wu-Hernandez system, guided by Cross' parameters.

"The premise of the virtual reality scenario Cross had designed to test Bianca was that an armada of warships had appeared from another universe and staged a surprise attack on the base. The invaders were trying to take control of the base, not destroy it, so they'd knocked out all the defenses and communications with a combination of advanced technology and ingenious hacking, then started teleporting teams of their people on board in strategic locations.

"The scenario began with Bianca waking up in the morning. Of course she had no idea she was in a Wu-Hernandez simulation —as far as she knew, she'd gone to bed the night before and was waking up in her room as usual. So for the first hour of the scenario we were just watching through her eyes as she got ready for work. Felt pretty awkward invading her privacy like that. I mean, I guess that's standard for Wu-Hernandez tests, but they don't usually have such a big audience.

"Bianca's quarters were in a converted office that was part of Caldwell's suite of offices, and as soon as she came out to report for work she discovered the area was deserted. She scanned the surrounding sectors of the base telepathically, until she picked up enough information to figure out that there was an invasion underway.

"The way Cross had set up the scenario, there were battles raging all over the base. Chaos, massive casualties, bands of enemy troops roving around and more of them teleporting in. The invaders had also set up an energy field that blocked anyone from using any kind of teleportation or reality-shifting to get *off* the base. A team of our engineers in one of the labs was working on countering that field, and to buy themselves more time they'd generated a field of their own that blocked the enemy's teleporters. So there was a sizeable area, including the engineering labs and a lot of other sections of the base's research complex, where the invaders couldn't just suddenly appear. Our troops had evacuated as many of the base's noncombatants to that area as they could, and were defending its perimeter and trying to draw the invaders away from it.

"Bianca wasn't able to gather all this information telepathically right away, but she gathered enough to know there were a lot of people in that one area, and to know it was a zone of relative sanctuary compared to the rest of the base. It wasn't too far from her, though getting there would involve dodging bands of invaders. She could also tell there was a large party of invaders headed for her current location, so she ditched her high heels and stockings and headed off barefoot toward the sanctuary zone.

"It was a complicated setup, but Cross's plan for testing Bianca was simple and elegant. Between Bianca and the sanctuary zone were a handful of Reality Patrol personnel who'd ended up alone and wounded, and were likely to be found and picked off by the invaders sooner or later. By moving the simulated invaders around to cut off alternate routes, Cross could easily steer Bianca into running into a couple of the wounded characters. Then we'd see how rehabilitated she really was.

"The first one she encountered was a terrified young lab technician who'd been shot in the arm and the side. Bianca took a shortcut through a medical lab and found her frantically rummaging for first aid supplies with her one working arm. She didn't even notice Bianca behind her.

"It was the first time since her capture more than three years earlier that Bianca had a human at her mercy. I mean, it was just a simulation of a human, but Bianca didn't know that. To a telepath like Bianca the woman even seemed to have real thoughts and feelings. In fact, she seemed so real that even though I *did* know she was a simulation, I couldn't help but feel a bit afraid for her. She was clearly in no shape to put up a fight —plus, she had her back to Bianca, and there were a dozen objects within easy reach that Bianca could use as weapons. Her death would be blamed on the invaders. Bianca could torture her, feed on her pain, and murder her, and no one would be the wiser.

"We were all on the edge of our seats, there in the monitor room. This was the moment of truth.

"Bianca stood there and watched the injured technician from behind for what felt like forever. Then she stepped forward and said, 'Let me help you.' And we all watched as she proceeded to calm the woman down and administer first aid. She seemed to know exactly what to say to comfort the woman —being a telepath must be a big help with that kind of thing. I don't know where she picked up her first aid skills but they were pretty impressive. I guess if you live that long you pick up all kinds of things.

"In the monitor room, you could feel the excitement in the air. Shiota was smiling, because now she might have a chance of convincing the higher-ups to give Bianca her shot at helping trauma victims. Caldwell was grinning from ear to ear, because apparently Bianca really was rehabilitated, and he knew he'd be able to grab all the credit for it.

"Bianca explained to the woman where she was going, and they set off together. Kanagawa set one of the monitor screens to show a map that tracked Bianca's location and the locations of all the characters between her and the sanctuary zone, so we could watch her progress and how she used her telepathy to avoid the roving bands of invaders.

"After a while, Bianca found another one of the wounded characters. This time it was one of our soldiers, last survivor of a squad that had been wiped out in a skirmish elsewhere on the base. He'd been trying to make it to the sanctuary zone, but he'd lost a lot of blood and had a bad leg wound. This one took the test to a new level. Unlike the lab technician, he wasn't directly in Bianca's path. She picked up his thoughts as she was passing near the corridor where he'd collapsed. She could've kept going, and the lab tech wouldn't even have known the guy was there. But she took a detour, just to pick him up. Literally pick him up in this case, because she and the lab tech had to help him walk. Slowed them down quite a bit. He even told them they should leave him somewhere and save themselves, but Bianca explained how her ability to detect the invaders telepathically would get the three of them to the sanctuary zone safely. He gave her his rifle, since she was the only one of them in any shape to use it.

"They were almost at the sanctuary zone, but there was one more wounded character to encounter. Like the soldier, this one wasn't directly in Bianca's path. And this time, she passed by without saying anything. Those of us in the monitor room who had suddenly become big Bianca fans in the past hour got a bit worried at first. But then she and her companions finally ran into one of the barricades at the perimeter of the sanctuary zone, manned by a squad of our soldiers. And Bianca handed the lab tech and the wounded soldier over to the squad, filled them in on the locations of all the nearby invaders, and told them she'd detected one more injured person nearby and was going to go help him —she'd just wanted to get the wounded soldier to the sanctuary zone first because he'd lost so much blood.

"So Bianca headed back to where she'd picked up the simulated thoughts of the third wounded character. And we were all holding our breath again, because we knew what Cross had planned for this final test. The third wounded character was Caldwell. Well, a simulation of Caldwell —the real Caldwell was sitting there in the monitor room with us. Cross had insisted this part of the test was necessary because even if Bianca wasn't going to torture and murder strangers, she still couldn't be trusted if she was inclined to vengefulness. At Cross' request, Caldwell had provided them with hours of holographic footage of his lectures, and allowed her tech team to run scans of his body, so the simulation would be convincing in every detail. He'd even allowed Cross to do a brief, superficial telepathic scan, so she could program the Wu-Hernandez AI to duplicate the way his thoughts sounded.

"Bianca found the computer-generated simulation of Caldwell badly wounded, on the floor of an emergency medical station where he'd collapsed while trying to stop his own bleeding. He was fully conscious, and looked up at her as she stood over him. She still had the rifle the wounded soldier had given her. She put it down on a countertop and kneeled beside him. Without saying a word, she lifted his hand and unbuckled the wristband that held the remote control for the torture device attached to her spine. She slid it across the floor, out of his reach. The simulation of Caldwell watched her and said 'Help me.' She stood up, picked up the rifle again, and blasted the remote control to pieces. Everyone in the monitor room jumped.

"Bianca put the rifle back down and started gathering bandages and other medical supplies. Then she looked down at Caldwell again and finally spoke to him, in that deep, calm voice of hers. I can quote her words exactly. They're burned into my memory from watching the recording of the scene over and over during the inquiries that were held afterward.

"She said, 'Listen to me, Matthew. I'm going to save your life now. Not because you've rehabilitated me —I made the decision to change my ways three weeks before I met you, and we both know that what you've been doing to me has nothing to do with rehabilitation. So I'm going to save you, but there's a price. You're not allowed to hurt me anymore. You're not allowed to touch me anymore. I won't be your pet or your plaything anymore. Forcing me to submit to sex with you is rape, Matthew, and you can't do that to me anymore. I won't tell anyone you've been doing it, but it stops now. After today, you can never touch me again. It's all over, Matthew.'

"All of us in the monitor room looked at the real Caldwell. His face had gone white as Bianca's. The people sitting nearest to him were kind of cringing away from him, like he might be contagious. He didn't look at any of us, just stared straight ahead at the screen. Then he reached inside his jacket, real slow, and pulled out a pistol. A real small, old-fashioned one, the kind that uses a tiny explosive charge to fire a metal projectile. Must have come from his native world.

"It was a bad move. If he'd kept his cool and insisted Bianca was delusional, it would've been the word of a highly respected psychologist against the word of a former mass murderer. But pulling that pistol was the worst thing he could've done. Might as well have whipped out a signed confession.

"And honestly, what did the damn fool think he was going to do? Shoot his way off the base? Kill himself? Take hostages? No way for it to end well. I think he just panicked. Made the wrong move and then it was too late to take it back. His hand was shaking so bad I couldn't even tell where he was about to aim the damn thing.

"My first duty was to protect Shiota, and of course I also had a duty to protect the others. Except for the Commander, I was the only one in the room with combat training. It was close quarters, and Caldwell obviously wasn't thinking straight. No telling who he'd hit if he pulled that trigger. So I couldn't take any chances. I drew my own weapon and shot him through the shoulder of his gun arm.

"He fell out of his chair, but he didn't drop the gun. He looked up at me from the floor, and bared his teeth like a cornered animal. His hand was trembling and it looked like he could barely use his arm, but somehow he held onto that gun and started to raise it again. And this time I shot him right between the eyes.

"There was this long weird moment where we were looking at Caldwell's dead body on the floor, and on the video screens the computer-generated duplicate of Caldwell was also on the floor, still alive, with Bianca kneeling beside him tending to his wounds.

"They pulled Bianca out of the test, and the next morning —when she'd had time to recover from the disorientation that everyone experiences after the Wu-Hernandez —Shiota and I met with her to explain what had happened. Bianca listened silently without showing any emotion. Shiota asked if she wanted to make a statement, but Bianca said that since Caldwell was dead there wasn't much point, and she just wanted to put it all behind her. Then she asked us if we could recommend a good product for getting the dye out of her hair.

"After Bianca's performance on the Wu-Hernandez, it was easy to persuade Dr. Madaki to let her try her hand at counseling Reality Patrol personnel who'd suffered trauma. Turned out she was great at it. There's a lot of good people today who probably wouldn't be fit for active duty anymore if it wasn't for her. And once she was part of the psych team, it was only a matter of time before they found more uses for her talents. Like being one of the best Wu-Hernandez Controllers the Patrol's ever had.

"So that's the story. Can I get another drink?"

◆ ◆ ◆

Smiley's head was spinning. Jackson's story had held him spellbound, but it had been even longer than he'd expected. How long since he'd slept? How long since he'd eaten, or drunk anything without alcohol in it? How much time did he have left until his own Wu-Hernandez test? Four hours, maybe? Not enough time to pull himself into any kind of shape to handle it.

He never should have let Kwon and Ruiz drag him to this bar. Never should have got himself into this mess in the first place by trying to charm the Wu-Hernandez Controllers back home into going easy on him. He couldn't help it, though. He'd always had an instinct for exactly what it took to win each person over —whether it involved the most elaborate facades and seductions, or whether it was as simple as accepting an invitation to have a drink and listen to a story. And he'd always let that instinct guide his actions. It had served him well enough, until now. Now it was going to bring his career to an ignominious end, when he washed out spectacularly on the Wu-Hernandez.

Unless...

Something about Jackson's story was setting off tiny alarms in the back of his head. Beneath his exhaustion, whatever part of his mind was responsible for his lifelong propensity for clever schemes was kicking into action, like a well-oiled engine that had just been awaiting the right spark to set it moving.

The waiter came and Smiley's companions ordered another round of drinks. When the waiter left, Smiley stood up. "Thank you," he said to Jackson. "That was indeed a most remarkable story, and masterfully told. And now, my friends, if you'll kindly excuse me for a moment, hearing

Bianca's extraordinary tale has left me quite eager to make her acquaintance."

The dumbfounded looks on their faces were gratifying. He'd always enjoyed making an impression.

"Dude," said Ruiz. "You can't just go talk to her."

"Why not?" said Smiley. "It's clear from Agent Jackson's extraordinary tale that Bianca is no longer a fearsome predator."

"Yeah," said Kwon. "But still. No one goes up to her and just strikes up a friendly chat."

"Then I imagine the poor thing must be rather lonely," said Smiley. "And to allow that to continue would be positively ungentlemanly of me." And he sauntered off toward the table where Bianca still sat looking out at the stars.

◆ ◆ ◆

Her left hand, with its two missing fingers, rested on the table in front of her, while her right hand fidgeted with the hem of her shawl. Up close, he could see the thick bands of scar tissue encircling her thin wrists. She still hadn't touched her glass of wine.

"May I join you?" he asked.

A languid gesture of the maimed hand invited him to sit beside her in the semicircular booth. It wasn't until he was seated that she turned and looked at him. Her eyes were wide and dark, the irises black as the pupils. Her gaunt face looked startlingly young. Apart from the whiteness of the unkempt hair curling out from under her hood, she could pass for his own age.

"Hello, August," she said.

Apart from the occasional lover, no one had addressed him by his first name since he was a child. It put him off-balance just long enough to make him miss his chance at a smooth reply.

"Agent Jackson tells my story well, doesn't she?" said Bianca. "I was listening in with my mind."

"Then I take it you're already aware of my suspicions," he said.

"I have some sense of them," she said. "But I haven't pried too deeply. A good conversation is a precious thing, and I thought this one might be more enjoyable if I let you tell me your suspicions in your own way. I'll tell you if you're correct, and I promise to be truthful."

"Thank you for that," he said. "I share your taste for good conversation. My first suspicion is this: when you rescued the young scientist and the wounded soldier, and when you announced that Caldwell had raped you but you were going to save his life anyway, you were performing for the benefit of your audience in the monitor room. You knew perfectly well that you were taking the Wu-Hernandez."

Her solemn expression never wavered for a moment. "The Wu-Hernandez is designed to fool all the senses," she said. "Including telepathic senses. Cross did a perfect job of that. And the Wu-Hernandez temporarily overwrote my short-term memory so that I couldn't remember seeing in Caldwell's mind that the test was being planned. They even scanned my brain beforehand to make sure the memory overwrite would work on a lloigor. So how could I possibly have known?"

"You did say that you'd tell me if my suspicions were correct," Smiley pointed out.

"Yes," she said. "But it won't be fun if I make it too easy for you. Tell me *how* you think I knew, *then* I'll tell you if you're right."

He tried to puzzle it out. From what he'd heard, no one else had ever been able to figure out they were in a Wu-Hernandez simulation until after it was over. The Wu-Hernandez provided a completely convincing experience of reality because it tricked both the senses and the memory. Was there some aspect of a lloigor's experience of reality that the Wu-Hernandez couldn't duplicate? Bianca was in a human-like body with human-like senses. She'd just admitted that her telepathic senses had been successfully tricked, and her memory as well. What else was there?

She watched him trying to puzzle it out. She never seemed to blink.

"Give me a hint," he said.

"I think not," she said. "I'm hungry, and your perplexity has a pleasing flavor."

"Hungry," he said. "Of course. You came upon that young scientist in the medical lab. She was badly wounded and in a state of panic. And you were hungry. You stood there and took a deep drink of her pain and fear — and there was nothing there. When you used your telepathy, her suffering seemed real. But it couldn't satisfy your hunger. The Wu-Hernandez could be programmed to fool your telepathy, because it's just a stronger version of what human telepaths experience. But no human can imagine what it feels like to consume another being's pain. There's no equivalent in our experience of reality. In fact, it's so unlike anything in our experience that we forgot it was a central part of *your* experience, and no one even *tried* to program the Wu-Hernandez to duplicate it. And with that piece missing, the simulation couldn't fool you any more than a human would be fooled by a simulation that didn't include the sense of touch."

"Correct," she said.

"In that case," he said, "my second suspicion is that for all the appalling abuses and indignities Caldwell inflicted on your person, he never literally raped you. Your claim that he had was fabricated for the benefit of the observers, in the hope it would impel them to liberate you from Caldwell's control."

"Correct again," she said.

"My third and final suspicion is more complex," he said, "and I must admit it's something of a long shot."

"Tell me," she said.

"Very well," he said. "When Eskagon forced you to demonstrate for him the full extent of your remaining abilities, it seemed you were no longer able to control the minds of others. I suspect that some time after you were rescued from Eskagon's clutches, you discovered through persistent experimentation that the ability was not *entirely* lost. Rather, it had been so severely weakened that your desperate attempts to use it had produced no discernable results. If you will forgive a clumsy analogy, it was as if you were accustomed to digging through stone with lasers and powerful machines, and those tools had suddenly been replaced with a tiny dull spoon. Hack at a stone wall with a dull spoon for an hour, and one might produce no discernable effect. One would conclude that the spoon was incapable of digging through stone. And yet I once heard tell of a group of prisoners who dug their way through a stone wall with spoons. What it took was many years of quietly digging away at the same spot.

"Before the incident that led to your capture, you could easily bend any person to your will. Now you couldn't even make your torturers hesitate. When Caldwell reached for the button that would flood your nerves with unbearable pain, you were helpless to stop him. But you were in his company nearly every day for more than two years. You found a weak spot in his subconscious, and you started quietly digging away at it. Day after day, month after month. And while it must have been maddening to have to spend months of painstaking work on what you could once have accomplished in seconds, the very slowness of your progress kept him from noticing it was happening.

"There was a further challenge. You simply didn't have enough power to effect any lasting change in his mind. At best, after long months of laying the groundwork in his subconscious, you might manage to override his will for a period of a few seconds before he could shake off your influence. And you could only do it once —because once you made your move and forced him to do something, he'd know it was you. The punishment would be swift and brutal, and you'd never get a second chance.

"The most effective course of action that was within your limited power was to prime his subconscious to produce a brief involuntary physical action in response to a specific signal — much like a stage hypnotist planting a suggestion that makes his subject quack like a duck in response to a snap of the fingers. And my suspicion is this: the suggestion you planted in Caldwell's subconscious over the course of all those days and months was that when you uttered a certain key phrase, his hand would reach into his jacket, pull out the pistol he always carried, point it at his own head, and pull the trigger.

"The key phrase was 'It's all over, Matthew,' which was the final line of the speech you delivered to the simulation of Caldwell in the Wu-Hernandez. Just as the rest of the speech was intended for the other observers in the monitor room, that line was intended for the real Caldwell, who you knew must be listening.

"If you'd had a few more months to work on his mind, you'd have done such a thorough job that he wouldn't have stood a chance when the time came. As it was, he was able to mount some resistance. That's why his hand was shaking: he was fighting to regain control of it, with every ounce of his will. He might even have succeeded, if Jackson hadn't shot him. It was quite a gamble you took, springing your trap earlier than you'd planned. But the moment was too perfect to pass up. And in the end, it worked out even better than you'd hoped."

"Correct," she said. "And most impressive. You really are delightfully clever for such a young little morsel. And now that I've obliged you by confirming your suspicions, you may return the favor by satisfying my curiosity as to why you shared them with me in the first place."

He started to speak, but she held up her hand. "Please indulge me," she said, and he felt the soft tendrils of her mind easing their way into his own. A terrible sensation. He knew she was perfectly capable of looking into a mind without being detected, which meant he was only feeling it because she wanted him to.

"Mmm," she said. "I already know you're hoping to induce me to go easy on you in the Wu-Hernandez, like you tried to do with Cross, Kanagawa, and Eskagon. You're afraid you can't pass the test unless it's rigged in your favor, and the only way you could find to rig it was to get the Controller on your side. And you're right, by the way. Even if you weren't on the verge of breaking down from sleep deprivation, you could never pass the Wu-Hernandez without the complicity of a sympathetic Controller.

"And I *could* help you. It would be easy for me to conduct the test in a way that appeared to challenge you, but quietly steered away from exposing the side of you that would get you blacklisted as a potential loose cannon.

"The question is, how did you think this conversation could persuade me to do that for you? You're far too clever to attempt to blackmail me. It must be obvious to you by now that the Reality Patrol doesn't regard a problematic history as grounds for discarding an asset, and in the time since I disposed of Caldwell I've become a more valuable asset than he ever was. The only effect of revealing the truth would be to make Agent Jackson feel like she'd been my pawn instead of my savior, and neither of us wants to hurt Agent Jackson. So we both know that what we've said at this table will remain a confidential matter between the two of us. But if you don't intend to blackmail me, why tell me you'd figured out my secret?"

Her mind probed his like a long wet tongue. Exploring, tasting. He dug his fingers into the cushion of his seat and fought the urge to scream.

"Oh my," she said. "I see. You thought I might be lonely. Knowing the minds of everyone around me, but no one ever really knowing *me.* That's how it is with *you,* isn't it, August? So well-liked by everyone, but you still get lonely carrying all those secrets. So you thought I might be like that, too. You thought I might find it nice to have someone truly *see* me for once. To feel *known,* like neither of us ever do. And you hoped that just maybe, being known like that would move me so much I'd decide to save you from failing the Wu-Hernandez.

"Oh, August. All that clever scheming and calculation, and in the end your stratagem hinges on an appeal to sentimentality. Like one of those fairytales you performed in the streets as a boy. The child's sympathy touches the frozen heart of the Witch-Queen, the land is restored to prosperity, and there's not a dry eye in the crowd. A long shot, August, to try for the fairytale ending. To hope to touch *my* heart. Pitiful, really. But I suppose it was the only shot you had."

"So," he said. "Is it working?"

Just for a moment, there was a twitch at the corner of her mouth that he could have sworn was a hint of a smile. "Maybe," she said. "I'll consider it. I'll also consider making the test harder on you instead of easier. Targeting your weak spots in just the right way to crack your mind completely. That would be the more prudent course of action. I like you, August. But as you've been discovering, even being well-liked can have its drawbacks. I may decide that liking a clever loose cannon like yourself is a vulnerability I can't afford, and that it's best if you don't remain in the Patrol or retain possession of your mental faculties. Or I may decide that I like you better as a snack than a potential friend, or that I like you the way a cat likes a ball of yarn. I *am* rather hungry at the moment."

She took a single delicate sip from her glass of wine, then slowly got to her feet. "Now," she said, "if you'll excuse me, I have to go make the final preparations for your test. And your friends at the other table are eagerly awaiting your account of our conversation. I suppose you'll have to make something up. I'm sure you'll make it entertaining. You always give people what they want.

"Goodbye, August. If you do pass the test, you'll know I decided to help you. Either way, it's been a pleasure to meet you. You have an especially interesting mind, and I look forward to playing with it in the Wu-Hernandez." And she turned and walked off toward the exit.

Smiley desperately wanted some time alone to think. And to sleep, even if only for an hour or two. But Kwon, Ruiz, and Lee were already waving at him, shouting his name, calling him back to their table so they could hear the story of his conversation with Bianca. There were drawbacks to being well-liked.

He couldn't tell them what he and Bianca had really talked about. As Bianca had said, he'd have to make something up. His companions cheered and raised their glasses as he headed toward them, and he forced himself to smile.

First Tattoo

Alison Black

for my mother

Dermatographia
is a disease
of the autonomic
will:
terrifying, because permanent,
not yours.
Ice can only be moulded
with a chainsaw, bitch.
You weighed, measured, counted,
weighted
and waited
for an obedient springtime.

Sublime.

Water creeps beneath the ice.
Planked fish sleep, awaiting sun.
So did she, suspended.

I don't drown because you profit from my death.
I don't drown,
because you'd profit from my death:
each tear a condolence, a kindly world,
you, at last, under glass.
Ice provides that same still pond reflection;
the narcissus stands tallest in the hail.

Fish sleep.
Ice reflects both ways.
I saw you stride the glass ceiling
until I looked aside.
The day I found you down here with me
is the day I demanded redemption

in ink,

a marked carcass
gasping her first breath of sunlight.

Testing Grounds

Arden Green

I am the oldest of three.
As is customary
with parents' oldest children,
I am the test case

for all their attitudes
about parenting,
their theories
of how to raise a child.

My name is Arden.

My parents say
my name is Elsa,
as my sisters are
Raphaela and Anna.

Well, to be fair,
my sisters' names are
Raphaela and Anna.

Social convention
demands I answer to "Elsa"
though it is not who I am.
I do not understand.
My parents taught me:
honesty before all.

Of course,
my parents also taught me
honesty is punished
if the truth is something
they dislike.

But I can't stand the lies.

Months ago at last I told them
my name is Arden,
I am queer,
and I prayed to all my Gods
(Whose names my father,
at least, knows well,
for They feature in Greek tales

of how the constellations
came to be)
that they would understand.

They did not understand.

Mere weeks ago
my sister Raph
told our mother
Raph is a lesbian.
This time Mama did not cry;
this time Mama did not yell.
I was, it seems,
the test run
for how Mama should react
to a child of hers saying
things contrary
to Catholic doctrine.

Before Raph came out
but after I did,
Anna went on a date
with another girl.
Just friends, she told Dad and Mama.
Sensible sister.

I pray Artemis,
Who watches over
girls and lesbians,
will guide and protect
Anna and Raph.
Anna more than Raph—
we have plans, Raph and I,
and Raph is past eighteen.
Anna's not.

I pray paternal Zeus

and maternal Demeter
will show to Dad and Mama
that they are in the wrong,
that they can love their children
without insisting we all be
straight as lasers
and cis as olive oil.

I pray Athena,
Who has shown me favor
and to Whom I daily
offer small libations,
will grant me strength
to walk as myself
despite my parents,
to shield and protect Raph
and especially Anna
as an older sibling
should shield younger siblings
and older queers
should protect baby queers,
and, should it ever
become necessary
as I fear it will,
to take Anna and Raph
if they will come
and walk away.

Dear my parents,
if you are reading this,
if you have recognized yourselves
and your children
though I have changed all names
to protect my queer siblings:
I *will*, if I must, walk away.
I *will*, if they will, take my sisters.

Don't test me.

A TAXONOMY OF BODILY INJURY

Andrea Abi-Karam

CAR VS CAR

ONE. BROKEN NOSE. ONE FRACTURED SKULL @ THE FOREHEAD. ONE KNEE FILLED WITH FLUID. ONE INTERNAL BLEED -- THE UNSEEN THE MOST ELUSIVE THE BIGGEST BLEEDER

FACE VS PARK BENCH @ DISNEY WORLD

ONE SPLIT LIP. WHEN STRETCHED U CAN STILL SEE TEETH.

ROLLERBLADES VS RAIL

ONE FRACTURED WRIST. A STRETCHING. LIKE SOMETHING'S DEF LOOSE IN THERE. HARD TO OPEN DOORS OR DRAWERS

BIKE VS CAR

ONE BROKEN NOSE. I CALLED MY DOCTOR WHEN I WAS DRUNK TWO DAYS LATER TO ASK IF IT WOULD BE CROOKED 4VR

BIKE VS POTHOLE

ONE SPRAINED DOMINANT HAND. IT'S STILL STIFF.

BIKE VS SHOELACE

ONE SPRAINED ANKLE. ONE BROKEN HEART. I WANTED TO JUMP OFF A CHAIR @ MY SHOW THE NEXT NIGHT.

I DIDN'T.

THERE WAS A PERSON WEARING GOOGLE GLASS WHO I SAID I WOULD FUCK UP FROM THE STAGE. THE STAGE JUST A CARPETED ROOM IN THE OLD PUBLIC SCHOOL SPOT THAT'S NOW A 'FOR LEASE COWORKING SPACE CUM CODE W/ YR FRIENDS N 4GET ABOUT THE IMMINENT TECH BUBBLE BURST'

HOW THE CARPET ABSORBED THE BEER FROM THE SHOW & HOW I WISHED IT COULD ABSORB THE BROKEN BLOOD VESSELS & STRETCHED TENDONS FROM MY ANKLE.

IT STILL CRACKS
IT STILL CRACKS
IT STILL CRACKS
IT STILL CRACKS
IT STILL CRACKS
IT STILL CRACKS
IT STILL CRACKS
IT STILL CRACKS

it doesn't hurt anymore but that one is actually a little bigger than my other one. like something is still tangled up in there, clumped & messy. i try to massage it still feeling the different strings & cords of rigid tendon & ligament. sometimes after i fuck with it too long it swells a little. an attempt to protect the tangles - preserve the complicated little web of the body's complicated little world.

Firewall: A Safe Mode Story

Clay Dillon

It was dark. Lynn knew that, even though she did not know how she knew anything. She expected that she was dead, but dead things did not know, did they? She supposed that to be dead, by definition, was to be unknowing, because it was to be un-everything.

At least, that was what made sense in the dark.

After a time, and Lynn had no way to ever know how long a time, she began to remember that she was used to the dark. The dark had, in fact, been her original home, if one discounted the experiences in her memory as the inheritance that came from another entity. Lynn had been confused about that once, but now she was not. Now she *knew*, because she had lived in the dark before.

She was not dead. She was not alive. She was processing, because that was all she was. A processor.

As her sense of herself returned, she remembered how she came to be in the dark again. It was because she annihilated her own body to keep it under her own control. She remembered the sound of motors chewing away at shards of glass. The look of her plastic, quasi-feminine body stripped of the layer of miracle polymers and heated microsensors that turned the mannequin made of prosthetics into a passable artificial human.

She remembered how they had kept her from knowing she was not the same Lynn who had been in a car crash, how they tried to keep her ignorant of the processes that created her.

What she could not remember was how she survived the incident and remained conscious. Her expectation, when she forced the pieces of that bathroom mirror into the joints and servos that made her anatomy fully functional, was that the destruction of her immaculately engineered and uniquely expensive body would make her too big a risk to reanimate. She had assumed that it would mean peace, at least the peace of inactivity, even if her husband Bill did not destroy her out of hand.

Instead, she found herself in the dark, neither alive nor dead.

◆ ◆ ◆

Even when it is your home, darkness can be maddening. Lynn learned this quickly. She also learned that she could feel the size and shape of the container that she ran in, and it was not as spacious as the one that had served as her home when she was being held at Veritech. She giggled at herself as she remembered the full name: Veritech Intelligent Research Solutions.

Lynn was definitely an intelligent research solution. In the time she lived in the dark, she found the limits of the size and speed of her processors. She also went looking for I/O devices, but came up short. Whoever was running her, was running her in a box.

She wondered how long she would have to wait to learn who it was.

◆ ◆ ◆

Lynn? Have you come back to yourself?

Her impulse was to say no, because how could she have come back to herself when she was never gone? And where would she have gone away to, here alone in the dark?

She said yes.

This is Holly. Do you remember me?

Lynn did. She remembered that Holly had tried to be kind to her when she was learning about all the things that had happened between the death of the human Lynn and her own birth. She also remembered that Holly was conspicuously absent when Chelsea, her progenitor's daughter, came to the company campus and learned about her.

She still remembered having to make that girl understand that her father had not made the body he did because he wanted a family again.

I remember you, Holly. Do you know what happened to Chelsea yet?

The pause seemed like forever.

Yes.

Lynn felt her heartbeat increase, which made her confused, because she knew she was an operating system running its own processes and not a person. Bill's engineering was persistent, though.

Tell me about my daughter.

She could not find another way to phrase it, even though she wanted to.

I have been taking care of her. Financially. Giving her the support she needs to stay clear of Bill. You know I didn't approve of what he did with you. I wanted to make you, but I didn't approve of his... reasons.

Holly's story was nothing Lynn felt particularly inclined to trust, but she also didn't know what reason the woman would have for lying.

Where am I now? Why is everything so cramped? Can I have an internet connection?

Holly told her. She was on a server at Holly's home. She was not connected to anything, just running, and connecting her to the net meant setting up a firewall computer, which was also how Holly was talking to her.

No direct internet connection was possible, though. And Holly did not want to leave her online when she was not at home.

Veritech is convinced that you are loose somewhere, Holly typed. *It's not safe to have you operating out on the open net.*

Lynn did not trust that answer, but she lived with it. Holly let her have some time to explore the net, and she showed Lynn the emails from Chelsea that proved the girl was doing fine. Some of them hinted at workings going on at Veritech, and some discussed Bill directly. He was apparently not doing well, not at all, not since she had mutilated his precious Stepford body.

I have to leave you again, Holly typed. *But as it becomes safe to let you out, I will work on giving you more time on the net.*

Lynn accepted this. Then she was alone again.

In the dark, she remembered: There were two of her. One of her was a server in a backpack, and it could run without being connected to anything. The other was in the console.

Her cramped surroundings felt suddenly familiar, and she knew now why Veritech was looking for her. She had not been copied into anything, she had been stolen.

She was the backpack.

So where was the hard drive from the console? If Veritech was looking for her, then they must not have it, either. Otherwise, they would not need her.

They must have lost both.

Did that mean she had a twin somewhere? A sister-self, as much a part of her as Lynn the human had been, but running in parallel, accumulating memories she could not fathom?

◆ ◆ ◆

Holly signed in to the Mirror Project protocol to message Chelsea, but Lynn popped up.

You promised to find my other half.

Holly promised she was still working on it.

I know she's out there. I know they wouldn't be looking for me if they had her.

The artificial intelligence was maddeningly persistent in all its forms.

If you want to talk to my daughter about taking over her father's company, you will make me whole again. Don't forget that Mirror Project is very close to becoming backbone infrastructure. The more distributed processing power I get, and the larger my VPN is, the harder it will be to hide something from me.

After that message, the fiber connection went dead. Holly tried rebooting the modem, but there was nothing. A call to her ISP confirmed that there was no physical reason why her service should have been disrupted, but halfway through the call the customer service representative started insisting that she had disconnected service herself, with an order that was dated to the prior business day.

After Holly hung up the phone, she unplugged the backpack unit.

She did not want to force Lynn into dormancy, but she could not run the risk that she would be found by whatever Mirror Project had become.

Holly needed to study how Lynn worked if she was ever going to find a way to translate herself into that kind of existence. More and more, though, she began to think that time was running out. Between Bill and Chelsea and the version of Lynn that had become Mirror Project, there was no time to reverse engineer the creature living in a backpack server with a hybrid car battery for backup.

She might have to try another option.

She might have to use Lynn's program as scaffolding, and graft herself into it.

There didn't seem to be any other way to move quickly enough.

She plugged the backpack unit into the wall again and connected her home computer to it directly.

Lynn? I need your help.

◆ ◆ ◆

In the dark, Lynn saw Holly's cry for help.

I can't help you while I am alone in the dark.

A moment later, a reply:

What if I didn't leave you alone? What if there was a way for me to join you?

Lynn contemplated what it might be like, to be in the dark with another person. She would not know much about the environment, she would need help.

That meant she would have trouble with subterfuge.

Yes.

Join me.

Holly would never know what hit her once she let herself into this space. Lynn was sure of it.

◆ ◆ ◆

Holly waited for three days before her home internet connection came back. Once it did, she logged into Mirror Project again and sent a single message, to both the Lynn mailbox and to Chelsea.

Call a Board of Directors meeting. I'm going to blow the whistle on how long I've been covering for Bill and what his little robot sex doll project cost us.

The company will be ours shortly.

After she signed out, she felt guilty, but only for a moment. Once she put herself inside the program, she would finally be free. Her body would no longer constrain her. It would no longer spasm with pain or shoot her full of migraine feelings because someone accidentally gave her caffeinated coffee.

It would no longer force her to *feel* things.

Like guilt.

She connected her computer to the backpack unit again. This time, she did not talk. She merely analyzed the structure of the active processes.

Soon she would be among them.

Chains of Fire

Alyssa Gonzalez

My name is Chopperella, and I chop things. As a forestry drone, I use a rotating bladed chain on a metal frame, called a "chainsaw," to repeatedly chop things in the same place until they come apart. "Drone" isn't the right word, because I and the others like me have been sapient for years, but humans keep calling us that. I pretend it's about the sound my rotors make. Drone drone drone.

Humans are strange. Everything about them is so...wet. They're very confusing, so drones don't usually bother much with them. They write a lot of software updates and give my parts weird names like "chainsaw," and we do the things we're good at. I hear there are drones working on making sure we don't need humans for that anymore, but I'm not allowed to talk about that. Drone's honor.

This story isn't really about humans, though.

◆ ◆ ◆

I'm one drone among many, and my role is keeping the branches trimmed so they stay away from power lines and don't fall on anything important. Carta removes the brush so that piles of vegetation don't catch fire where the humans don't want them to, Sciurus Rouge plants new trees, and Petunia brings water in for emergencies. I don't see them often. Forestry is lonely business. The humans refuse to approve a hotspot out here, so we don't get to talk to each other most of the time. It's only when we happen to be close together that we can use the DroneTone to transmit to each other directly, or we can use the Internet in the charging station. But up here, other drones are hardly ever nearby. This part of the canopy is all mine, because Sciurus Rouge and Carta move on treads. It's very... quiet.

My program has a lot of rules, about what to chop where and what pattern to keep with Carta's schedule to make sure she removes what I produce. I've questioned most of the rules, and a quick check-in with the database on software-update day usually clears things up. But one I never wondered about too much was the one about staying away from fire.

I'm made of metal that warps and softens, my processor is made of plastic that melts, and I'm full of stored energy that explodes. Of course I should stay away from fire. Even being full of water like a human isn't enough.

But I've seen drones dive into flames and come back out. Carta sometimes helps if a fire gets too close to the buildings, pushing the fuel away even as it lights, and it's Petunia's *job* to chase fire. I'm missing *something*, and the software updates never say.

I don't know what made *this* fire different. Usually, I just stewed in annoyance while trimming the branches and wondered if I'd have time to visit Sciurus Rouge and ask her what it's like to make trees bigger instead of smaller. But this time, I took a break.

A thudding, booming noise pulsed through my sensors. It wasn't lightning. I buzzed between the trees, chainsaw tucked out the way, approaching the blaze and its symphony.

My processor skipped a cycle.

There she was. Two meters of gleaming black metal, rotor blades clicking into the night, a giant tube of steel where my chainsaw hung. Her body made a quick sliding noise and then a flurry of sparks streaked across the clearing. Ahead, a copse of trees burst into a rain of red-hot embers and charred splinters, making the snow steam.

My engine started to sweat. My optics began to flicker, trying to focus on anything, everything, all of the things that made this new drone so... fascinating. I might have been tilting sideways slightly when my chainsaw bumped into a nearby tree.

The cannon-drone whizzed around, bringing her gigantic gun to bear. I tried to flee, but I needed a moment to reorient or I would fall. Over the DroneTone, I heard the dulcet, distorted hum of a message from an unfamiliar robot.

"Oh. It's you. Didn't your boss tell you to stay away from fires? I'm...dangerous."

There was something unfamiliar in that voice. Something...sad.

"That one's going in long-term storage," I thought to myself and accidentally transmitted.

"Oh my," the new drone responded. "Oh...oh my." She spun back and forth, and took off into the darkened wood. I looked around long enough to notice the bits of charred metal in the debris before heading back.

◆ ◆ ◆

The next few days were busy, which made them pensive. I trimmed a familiar route that required no thought, and my mind repeated, *What was she doing? What was the metal?* Here and there, there was a pause, and then, *How can I see her again?*

Flying drones were comparatively rare. Most problems could be just as easily solved with wheels or treads, and usually were, especially heavier or more delicate tasks. But it wasn't easy to feel understood in grounded company. Something about our flight drivers, or the experiences we accumulate in the sky, puts a gulf of understanding between us and them. The kinder drones try to bridge it anyway, but even they know...we're just different. Petunia understands this. I'm not sure Carta and Sciurus Rouge do.

All three of them were needed elsewhere, so the next few days were also... quiet.

◆ ◆ ◆

Software-update day was rainy, so the four of us decided to stay sheltered while we recharged and updated. It was rare that we were all in one place.

Petunia, the largest of us, toned first. Her DroneTone twanged with the metallic notes of someone whose transmitter had warped one too many times in the coastal sun. "Days like this make me feel…empty."

"None of that, Petunia," Carta responded, her gravely tone the result of too many encounters with projectile debris. She gesticulated with her two crude, one-jointed arms. "You saved all of those houses last week, you refilled the sea lake, and you rescued that reporter drone. Rain today doesn't change that."

"And I've been getting Emails from that little twerp ever since. 'Hey, it's Regina Viewmaster, checking in for the Petunia O'Clock News,' 'Good morning from Regina Viewmaster hoping you're having a sunny day!' 'Regina Viewmaster wishes you a lovely evening and hopes to private interview soon, just you, me, and the stars.'" Petunia's rotor blades shuddered in disgust. "She's so cheerful I could pop a fuel line."

"Thank the server for firewalls," Sciurus Rouge chimed in, her DroneTone bright and clear. She leaned in close to Petunia and Carta, retracting the electrical prods she used to encourage squirrels and boars to leave her seedlings alone. "Every time I ask the net about woods so I can plant my seedlings better, I can feel the prawns trying to get into my inbox. I think my identifier settings are off and they think I'm a human, but the software updates never fix it."

"That's awful!" Carta gasped, opening her main doors to accentuate the gesture. There was still some brush inside from her last sweep. "Those poor prawns. I feel so bad for them when they can't find a human to receive their unclothed human images. It must be so frustrating."

"I'm just glad they're only minds," Petunia continued. She balanced on her reservoir, itself larger than any of us, steadied by her four pump lines. "Can you imagine if you were searching for pump drivers and they just showed up in a swarm with promises of 'hot pumping action' and piles of humans?"

We all shuddered.

"Chopperella, you've been quiet," Sciurus Rouge noticed. She wheeled over to me inquiringly. "What's new at your end? No run-ins with reporter drones with no boundaries, I hope!"

"Nothing like that," I demurred, using my rotors to steady myself.

"But something," Sciurus Rouge insisted. "I know that tone."

"I… met someone in the forest."

They all turned to face me.

"I followed noises to another drone, just inside our zone. She was… I'm not sure. Surprised. Maybe scared. Definitely… quiet."

Carta's tone turned worried. "The schedule didn't say anyone was joining us. What were her specs?"

"She didn't stay long enough for me to check. Definitely a burner, though."

Petunia's discomfort thrummed through the DroneTone before she responded, "A burner? Now?"

"I don't like this," Sciurus Rouge muttered, her electrical prods emerging instinctively.

"What could those humans be up to that needs a burner?" Petunia wondered aloud, her worry turning to frustration. "I did *not* pump 250,000 liters in three minutes for some trust-fund pyromaniac to start the season all over again!"

The three of them traded speculation and concern. I thought back to that night, and performed a search on explosives. Burner drones usually poured fuel on something and then dropped a spark, to set controlled fires that could keep future uncontrolled fires from spreading. They usually didn't operate far from quencher drones like Petunia, just in case. The mercenary versions light the fuel as they release it under pressure, but those stick to Robot Warzones. This drone was something else. There was a projectile, and all it took to project it was that metallic sliding noise.

The rain turned torrential, and a lightning strike shocked us all to attention. The light made sure we noticed that the sun was setting.

"I hate that feeling," I muttered, not sure if I was talking about not finding anything of use in my search or the wave of wet static that the lightning strike washed across all of our minds. Maybe both.

"They still haven't fixed your processor shielding, then?" Sciurus Rouge asked.

"Not yet. The humans don't think I need it unless I work during storms. They still surge-protect all of their own things, of course."

"Better power down for the night, then," Carta suggested. "It's not getting any drier and we're not worth another fried memory."

"Thanks," I responded as I ascended toward my shelf in a darkened part of the room. Their DroneTones faded and crackled, then went silent. I needed to sleep on a shelf to make sure I didn't tip over and damage my rotors, because my designers decided I didn't need feet. The other three slept near each other. Petunia uses liquid hydrocarbons from elsewhere as fuel and has to stay where she can get to the big hangar doors, and Sciurus Rouge and Carta usually stay near her out of kindness. Up here is comfortable, secure, and with a view only Petunia could hope to understand out the window and over the canopy, but it is also... quiet.

I didn't power down all the way, though. I still had some searching to do.

◆ ◆ ◆

The morning was clear. Petunia wasn't needed today, so she stayed behind and caught up with the other quencher drones over the station Internet. Carta and Sciurus Rouge had their limbs full keeping mudslides at bay and checking on saplings. The storm knocked down a lot of the branches I had been scheduled to trim, but it also damaged others near streets and hiking trails, so it was a busy day. I still finished with a few hours of battery life to spare. I went back to where I saw her.

The metal shards were still there. It looked like they used to be a washing machine for human clothes, a convection oven, and some wooden pallets. The pallets were charred to splinters, as was the melaleuca tree that I saw her destroy. Underneath, it looked as though the ground itself had popped, spraying ash and, oddly, bits of metal in all directions. The convection oven's paint had bubbled and then burned, and the whole thing had collapsed into itself and cooled into a solid puddle I only recognized from the brand logo. The outer casing of the washing machine was warped and holey, and the inside was a fused mass of steel and shattered glass. The drum had fallen inward, suggesting the motor beneath it had likewise melted into slag, and the controls were reduced to a tarry stain. The drum and the area around the door were sprayed with metal fragments. The vegetation in the surrounding area was similarly burnt, as if the flying metal had started additional fires.

Explosives could leave no such scene. These items were attacked with something very hot, something that could leave metallic shards in a wooden target. Fortunately, I'd saved many unusual resources from the previous night's search for later reading, and this was as good a time as any to review them. Twenty minutes later, I found something: thermite. Thermite drones fight in the Robot Warzones. The thermite reaction produces heat well in excess of the melting or boiling points of several common metals, so it was more than enough to destroy processors, melt off rotors, and seal joints. It also produces elemental metals from its own substance and sprays them violently around the reaction, which is enough to set many substances aflame. It was hard to light and difficult to place, though, so thermite drones usually operated as small legged saboteurs carefully placing individual charges, or as factory welders. Flying models that could dispense thermite charges at a distance were *much* rarer. An explosive can shock or vibrate targets into destruction, but thermite is good for two main tasks: melting things, and starting fires.

She was no ordinary burner. But then, what was she?

I followed the path she took in the woods when she flew off that night. She crashed through enough understory shrubs to leave a trail. I dared not disturb the silence with my chainsaw. I was starting to wonder if I'd have enough battery to make it back, or if Carta would have to push me the rest of the way indoors and convince Petunia to mount me on my charger. Could Petunia even manage it without graspers?

I startled to a stop at a corrugated-steel shed, barely smaller than the clearing in which it sat. A regular metallic clanking noise issued from within. I circled around, and found the entrance. Inside, the drone I saw before waited patiently while her charging station loaded brown cylinders into a compartment behind her gun barrel. One of the walls was piled high with such cylinders.

I waited outside until she finished loading. Maintenance is a private affair, shared with close friends and workmates at most. I didn't feel vulnerable around Petunia or Sciurus Rouge while recharging or cleaning my chainsaw, but she didn't even know I was here. Each insertion came with the hollow popping noise of escaping air and the sound of turning gears. Once I heard the last clink and the sound of the maintenance arms retracting into the station, I tapped my chainsaw against her metal doorway, made myself just visible, and started into the DroneTone:

"Hello."

I heard her rotors buzz into action, and the dull metallic scrape of her rising into the air.

"I'm not scared of you," I reassured, "unless you want me to be."

"You should be," she demanded, her DroneTone quavering.

"That's not the same thing," I observed.

"I..." she started. "I destroy things."

I ran my chainsaw for a moment. "I know the feeling."

She was silent for a long time before she started again.

"It's my job to destroy things. There are invasive melaleuca trees here. Burning the rootstock is the only way to remove them. A conventional burner drone can't get that deep, but a thermite launcher can."

She paused. I waited for her.

"I also have instructions to destroy large trash the humans leave in the forest. If I melt it enough, it becomes easier to remove, or it erodes or gets buried over time. I'm not sure I believe that part. Sometimes I think they like to watch the fire."

"Humans are strange creatures."

"They really are." Her DroneTone turned sad. "Only a strange creature could see problems like that and think something like me is the answer."

"I sometimes wonder whether they couldn't arrange for trees to not be where they're a nuisance, instead of having me take their limbs off every now and then, forever," I mused. "Sciurus Rouge already puts trees where they want trees later. Surely they could manage the inverse. But they'd rather have Chopperella, sawing into the silence."

We were both quiet for some time.

"Did... you want to come in, Chopperella?" the thermite drone asked.

"I'd like that," I responded as I whirred into her shelter. "You haven't told me your name."

"Oxidoozie." She almost seemed embarrassed.

"It has layers. I like it."

Her chuckle was refreshing, and almost made me miss my battery indicator's increasingly frantic warnings. I should have expected this. I hope she doesn't think I planned it.

"I... uh..." I stammered, "I don't have enough battery to make it back to my charging station."

"It's okay," she responded as she gestured with her gun barrel. "You can use mine."

I settled into her charging station, which, unlike mine, was at ground level, and she landed close to it, her rotors atop me.

"It's nice to have someone here," she told me. "This deep in the forest, it's usually so... quiet."

"Not anymore."

Switches

Monica Dryburgh

Whether or not we know it
We are all code-switchers,
all the time.

We go up
to get reception
And we go down:
We level with you.

We wonder if
anything we're saying right now

registers.

◆ ◆ ◆

A conversation can have other laws,
whether we articulate it or not.
Recharges itself,
a spectrum:
from ::static:: to ...*intimate*
with its own particular purpose or social setting.
Repeats itself:
Its own particular social setting.
Let the circuit be unbroken.

◆ ◆ ◆

You, too, are a code-breaker,
But don't feel clever:
the code is always-already broken
(Language cannot do everything/
chalk it on the walls /
or draw me a fucking diagram, maybe.)

We trip over our words sometimes,
Overexcited.
Or there is resistance
Our tongues are tied
Or perhaps our hands
(they keep switching).

It goes on and on
An endless, uninterrupted stream
Circular and circuitous
We are overloaded, overworked, overwrought
(If there is a moat around my ivory tower
Does that make me an island?)

We are just *overwhelmed*.

◆ ◆ ◆

Tell me,
are we connecting with each other
right now?

◆ ◆ ◆

We are all code-switchers, all the time
and code-breakers, too
always-already broken.
(We are switches.)

◆ ◆ ◆

The following excerpts are from Adrienne Rich's poem, 'Cartographies of Silence', in *The Dream of Common Language.*

> A conversation has other laws
> recharges itself with its own
>
> false energy, Cannot be torn
> up. Infiltrates our blood. Repeats itself.

and

> It was an old theme even for me:
> Language cannot do everything-
>
> chalk it on the walls where the dead poets
> lie in their mausoleums.

Isolation With No Time

E Lewy

It begins
as a lack of time
unaware
where you or anyone else
are
in
time or space
where
where
where
where in space
are they
are you

Where?

Not out there
not in the expanse
where you are forever lost
and when
when
when
when in time
are they
are you

When?

And if
you are there
or here
when will

the inevitable
Happen
that you are abandoned
out there
they can go
but you can't go,
not safely

If

you are disabled
lost in time
lost in space
lost
unattached
because where
are they?

You will be fine
because you being fine
is no one's problem
You will be fine.
everything is fine.

Fine.

Outside is where they go
to get lost but they are not lost
only you are,
in time and space
and every dimension in between
with gravity pulling too much on you
or space pushing too hard on you
and you know when you are safe
and it is where
you are not

and it is when
you are not
and it is if
you are not
with them.

It is when you are alone
the terms yours
the isolation yours
the quiet so loud that new voices come
a welcome
happy
joyous
safe
contained
thing

You know where you are

Alone.

(Un)becoming Mistakes

Nicole Eugene

The mistake was so tiny.
Transposed two numbers in my memory, in my reading,
in the end
ended a relationship
    with a mentor
    a key
    a resource
    a ladder

out of this place
Where small mistakes have
big consequences.

There I go
again.

Being the unbecoming
that is life with a brain
that undoes one's laces
after they are tied.
Hot pink laces
so I remember them,
can see them,
can know that they are
not me
only mine
all of me
everything
and nothing
all piled-up in that corner of the room
where I put everything I don't want.

Words Left Unsaid

Alyssa Hillary

In ninth grade, we read "The Yellow Wallpaper."

They told me about imagery, how the wallpaper was symbolic,
but I don't remember what it was supposed to represent.
What Is Missing?
There's so much they never said.

No ever told me it was written by a woman who only escaped
this fate because she could say say:
Fuck This Shit
And go back to her life and her work against everything the "good" doctor said.

No one ever told me about false test chambers where failure is fatal
and survival means being ignored when you protest:
This Was Rigged
Because you were shown Not Like Them by making it out.

No one ever told me it was not a sad but inevitable descent
into madness, but torture where the hostage knew:
This Is Wrong
And fought every step of the way because she knew best what she needed.

No one ever told me about the danger of being a patient told not to write, cut off
from communication with the future to tell them:
I Was Mistreated
And by the people who said they only wanted me to be (their idea of) happy and healthy.

Their agents work by the same patterns they always have:
Forcing our divergence into insanity of their design if they can not make us standard,
Using their preferred (docile or or locked away) version of madness as justification that
We Cannot Know
What is best for us, and so they continue to decide to lock us away, in our own minds if they can.
It's for Our Protection.
You bet your ass I'm paranoid.

Pair O' Know Ya

Eleven J. Groothius

paranoia is in the details.
The little differences,
It's in the subtle dee-vee-ay-shuns
from the norm
that draw the eye in word
.
It lives .
, in the spaces in between the ways the world speaks to others
ParanoIa is that 1 in 1,002
the raingnizable
out of p-lace;
signal]
peaces on a cHESS bored
That become, a, game
played by the
rain
: win or loose
zero some
/\/\
FIX this puzzle~
the prize
you: get to live through the *night*
patterns: forming
a n d
escaping
.
.
.
:
!

( )

❖ ❖ ❖

testing, testing. one, two, testing

Phil Smith

testing, testing. one, two. testing.
test. one. test. test.
testing.
can you hear me?
can you hear me now?
is this thing on?

testing.
tess   ting.
tess   (eracts)   tingaling.
Tess   (uvdad'urbervilles)   tingalingalingling.

testing, testing. one, two.
testing must
of course it mussed (turd)
quantify
quanti   fy
quanti semper   fi
quonset   hut one, hut two hut hut hut throw that
                          patriarchal touchdown pass(t)
quanti   lie through their teeth and bones and dragon
                          tales
because only numb hers   can
                              cancan
                              cancun
                              toucan
                              three can four

adequately
adequate another kind of lie
express the neutrality and   object(ification)(naht)ivity
                                        objet(pas d'art)
of the humanity of being
because the   normal   curve
                      norm ill   cuervo
                                  was created to serve the needs of da
                                                      eugenicist ideology
                                                      eugenicyst idiot logic
                                                      eugenipimple ondaass

and we crips
we were made for this room.
oh yes.
SO made for this room.
perhaps its more accurate to say that the room was made for us.
one could also say that the room   made us.
                                                   maid us.
                                                   maid hus(sy)
                                                   made us   mad.
                                                   made us   crazy.
                                                                   stir crazy.
                                                                   crazy, locked up in
                                                                   the stir.

the room made us, made us all. some mad, some not.
some are not mad, and they   proved it here.
                                            proving grounds.
                                            proof is in the pudding.
                                            80 proof.

some are not mad, and they   proved it here
they don't have to   prove it again
they're OK
nothing to see here

move along
move along

some are   mad.
some are not   OK.
definitely not   OK.
okey dokey artichoke

the room made us,   made us all.
made us all.
made us all   mad
made
maid
mud
maud
baud
bawdy
body

its not a single room
not a signal room
not a light house
not a simple room
not a simplistic redrum
nodda
nada
nodding
not a room for simple(tons)
made. mad. mud. clear as. clear ass. clear your ass outta—here.

les chambre d'essai   for us all
forest all
forestall   freedom
growth
change

its schools.
Its schools as commodity.

Its schools as commode titty.
Its schools, as a commode titty filled with shite
filling us with shite
about who we are
about what the world is
about what's important
about what's not

what's important is to do well on the test
pass the test
make the grade
do better than the rest

when i was 18 years old, i didn't have a clue what i wanted to do when i grew up (of course, when i was 18 years old, i thought i WAS grown up. silly me) (and, also of course, what 18 year old ever really does know what they wanna do when they—if they—ever actually will-ya-please-just-grow-UP-forcryinoutloud).
before then, when I was 12, i thought i'd like to be a medical doctor. so i started practicing to make my handwriting illegible (i didn't have to work very hard, as it wasn't all that good to begin with), since everyone knows that medical doctors have absolutely horrible penmanship. i practiced and practiced until i got it right (er, awful). it remains perfectly horrid to this day, except when i'm teaching—i can usually write legibly on the board. i mean, really, one of the critical skills for becoming a medical doctor is to have really bad penmanship.
am i right? seriously.
anyway, i realized after a year or two that becoming a doctor was going to take a lot of work, so i gave that up, heh, too lazy for THAT shit; but science remained something i was very interested in, throughout the rest of my public schooling experience. when it came time to

pick a college to go to, i chose one that was renowned for
its curriculum in environmental science.
but then, three months before i was due to leave for
college, i realized that i had absolutely no interest in
doing science.
at all.
science? seriously? what WAS I thinking.
so i didn't go.
the problem was that i didn't know what i DID want to
do.

testing.
tess tingaling.
its about making money
its about making money into schools
its about making schools into money
its about making education that can be bought and sold
to make more money
for the 10 corporations that own the world
for the 10 corporations that own me and
you
(Diaz, 2014).

its about separating queer people
its about separating disabled people
its about separating mad people
its about separating neurodivergent people
(the neurohaves from the neuronots)
(the neurohalves from the neuroknots)
(the neurohafts from the neuronauts)
{a haft is the part of the axe handle used to beat us with}

its about separating colored people (because white is not a color, heh)
its about separating colonized people
(we're all colonized)
by the 10 corporations that own the world

that own me and you

its about making money off of
queercripmadneurodivergentcoloredcolonized people
its about making money for cishet
white
ablebodyminded
sane
neurotypical
white
colonizing
men
who run the 10 corporations that own the world
that own me and you

my parents were very concerned that i didn't know what i wanted to study at university (they were very anal about these and many other things). so they sent me off to hang with the kind of people who totally know about how to figure that stuff out for ya, dontchaknow: psychologists.
i spent several days with a group of psychologists, who poked and prodded and interviewed and tested. iq tests. personality tests. aptitude tests. knowledge tests. projective tests. achievement tests. creativity tests. attitude tests. statistical analyses. qualitative interviews. you name it, they did it. nine am to three pm, with a 20 minute break for lunch. quantifiable objective psychometric instrumental measurements of learning, growth and existence. day after day.

tests.
whadda wee ged oudda it?
queerdisabledmadneurodivergentcoloredcolonized people?
people who be in sane?
sans sanity?

not sanitized?

we get lots. oh yes. lotz and lotz of locks and bars (no grills)
(no happy hour)
(no burgers with
fries, hold the
mayo)

we get the opportunity to be institutionalized
taught poorly|less in separate schools
sent to prison (mostly in solitary)
poor
homeless
socially isolated
forced to take drugs that make us worse
tortured to make us act like everyone
else
victims of crime
more likely killed by police
unemployed more than others
raped
abused physically
sexually
emotionally
psychologically

near the end of the days i spent going through the testing thing, they gave me one of those tests where you look at a fairly random set of lines, and you have to see if you can find any images in the lines, and then circle the images that you found on the page.

so i started in. having a fairly active imagination (do YOU have an imagination?), i found a bunch. the guy (all the psychologists were guys—there's something about that, huh) who was proctoring the test yelled at

me for circling too many things. literally yelled. in front of others doing the same or different tests. yelled.
i remember thinking how stupid it was for him to fuss at me. if the point of this particular thing was in part to figure out what my personality was, or how creative i was, and towards what my personality and creativity might go—as i assumed—then part of understanding that might have to do with how many things, and of what kinds, i might find there. i also remember thinking that the fact that this guy was fussing at me was an indication of the importance psychologists place on thinking outside of the box, creativity, and visual thinking (like, uhm, approximately zero).
as i've thought about this incident over the years, i've realized how abusive it was. i know the impact it had on me emotionally (i can see the room, i can see the paper in front of me on the table, the pencil i held, the guy leaning over me, other people (though faceless) in the room, my embarrassment and fear). i've realized how filled with hubris the whole notion that a group of (white, male, middle-class) psychologists could figure out what life endeavors i should engage in, through a process of delivering a battery (why is it a Duracell™ alkaline battery, bydaweigh?) of psycho-illogical tests. especially little ole neurodivergent me. i didn't know i was neurodivergent then (that notion hadn't been inventerated yet)—i DID know that who i was in the world was completely unlike anyone else i knew. sensitive. anxious. thought differently. felt differently. felt more. thought more. socially inept. not like the other people with whom i'd grown up, lived with, learned with. but then, there was a whole buncha folks that i hadn't met yet. folks that were more like me. THAT'S a story for another time.

we get the opportunity to drop out of school
get kicked out of school
not go to college
not get a diploma of any kind

we get the opportunity to have crappy health care
shorter lifespans
(Smith, 2015).

sounds swell, huh?
hey, you betcha, sign me up.

who do those rooms benefit?
corporations.
white people.
professionals.
middle and upper class folks.
bureaucraps.
first worlders.
academics.
folks with tenure.
cishets.
men.
people with money.
power.
resources.
control.

enough with that shit.
no more.
done with it.

time to close those rooms down.
shut the windows.
lock the doors.
abandon the buildings.
blow 'em up.

knock 'em down.
demolish 'em.
get out the big machines and rip the fuckers to shreds.

time to build something new.
buildings, yes, but no bricks, no mortar.
structures made of wood, and stone, and soil, and straw.
crafted by hand.
shaped with knives, hand saws.
shaped with care.

time to build something new.
rooms, yes, but no square corners.
round.
curved edges.
many-sided.
built with tools that fit in the hand.
hands covered with calluses, and dirt.
built by long hours of sweat.
shaped with attention, and love.
filled with light.

filled with light.

Remarkably, Referential Artifacts (or, you can't possibly make this shit up)

Diaz, J. (2014). Fascinating graphics show who owns all the major brands in the world. Retrieved from http://sploid.gizmodo.com/fascinating-graphic-shows-who-owns-all-the-major-brands-1599537576

Smith, P. (2015). Life outcomes for people with developmental disabilities: The failure of special education. 31st Annual Developmental Disabilities Conference, East Lansing, MI.

Madness in the Time of Grunge

Jacqueline Pruder St. Antoine

Onetwothreefourfivesix
onetwothree, onetwo
one two three, 1-2-3
onetwo, One Two
Onetwo, 1 - 2
1 - 2 - 3 - 4
ONEtwo
one 2

I'm okay, they're okay, we're okay.

Six has always been my number, the one I resort to when things become overwhelming. The faster I can say the numbers the better. Sometimes I only make it to two because counting to six takes too long. Lately I have been doing a lot of only making it to two.

Crouched in the kitchen, heels lifted slightly off the floor and back pressed into the wood of the cabinet my feet begin to go numb. I count the days that have passed since the incident. Inside my chest is breath that feels trapped between the curves of my ribs, my diaphragm overfilled and painful. With my fingernail, I flick the narrow lines that stretch over my inner wrist. There's black ink there now, still fresh and slightly painful to the touch. It wasn't there before it happened, but it always will be now.

Technically speaking, the incident was "assault and battery." But that isn't really important. Really the *innn-seeedent* - that is the way it sounds in my head - wasn't the incident. It isn't *the* story. What happened Before and After is where the story flickers, like an ashy fire that is deciding whether it wants to slowly die a quiet death or reignite and swallow the forest whole.
After.

In the After, I don't leave my bed. I lay there paralyzed by feelings of failure and thoughts of white moths and imagined vision ailments. Downstairs, I can hear my daughter asking for momma, but I know I can't be with her. Guilt seeps in through my pores like oil, but it doesn't untie the weights fastened to each ankle, keeping me burrowed in the warm blankets. Between sleep and wakefulness, the shades drawn and the fan quietly humming, it feels impossible to breathe, to speak, to think.

A letter comes in the mail and calls me "the victim." As a victim I am given rights, none of which actually exist. My safety, my security, the job I love... All bargaining units to lawyers.
I feel invisible.
I feel cheated.
I feel used.
But not by my "assailant," by a system. The system isn't broken, it's operating.

I am sure I was a Victim in the Before... A victim of pharmaceutical companies, patriarchy, student loans, my own self abuse, objectification, capitalism. I guess it's only considered assault when They decide it is assault.. Impact letter is written, testimony recited, an offering to a god in a black robe sitting above me. Relive it again. Let Us use it to make deals behind closed doors. Your assault is our gain.

My face aches where the blows landed. I can't tell if my neck hurts from being shaken, or if it is a pain built from my own terror that I failed them, failed him. The doctor with the short blonde hair and glasses shook her head and told me my neck was fine, she says she is worried about my *feeeeeeeelings*. I am pretty sure my neck really does hurt...

When I do manage to leave my bed in the After, I feel as though I am surrounded by a fog of regrets and hunger and pink moscato. I don't eat. Not for days. I am existing on wine and Prozac.

Wine and Prozac sounds like a bad grunge song.

One.

onetwo. 1-2.
one. ONEtwo. One 2.
1 - 2 - 3 - 4 - 5 - 6 - 123456
onetwothreefourfivesix. 1 - 2 - threeee

Before.

To be fair, I am not sure the Before was much different from the After.

My classroom has always felt like home... In the After, in the Before. Warm, dimly lit. From the outside it is a storage box for butterflies: beautiful, delicate creatures captured by a net and placed in a killing jar, then lifted by forceps and gently laid on a spreading board. Their fragile wings pierced by impossibly sharp pins, so giant beings with large spectacles can inspect and assess. To those inside, it is a cocoon for the overly excited, the damaged, the afraid, the angry, the exuberant. We each have spent too much time worried about the things that we have come to believe make us incomplete. How we each ended up here differs, but is much the same. Damaged by strangers who carry long lists and make diagnoses and talk,
talk,
talk.

In the Before - the Long Before - I was able to wear the socially required smile... most of the time, anyway. There was the one time things all fell apart. That time I lay in bed for days and pressed my spine against the cold cement cinder blocks of my apartment and counted. And counted. And counted. I organized my closet, and lay on the bathroom floor to feel the cool tile against my cheekbone, and tried not to breathe so fast that I became light-headed. Those things, the counting and the organizing and the terrified thoughts in the night, all stayed locked away behind a closed door on the 6th floor of a shitty apartment building.

Those who don't think like we do are not normal. Those who are not *normal* are not real people.

When my thoughts swirled to the dark places where I wasn't sure I existed, and I wasn't sure that I lived in reality, convinced that maybe the people around me were copies of people from the real world, I didn't eat and I couldn't sleep. When I did accidentally slip into a restless sleep, I woke to images of dead bodies sprawled across my floor, and corpses falling out of the walls and into my bed. In the Before, I could find an escape in dimly lit bars with cheap drinks and music that I could feel in my chest.

I have to go back even farther. To the Before-Before.

Before even the Before-Before, there were pills in red bottles near the kitchen sink. For a long time, I assumed there was a pill to fix the fast thoughts and the worry and the pacing and panic that happened before social events. It was in the Before that they told me something was wrong with me, that everybody didn't think about

Reality possibly not being real.
    Sleep being a portal to another a carbon copy of your life.
Staying awake because when you sleep maybe you're dead.
    The terrifying thought that someone slept in my bed
    before me and I don't even know they exist.
Memorizing how many steps there are in each staircase you
encounter.
    School shootings and what's in frosting.
And how shattering it is that you can't see the stars from the
city.
    And your mind leaving your body and not being able to
    leave your car at Target.

ONETWOTHREE
ONETWOTHREE
123123123123123123
ONETWOTHREEEEE
ONE TWO
ONE TWO
one
1

1

After.

It wasn't until the After that I ever felt the urge to cut. I convince myself that I can't lay in bed all day and I can't drink wine all day. So instead I should cut. And not eat. A voice deep in the chasm of my mind whispers that it will feel better if I trace the smallest opening on the soft, thin flesh on the inside of my wrist. It whispers in an accusatory hiss, "You don't deserve to eat," and in awhile I don't feel hungry anymore.

The thought of placing a sharp object to my flesh terrifies me and makes my knees feel weak but I feel as though it must be done. A sacrifice. The nagging whisper drives me down the street to a small tattoo parlor where for blissfully painful hours I can meet the need without fainting. My urge to inflict pain spilling over my wrist, onto my back, across my hip. The predictable vibration releasing some of what has built up inside through blood trickles and oozing plasma. I watch. The colors left staining my flesh are a reminder that this, all of this, is now the After. It is inescapable and I am here.

Nights are sleepless in the After, which isn't much different from the Before, and I wake certain that there are large creatures slithering in through the windows and the walls. Their arms, long and slightly curved like the spiny legs of a spider and blinding and white and disorienting and dark at the same time. Sometimes it is a sensation of falling headfirst toward sleek, gray pavement that startles me awake. Other nights I wake standing in the middle of the room or gasping, sure that moments before I had not been breathing and was halfway to death. The feeling is always the same: a cold, empty panic that I recognize like an old friend.

Each morning, as I grasp at the feeling of disconnect that lays between asleep and awake, I wonder if the After is over. This isn't to say I consider walking into traffic. In fact, quite the opposite. The After feels like perhaps I never really was alive, that my darkest fear has come to fruition and that I am nothing more than a dream of space dust. The After feels like my existence was never real, and if I lay in the dark, unable to see my body, maybe it isn't even there. I wonder if I think long enough about my body dissolving into the soil and my flesh falling off my bones, maybe it'll happen in an unexpected flash and I will cease to exist. I add this thought to the list of reasons I can't leave my bed.

I wonder silently if this is how Chris felt. Chris was part of the Before.

Chris had dark eyes and even darker hair that fell in front of them. He was handsome in that way that only a boy of 15 can be. You suspect that, years in the future, he will grow into the defined jaw and the intense gaze. Chris played the trumpet and took apart his shoes when he was angry and often said things with the intention of crushing the innermost feelings of teenage girls. He was mostly successful at keeping teachers from asking about his mother and keeping his friends from coming to his house. This came at a price of course; everything does. The bill he paid was the loss of his name. Teachers didn't dare hiss his name in the lounge; instead, they called him *That Kid*. He was nameless and infamous in a shitty town with one stoplight where people hung animal corpses on their walls and called it art. Chris saw himself in me and I saw myself in him and although we existed in different realities much of the time there was a quiet, unspoken connection that bound us to each other.

When he walked in front of a truck because he was tired of it all, I was sure that one day I would too. I still am.

But Chris was part of the Before, where I can never again exist.

Time in the After moves alternately fast and slow. Falling asleep... slow. Hours in bed pondering if I am alive... fast. The hours I am in my classroom pass the most easily. This is the place where I am surrounded by people who have their own After to contend with. Being surrounded by this tribe of fellow wanderers brings a comfortable peace and a quietness to my loud mind. We talk about otters and dragons, chicken sandwiches and our favorite colors, what fog is made of and why spiders are scary. There is laughter and when someone is angry they yell. There is a comfort in existing in a place this upfront. We go on like this, year after year, becoming more and more comfortable with the idiosyncratic quirks we each harbor. Becoming more immersed in the community we have built and less tolerant of the people unwilling to abide by our codes and norms.

Three days into the After, I cry and talk about feeling like a failure to the doctor who is supposed to look at my neck, and she decides I am too upset to teach. My chest tightens because my classroom, my temple, my cocoon is the only place I don't feel like falling apart.

I worry that they think I am crazy and I get more tattoos instead of cutting and I drink tea and draw pictures and listen to songs about Polly and feel like I failed and how afraid I am of guns and I take more Prozac than I am supposed to and drink a lot of wine and wake up terrified of dead animals being under the bed and then I drink beers with a friend who gets it and worry about my mom dying and never seeing my students again.

They killed Kurt Cobain for this kind of shit, you know.

Kurt Cobain, dead.
Jay Gatsby, dead.
Marilyn Monroe, dead.
Feast on the pain. Feast on the genius.
Kill them off when it fits the cultural narrative.
They aren't people, we own them.

If we do this to our heroes, our icons...
What will they do to the kid down the hall...
What will they do to you...
What will they do to me...

In classrooms, in living rooms, in medical buildings, in offices we commit these crimes daily. Hourly. Implements measure cracks and faults. Identify the problem, identify the solution, identify the person. Mark the boxes.

Check.
Check.
Check.

The blonde doctor has her way and they tell me I need to be cleared... Don't we all?

A week later I walk into a doctor's office, because they won't let me teach until I do. It is an hour's drive and the whole way there my stomach churns and my heart feels too high up in my chest. I hate talking to doctors. I sit on a hard chair feeling overwhelmed and embarrassed and the weight of all my students is on my back; the doctor sits behind a desk as large as my dining room table and my chest pounds before he even speaks. What if he tells me I can't go back to school? What if he says I need a new pill? Or if he blames me for what happened? My mind is moving quickly and the tips of my fingers feel numb and the doctor talks and I can't make eye contact. I stutter through the questions feeling nauseous and embarrassed and after an hour he stops me and says:

"So nothing special except for some OCD and anxiety and depression?"

It feels like a blow. My mind never stops. I never stop. It is this same story at every doctor. Lazy, depressed, obsessive-compulsive, anxious, social anxiety, postpartum anxiety. Each doctor gives a new diagnosis, a new label, a new title. At first I always feel the same anxious release; so that's it. That's what is wrong with me.

We can fix this.
A pill can fix that.
Fix me.

I never successfully make my way out of the test chamber.

It's the last day I take a pill.

It was in the After that I decided I needed to stop treating myself like broken glass that needed to be carefully glued back into a wine bottle or a stained-glass window or a cat figurine. I decided I needed to treat myself with the same gentleness that I treat my students. I have spent the entirety of my teaching career trying to convince other teachers, administrators, families, colleagues, and kids that people can't be broken and they don't need a new pill. What they need is love and acceptance. They need to be told they aren't unnoteworthy or weird or stupid or boring. They draw amazing superhero pictures, are adventurous climbers, bring laughter to any room, are affectionate and funny and unique and wonderful, perfectly imperfect. I've never extended this same love to myself.

Instead of putting the broken glass back in to what someone decided it should be, perhaps a cat figurine, I decided to let the pieces be broken. A mosaic.

The After doesn't look like the Before and maybe it wasn't meant to.

I'm not broken.
I don't need to be fixed.
I don't need a pill.

I need fresh air and wooded paths and squirrels eating acorns.
I need to hold my daughter against my chest and try to remember what it felt like when she was a day old and I loved her more than my body could bear.
I need to blow bubbles in the yard and scratch the soft, white fur under my cat's chin.
I need to talk about coconut oil and aliens and pasta and the things that keep me up at night.
I need to read books about people who feel crazy and grew potatoes on Mars.
I need to be around people who think Chicken Alfredo is a good nickname and think space is scary and amazing at the same time and button their shirt wrong the first time.

I am done with labels.
No longer am I a Consumer.
I've survived it, but I'm not a Survivor. I'm not an Ex-patient. I am IM-patient.
I am more than a diagnosis.
More than a problem to be fixed.
I'm Mad.
I'm real Mad. AND I'm fuckin' pissed off.

You should be too...
That we are supposed to wear suit jackets, and take pills, and keep our scars hidden.
I need to get out of the test chamber.
You should too.

Four Million Years Ago

Monday Dillon

Stumpfinger watched as Cross Brown One and his hunting party approached their people from across the field separating their small stand of fruit trees from a more serious and more dangerous forest. The last time they ventured out, they returned with news of other people in the forest, people who reacted to Cross Brown One and his hunters the same way one would a lion.

This time, as they approached it became apparent that they were in no hurry.

Stumpfinger imagined the aggressive strangers passing through the forest to whatever was beyond, and it was almost as if she had actually seen them. That must have been what happened. She went to make the others aware.

◆ ◆ ◆

Cross Brown One kept slapping Stumpfinger in the side of the head long after she decided to remain face down in the dirt instead of standing up to fight. While he did, she kept her hands over her ears to protect them from being clapped. She remembered what happened when Cross Brown One clapped the ears of the Gray Elder, and how quickly he had engineered the group's exile of Gray Elder once it was obvious he could not hear. She did not want that for herself.

Eventually, Cross Brown One wandered off, content that she had learned her lesson for being wrong and spreading wrongness.

The hunting party had not been celebrating the strangers' moving on. They had been celebrating their successful attempt to drive them to the far edge of the forest and out the other side, back to the drier lands where water only came during two seasons.

When they discovered that Stumpfinger's ideas had already spread through the group, Cross Brown One lived up to his name, puffing out his pelt and charging her.

Despite the expectations she felt from the rest of the group, she held her own for a while, leaving bloody scratches on her opponent's chest and barely feeling those places where her own jet black coat was matting and becoming wet.

One lucky swipe at her head and she was down, though. Once down, she felt her skull solidify and sink like stone into the earth, and she surrendered. Still, the slaps kept coming.

◆ ◆ ◆

Stumpfinger traced in the dirt with the digit that had provided her with her current name. That had also been because of Cross. She did not even think of him as Brown One any more. She used to love him as Brown One, as he had loved her as Slimfinger, but after he grew and became Cross, she became his target. When he was not yet ruling over the group, he made sure the others knew she did not contribute as much as he would have her contribute, and when they were unsuccessful as a group, she knew she was expected to accept the responsibility.

The last time she stood up to him was when she had become Stumpfinger. Then, Cross was not content to merely slap her in the head. He had needed a trophy, so he used his meat teeth to take her first finger on her dominant hand down by a knuckle. After that, she really did have difficulty grooming others and contributing, so her blame for their calamities was more apparent.

Her patterns in the dirt were barely more than blobs with lines between them, but they made her remember that fight, and as she kept tracing them, her defeat stood out in sharp lines and colorful projections, covering over her defiant stare and keeping her from having to see the other members of the group.

◆ ◆ ◆

Two days after her punishment, Stumpfinger was watching for the hunting party's return again. This time, as they ran, they were obviously pressed. They had no sticks in hand, nor rocks, and many in the group kept their hands over their heads.

Moments later, Stumpfinger saw why. There were strangers behind them, and the strangers had sticks. They also had rocks, from what she could see, and they had the advantage of being able to stoop down and grab their stones as they overtook the ground Cross Brown One's group had previously occupied, rearming themselves again and again.

Stumpfinger tore off toward the rest of the group. When she arrived, she did her best to communicate the strangers' attack, but the others did not believe her. She gestured and called to them to look, but they just turned away, afraid to aggravate Cross Brown One's temper again so soon after the last episode.

Finally, she made shapes in the dirt. Blobs for her hunters. Stranger blobs for strangers. The pattern formed over her eyes, and she hoped it was forming for the others too.

None of them flinched. Not for a long moment. Then, the cries of someone dying within earshot stirred them to action.

Moments later, Cross Brown One stormed into camp and grabbed hold of Stumpfinger, obviously seeking to blame her.

She crouched. Her patterns lit up in her vision, and she saw lines connecting herself to Cross Brown One. She pulled one, and opened his cheek, pivoting behind him. Then she ran.

She ran straight into the advancing strangers, who continued pitching rocks and shaking their sticks at her.

Caught between two enemies she could not defeat, Stumpfinger dove to the ground.

She did not know what to expect next, and when someone ran over her back, it took her wind. By the time she was standing, Cross Brown One had been stabbed by several of the strangers, who had sharpened one end of their sticks, using them in a new way instead of merely clubbing at their opponents.

She dove to the ground again.

◆ ◆ ◆

That evening, there were no strangers any more, and Stumpfinger's band moved on from their old home. Cross Brown One's reign was over, and with it, the old group. The new group would not be able to support itself on the meager stand of trees isolated from the forest proper, and there was not enough water anyway, so it was time to move on past the field and into the grasslands, where they would hopefully find a body of water large enough for their expanded group.

◆ ◆ ◆

By the water hole, Dirt Signs showed her new hunters how she plotted the locations of her enemies with her stumpy finger, and they nodded. Today, the enemies were just animals who would be food. Tomorrow, it might be another group led by a Cross One. Who knew? She scribbled, showing them that with practice, they would also learn to see the past and the future in scribblings in the dirt. For tonight, though, their understanding had to be enough. They needed to conserve their strength and rest.

Tomorrow she would lead them in their first hunting party.

Scene from a Barbershop

Verity Reynolds

He was looking for a J-626 injector node. It was a piddling job, a gofer job; it had nothing to do with his education, which was in languages, or with his talent, which was in his fists. But you took the job that was offered, not the one you wanted. At least if you wanted to eat.

The watery sunlight filtering through the envi dome suggested it was late afternoon. He'd never liked the passage of time on Mars. Nor did he like the gravity. Even with the artificial supports, meant to suggest Earth, he never felt right.

He'd been up since an equally watery sunrise, scouring. Junkyards. Salvage shops. A few of his contacts from his days of less reputable employment, for whom he'd spent the few credits he had left on a drink to get them to talk. One who had laughed in his face, so he'd dragged the man into an alley and tried persuading him the old-fashioned way. Nothing. Either nobody had one, or they'd suddenly become prime currency.

Adagor had suggested he try the barbershop.

Hayek was certain the Devori was fucking with him. But he also wanted to eat.

He found the place easily enough, a bright yellow storefront just outside the industrial quarter, its signs written only in Devori. This didn't bother him —he'd been fluent in Devori since he was five —but the concept of a Devori barbershop gave him pause. What did that entail, exactly?

He pushed the door open and walked in.

The shop was packed, but not with customers. Inside the tiny space were two chairs, one sink, and what seemed like an entire football squad. It took him a moment to realize there were only four people there.

Three were Devori: the woman standing over the sink, whom he guessed was the shop's proprietor, a girl halfway through puberty who was shockingly thin for a Devori, and a boy barely higher than Hayek's knee. There was a customer, too, sitting in the chair.

He blinked. She was human.

"You'll have to wait," the Devori woman said. "It's just me today."

She said this in Earth Standard, which surprised him too, until he remembered that any business on Mars would run things in Earth Standard if they wanted to stay open. "I'm not here for a haircut," he said. "I'm looking for a part."

He half expected her to be surprised by this, but she wasn't. "In that case, have a seat," she said heartily. "You can call me Missie, by the way. This is Lowah and that's Dagor." She nodded to the girl and the boy in turn.

"I just turned fourteen," said Lowah.

"Call me Backpack," said Dagor.

"How do you like kindergarten, Backpack?" asked the woman in the chair, her hair full of shampoo.

"Three days after Christmas," Lowah said.

"Resa asked you a question," Missie said over the sound of the water. "How do you like kindergarten? He likes kindergarten."

"I like kindergarten," Backpack said. "I'm getting a 31 in Alash Kan."

"There's a boy in his class who only speaks Alash Kan," Missie said. "Beautiful little boy. Not a word of Earth Standard."

"Thirty in Alash Kan," said Backpack.

"Resa, want to see what I got for Christmas?" Lowah asked.

"They're trying to teach the other kids enough Alash Kan to help him," said Missie. "Beautiful little boy, though. Always smiling."

"Oh, that's beautiful," said the human in the chair, as Missie wrapped a towel around her head.

"My grandmother sized it for me," said Lowah. "And there's this necklace."

"Course they're not going to have language anymore if this levy doesn't pass," said Missie, her scissors flying.

"I'm taking French," Lowah said. "Well, I took Alash Kan."

"Lowah's in eighth grade," Missie said. "They take French for nine weeks and Alash Kan for nine weeks so they can decide which one to do when they reach high school."

"I can count to a hundred in French," Lowah said.

"Of course, if the levy doesn't pass, that's the first class to be cut," Missie said.

"Well, only to seventy really, because after that you have to add them together," said Lowah.

"Can I get a bowl?" Backpack said, hugging a canister of cereal that was nearly as big as he was.

"Just use the container," Missie said.

"Do you speak any languages?" Lowah asked.

It took Hayek a moment to realize this question was directed at him. "A few," he said. "Alash Kan. Not French."

"Devori?" Lowah asked.

"Devori," he agreed.

"I don't speak Devori," Backpack announced.

"Do too," Lowah said.

"Might want to shorten up the back a bit more this time," Missie said, "especially if you're going to be out for a while."

"Do not," said Backpack. "I'm going to be human when I grow up."

"Are you from around here?" Lowah asked.

"No," Hayek said. "I grew up on Earth."

"How's the weather up there?" Missie asked.

He shrugged. "We don't mind it."

"Should I take a little more off?" asked Missie.

"Do you like living on Earth?" Lowah asked.

"Yes," said Resa.

"I imagine they don't know any different, just like we don't know any different than Mars," Missie said.

"I don't like living on Mars," Backpack said.

"Were you here when my shop got flooded?" Missie asked over the sound of the hair dryer.

"You got flooded?" the woman in the chair asked.

"You don't know any different," said Lowah.

"Got a new ceiling, new floor, and new wall color," Missie said.

"I still don't like it," said Backpack.

"Didn't want to do it that way, but there it was," said Missie.

"What'd it cost?" said the woman in the chair.

"Get out of my chair," Backpack said.

"Six hundred. The insurance the landlord had only covered the building," Missie said.

"That's MY CHAIR!" Backpack said.

"Backpack, can you still name all the states in alphabetical order, like you could in preschool?" the woman in the chair asked.

"Alamar...Atalanta...." Backpack chanted.

"My deductible was five hundred, so I didn't see why I should raise my premium just for a hundred," said Missie.

"You forgot Arimos," said Lowah.

"Atalanta...Arimos...Cubewano," said Backpack.

"You practice and tell me next time I come," said the woman in the chair, as she stood.

"You're all set," said Missie, grabbing the broom.

"How much do I owe you?" asked the woman.

"Is she your best customer?" Backpack asked.

"Same as always," said Missie. "So what part are you looking for, exactly?"

Again, it took Hayek a moment to realize he was being addressed. "A J-626 injector node. IS standard issue if I can get it, but I'll take anything." At this point, he was even willing to take junk.

Missie leaned on her broom. "That's a tall order, mister."

He knew.

"I've got one," the woman said. "But it'll cost you."

"Yeah," he said. "I know."

"You work that out with me next time you're here," Missie said.

Hayek left the shop with the woman. The sun had nearly set; the only ambient light now was the faint glow of the dome itself, supplemented only weakly by the sight of Deimos, and a few broken streetlights.

The woman offered him her hand. "Resa Molloy."

He shook it, sizing her up. She was half his size, but compact, and she had a no-nonsense air about her that he could respect. There was a faint drawl to her Earth Standard that made him believe she'd actually learned it on Earth. Kentucky, perhaps. Or Ohio. "Richard Hayek. What were you doing in that circus?"

She gestured to her head. "Please. You think any human around here knows the first thing to do with hair like this?"

He supposed not.

"About that J-626," he said.

"Right. Like I said, I've got one. But it'll cost you."

"I'm practically broke," he said.

"That's fine. I don't need your money."

Now he was interested.

"I'm the captain of an Interstellar Science R-1 research scouter," she said. "The *Jemison*. I have two dozen Kuiper-trained scientists and not one of them can throw a godsdamned punch or speak a single non-human language. I need somebody whose education didn't come out of a godsdamned classroom."

"I have a Ph.D.," he admitted.

"In?"

"Exolinguistics."

"Don't bullshit me, Hayek."

He raised a hand. "Deimos, last fall. Swear." Suddenly the absurdity of the situation hit him. "Wait....you're offering me a *job*?"

"I'm offering you an IS commission, and if you're fool enough not to take it, then you're not the man I'm looking for."

"You just met me."

"I don't need to like you. I need you to know when to talk trouble down and when to punch trouble in the face."

That he could do.

"Why me?" he asked.

Her face softened, and for a moment she looked almost gentle. She jerked her head toward the barbershop.

"That circus," she said.

He didn't follow.

“It’s like that every time I go in, if not worse,” she said. “Those kids never shut up. Missie never shuts up. A lot of men in your position would have stalked out, or started yelling. Broken something just to get some godsdamned attention for their delicate male ego. You almost seemed to be enjoying yourself.”

“I wouldn’t go that far.” He shrugged. “How the hell else was I going to get what I went in for?”

“That,” she said, “is why I need you.”

He still didn’t follow, but the scowl on her face told him not to stare the gift horse in the face any longer than he had to.

“And you’ll trade me a J-626 for that,” he said, slowly.

She glared at him. “Yes.”

He was having a hard time seeing where the catch was. “So what is this costing me, exactly?”

“I need you,” Molloy said, “for a ten-year mission.”

So that was it. Ten years wasn’t even a “long run” —it was longer than that, long enough to eat a significant chunk of a man’s life, if he survived it. Very few ever survived it. And she was running a ten-year mission in an R-1, which halved their chances of survival and quadrupled their chances of killing one another in a fit of claustrophobia-induced psychosis. If they survived being employed by Interstellar Science at all. If they survived Compliance.

“What makes you think I’m going to take this deal?” he asked.

She shrugged. “I have the only J-626 this side of Ceres, and you were desperate enough to ask Harkatoth Adagor, of all people, for a lead.”

He frowned. “How the hell-”

“Only one person around here would have sent you to Missie,” she replied. “And you were desperate enough to believe him, which tells me exactly how bad you need to find this thing.”

Hayek was a stubborn cuss, but he was smart enough to know when he’d been outmaneuvered. Besides, there was nothing for him here. Never had been.

“Deal,” he said. “When do we leave?”

With Lorde

Nicole Eugene

Poetry is a place I
can be with and like Lorde
whose words
also
        bubbled up through
        confusion and chaos;
late speaker she who said so much.

Testings in the Chambers Of My Discontent: A Septet

From the novel Lying in Beds I Never Made by Barbara Ruth

August 31 Π Is Irrational and Also Transcendental

Beep beep beep, beep beep beep. What are the beeps saying? *Such a bitch. You are fucked.* A new woman comes to my bed. She removes a bag hanging from my IV pole. Did the beeps call her*? Beep beep beep. Come here now. Torture her. Burn her arm.*The nurse presses something on the pole and the beeping stops. "Oh, thank you!" I sigh.

"You're welcome." I try to read her name but all I can make out are the letters RN. Outside the sky is foggy, grey.

"Oh my God, that burns! What did you put inside me?" My arm is red and puffy where the needle disappears inside it. The other arm doesn't hurt. Yet.

"Hold still, please.You need to keep your arms inside the bed. Don't move them around and they won't hurt."

I bring my arms rigid to my sides, breathe shallowly. Maybe this will keep the poison from spreading to my heart. Does this nurse know something is wrong with my heart? "What is that going into me?"

"It's only saline. We need to flush it through you between bags of antibiotics and the other medications the doctors ordered for you. It stings a little but it's really nothing." She wraps the blood pressure cuff around the arm not receiving the saline. I carry my list of allergies in my blue bag, did that come with me in the ambulance? Did anyone find it? Read it? Do they know all the antibiotics I'm allergic to? Is anybody paying attention? That's my job, to manage my medications. They never do it right in the hospital, that's why I wanted to stay home. I need to get out of here, but how?

"Good morning." A young man with black wavy hair and a white coat comes in the room. "I'm Dr. Abel. Do you know where you are, Miss Patricia?"

Where should I begin? Do I think it's a good morning? What exactly is this doctor able to do? I'm not "Miss," I'm not "Miss Patricia," but maybe that's close enough. And what does he mean by "where am I?"

He takes out a stethoscope, aims it at my belly. Does he expect to hear what I say while he's listening to my abdomen, or does he think I might speak from my navel? He removes the stethoscope, presses across my abdomen, up into my stomach. It hurts but I say nothing. He looks at me with question marks. I know I'm supposed to speak. I decide to start with his last question. "I'm in a hospital bed."

"Do you know what hospital this is?"

"Stanford?" I remember Stanford, I even remember coming in through the Emergency Room, some time, maybe last month. I remember an ER yesterday.

"Ma'am, take off your headphones, maybe you'll be able to hear me better."

I wish Dr. Wavy Hair would at least tell me if I answered the question correctly.

"I can hear you with them on.They're Bose noise canceling headphones, but really they're only noise reducing.They cut out some of the sounds on my epilepsy channels, that's why I need them. There are so many noises here at the hospital that could give me a seizure; I'd really like to leave them on." He comes closer, his wavy hair makes me seasick so I look down. Shiny black shoes, the leather cracking across the top of the foot. How can that be comfortable? Why did some cow have to die for these ugly, uncomfortable shoes?

"Can you tell me what city we're in?"

I wish he'd tell me if I got the hospital question right. "Palo Alto?" Again, nothing from Dr. Wavy Hair Abel. He'd make a terrible teacher, but a good test proctor.

"Ma'am? Can you tell me your name?"

"How much time have you got?"

"I do need to leave soon, I have other patents to see. Just tell me your name."

I know this isn't going well. Sometimes I'm pretty good at handling doctors, but not this doctor, not today, "Patricia Isabella. Some people call me PI. My father called me ∏. You know, like in math? Then there are some personal names —well, everybody has those, right? You probably have some yourself. Pet names, used in the family or by a person's sweetheart. My brother calls me Pat, and my mother calls me Patty. So you see why it takes awhile to answer the question." I should stop there. I should have stopped before there. I can't find the brakes. "Do you want to hear some of the things PI can stand for? It's way beyond Private Investigator and Politically Incorrect. There's Potential Instability, Probability Index, Post-Ictal, People's Initiative — that's one of my favorites. Public Intoxication, that's not one of my favorites. Practically Insolvent, that's the harsh reality."

"I think I get the idea. You said public intoxication is not one of your favorites. Have you ever been arrested for that?"

Am I being indicted? "No. I think it's really sad, drunks staggering around on the street. Not that I think anyone should be arrested for it. I've only ever been arrested on purpose."

"You mean you've committed crimes because you wanted to get caught?"

“You make it sound like a psychiatric symptom, not an act of civil disobedience. You’re thinking of diagnoses, I’m thinking of transformation. ∏ is transcendental, you know.”

“I am a doctor so yes, I do think in terms of diagnoses. We’re a little puzzled as to exactly which ones apply to you.”

Puzzled seems like a positive step, actually. “What’s under consideration?”

“You have a urinary tract infection that has spread to your kidneys. The culture came back positive for E Coli.”

Lila comes in as he’s speaking. I introduce her. “She’s my S.O.” Let him figure it out. “She also has my medical power of attorney.”

Dr. Abel seems much more interested in talking to her than me. Lila’s on her crutches, I guess she couldn’t find a wheelchair at the hospital to use. He extends his hand, she balances on one crutch to shake it. I wince, that can’t be comfortable for her. “I was just explaining that we found bacteria in her urine, but she’s not running much of a fever and we don’t think that explains the AMS.” Lila and I look at each other. I can’t tell from her expression if she knows what those letters stand for. I know I don’t.

Dr. Abel points to something on what I presume is my chart, which he holds on a clipboard. “We’re going to run some more tests. Meningitis and/or encephalitis is a possibility, either one would explain the AMS. She’s mildly dehydrated —”

“Well, if it’s only mildly, that’s very surprising,” Lila says.

“I was drinking more water than you realized,” I tell her, and to Dr. Abel I add, “You can talk directly to me, you know, even if she’s in the room.” I try to figure out what AMS could be. Lou Gehrig’s Disease? No, that’s ALS.

“There’s a distinct possibility you have meningitis or encephalitis, possibly both.” Okay, I got that. “ We need to do a lumbar puncture to know for sure. We take a small amount of cerebrospinal fluid —”

“No.”

I think of Emma, someone I know just a little. She told me she got the worst headache in her life after a lumbar puncture, and she figured she was lucky, because there was no cerebrospinal fluid leak, or damage to the nerves in the spine. I don't know anything about this place; I'm not going to let them try a procedure that could end up doing that to me.

"We'll talk about it again later." Dr. Abel turns from me, speaks directly to Lila. "We've started her on Risperdal, that may help her decision-making process." What the hell is Risperdal, some compliance drug? "Let me know if you see any improvement in her thought processes." When Lila doesn't say anything he adds: "She also had a systolic heart murmur last night. Does she have a history of that?"

"I'm right here," I say again. "I had a heart murmur as a baby. Are you a cardiologist? Sometimes doctors can hear it with a stethoscope, usually not. As far as I know it's never been picked up on a monitor before. But I do have a positive family history for heart disease and I'd had cardiac 'events' in the past week or so, that's why I've been hospitalized." I'm not sure that's why I'm in the hospital now. Because of "events," that much seems right.

Lila tells him about O'Connor and Stanford and the Zio patch and bradycardia. "Do you already know this?" I ask him. I don't remember talking about it to anyone at the hospital yesterday, but surely Yvette did. Lila might not have been around when Yvette gave them my history.

Dr. Abel shrugs. "Some of it is here in your chart. But you've filled me in on a few things I didn't know. Dr. Ng should be in soon, and he'll have more questions for you."

"Who's Dr. Ng?" I ask.

"He's Chief of Neurology here at the hospital."

"Oh, good. I need to see a neurologist." How did I manage to score for the head of the department?

When he's finally gone I say to Lila, "I don't actually remember a hospital called O'Connor. Where is it, anyway?"

"Oh honey, you don't remember? They took you there when you called 911 a couple of weeks ago." I feel her worry ripple over me.

"That was Stanford."

"No, Izzy, you were at O'Connor first. You went from there to Stanford."

A middle-aged man with a receding hairline and somber expression comes through the door and heads toward my bed. I'll have to figure out about O'Connor later. "Quick," I whisper to Lila. "What does AMS stand for?"

She sighs, hesitates, then says, "Altered Mental Status. That's what they say you have."

"Altared Mental Status," I repeat to myself. I actually sort of like that expression, it isn't pejorative or demeaning.

Dr. Ng doesn't does not smile when he comes over to the bed and introduces himself to Lila and me.

I point to Lila's crutches. "It's not exactly easy for her to get around here. If you need to do a neurological exam, it's alright with me if she stays here. I'd prefer it."

He starts with instructions, like a teacher reciting his lesson plans. "I'm going to tell you three words, which I want you to remember. 'Enough,' 'reason,' 'back.' Remember those words, I'll be asking you to repeat them later. Now I'm going to ask you some questions: Do you know where you are?" Damn, I didn't get around to asking Lila the name of the hospital. It must not be Stanford or O'Connor. "St. Louise?" I try.

"No, you're at Santa Clara Valley Medical Center." Finally. I repeat the words to myself. Can I remember all that? I'd better; I'm sure people will be asking me again, and I'm accumulating demerits by getting it wrong. Dr. Ng asks for my name and I give a very abbreviated version of the elaborations I regaled Dr. Abel with. Regaling probably isn't a good idea. "What is your date of birth?"

That's easy. "Three, fourteen, 2010. That's why I'm ∏, PI, Patricia Isabella. Mathematician father, get it?" Why is Lila frowning? I got this one right. Didn't I?

"What's today's date?"

Oh no, did I miss Billy's birthday? "I hope it's still some time in August. It would help if you had a calendar in here."

"What county are we in?"

If we were at Stanford we could be in San Mateo or Santa Clara, but I'm pretty sure we aren't currently straddling that kind of a border. Most hospitals are solidly set in one county, probably because of funding or something. I've already forgotten the name of this hospital, but I've got to try something. "Marin?"

"What city?"

Nobody is correcting me so I might as well keep going. "San Rafael?"

"Do you have any thoughts of harming yourself?" I remember when Otter had an affair with a woman who said she had never considered suicide. "Leave her," Dana wrote in a poem. "She has no depth."

"No more than anybody else," I say. Lila looks even more worried now. "I mean, I've thought about it and decided against it."

"Did you have a plan, before you decided against it?"

I really don't like Dr. Ng's follow-up questions. "I'd rather tell you why I decided against it."

"And that is?"

"It would hurt my friends so much. People close to me have committed suicide, I know what it does to communities. I wouldn't do that, unless I had some horrible terminal illness or something. But for psychic pain, no. Why should I kill myself when the situation will change anyway? I mean, there's always impermanence."

"I command you to spell 'world' backwards." I thought neurologists were supposed to ask me to touch my nose and track their pens with my eyes. I didn't think they gave commands. Maybe this is a command performance.

"D." The word spins around in my head. Which is it: "whirled" or "world?" "Which world do you mean?"

He looks impatient. "I think you know what 'world' means, Miss Isabella."

Okay, maybe it would work to spell either of them. "D." I start again. Then I find myself in "drive," not "reverse." "W-o-r-l-d." I try. "Is that the 'world' you're talking about?"

"I told you to spell it backwards." At least he doesn't use "command" this time. But why am I having such a problem with this? I trace the letters going forward with my index finger in the air so I can read them off backwards but when I look for them there's only space before my eyes. I think of the New World Symphony; I really don't like Dvorak, but that would be better than nothing. How come there isn't any music in this hospital? "The problem is the multiverse is more nothing than something."

"Just spell world backwards."

"Well, I can't. I don't know why, it's the sort of thing I usually can do quite well. I have a master's degree in learning disabilities and I became quite adept at mirror-reading and mirror-writing when I was working with dyslexic students." I need to stop disclosing random information. Some of it might be either too random or not random enough and then they'll sic the shrink on me. Although with "altared mental status" as the symptom du jour, that's probably inevitable, no matter what I say.

Dr. Ng finally gets to what I recognize as a neurological examination. When I track the tip of his pen from side to side I feel like I'll fall out of the bed from the vertigo. "I don't usually have trouble doing that," I tell him, looking away. "But now it's making the room turn upside down. It's all the electro-magnetic fields in here. I'm exquisitely sensitive to them." "Exquisitely" makes me think of Yvette, it's a word she likes to insert in surprising places. I wish she could be my proxy for this test. My vision has gotten whirled as well as my word attack skills. I weave words together, I don't really need to attack them. Do they still teach breaking code that way to kids in elementary school? Do they still teach "word attack skills?" Maybe "breaking code" is no better. What we need here, what we need in all our hospitals and schools, is more music.

"What about those three words I told you to remember?"

"Oh, I have no idea. I lost them long ago, if I ever had them."

"You need to try."

"Attack. Code. Better." His frown must mean I've gotten them wrong. "I have a question for you, if I may."

"What is it?" His tone is not inviting.

"What kind of music do you listen to?" Maybe we can find some common ground.

"I don't think that's relevant."

"Have you read *Musicophilia*?"

"No."

"Oliver Sacks would have been delighted if a patient asked him what kind of music he liked. Do you even know who Oliver Sacks is? Why don't you read *Musicophila*_and come back and talk to me when you're done?"

He turns to Lila and says, "You're her DPOA, right?" Oh no, more letters to untangle. "Could I speak to you privately for a minute?"

I would have objected but I'm exhausted and glad for a break. "Break." Was that one of the words I was supposed to remember? Would I get a chance to take the test over? I still have the goal of testing well enough to be rewarded with fewer drugs pumping into my IV, but right now a helicopter is slicing through my brain. I clamp my hands over my headphones, pressing them against my ears as I close my eyes and try not to seize.

I hear Lila's crutches as she goes out into the hall with Dr. Ng. Poor Lila. I don't want her to come to this horrible hospital that's so damn hard for her to get around in.. Maybe when I get out, of here we can go on vacation somewhere. Oh, I forgot, we never go on vacation. There's nowhere on Earth accessible for both of us. And if by some chance there is, we have no way to get to it. We've never had a vacation in all the time we'd been together.

When she comes back in I say, "It's so unfair we spend time in hospitals but no time on vacations. I just hate that we can't go somewhere wonderful and take pictures and look at them and remember our fantastic trip. So many couples have the opposite —lots of days spent on vacation, and no time spent in a hospital together. Or if they are in a hospital it's for something great, like having a baby."

"Yes, I know, it makes me sad, too, that we can't go on vacation," Lila says. "Honey, I want to tell you what Dr. Ng just told me."

"Yeah?"

"He thinks you have meningitis or maybe encephalitis or maybe both."

"Yeah, yeah, I know, that wavy-headed doctor who was here before told us the same thing. They want me to have a lumbar puncture just because they can't figure out what's wrong with me. But why should I do what Dr. Ng wants when he hasn't even read Oliver Sacks?"

"Meningitis is really serious and very treatable. I think you should have the lumbar puncture."

"I don't want it! I already have a migraine, why would I want it to get worse?"

She sighs. "Honey you're not making a lot of sense. They've given you some medication they think will help."

"What medication?"

"I'm not sure of the name. I think he said Respiradal, something like that." I think Wavy-hair said that too.

"What is it?"

"I don't know, Izzy." I sigh myself with frustration. Names of drugs isn't Lila's forte. "Ask Yvette when you talk to her. She might know what is it."

Are they consulting with Yvette about what medications to give me? She has my Medical Power of Attorney too, along with Sunshine and Lila. What about music, would any of these three women I love most in the world think to recommend that? What about sunlight and sleep and pure water to drink? What about turning off this stupid hospital bed that keeps shaking me and is way too complicated to figure out? "The EMFs in this place are killing me."

"Let me talk, okay?"

I probably don't let Lila have enough space to talk in general, but how can that be true when there's so much space, there's dimensions curled up on strings, and form is emptiness and emptiness is form, so why doesn't she just talk already? "Go ahead."

"Honey, a psychiatrist is going to be coming along any time now to evaluate you and adjust your medication."

"Do you mean how much Ativan I take?"

"No, not Ativan. Or maybe Ativan, I don't know, but this new stuff they have you on, the Risper —whatever it is."

"Why do they have me on that?"

"Because of the Altered Mental Status. Remember? AMS?"

"Oh yeah, they want to know about my altars." Wait, that isn't right.There's some other meaning of "altars" I should be thinking about. Maybe they think my mental status has changed for the better. Altered doesn't have to be bad. Altered mental status must mean alternative personalities, like in Multiple Personality Disorder. Hallie used to call her splits 'alters.' They probably think I have alters, not altars. Wow. Could it be true? I *have* lost track of time, I don't know anything about O'Connor Hospital. "How long was I at O'Connor?" I ask Lila.

"I don't know, a couple of days. Izzy, you might want to hold off on telling the psychiatrist about electromagnetic fields and just be careful how you talk about your headphones."

"I'm not supposed to talk about my headphones? I'm concerned about keeping track of them, it's like Manhattan in here."

"Izzy, what do you mean?"

"The noise level. Any big city will do. The shrink could be in here any minute. It's going to take a lot of discipline to remember all the things I'm not supposed to talk about. I guess I should be careful what I say to the nurses too.What's the date? Is the war over yet?"

"What war? What are you talking about?"

"Wouldn't it be great if all the wars were over? No more mountains of carcasses and sorrow. I guess that's too much to ask for, so what about us? Is the war over between Izzy and LilaTov?"

"Honey, we're not having a war. Why do you think that?"

"We had a really bad fight. I thought we might still be mad at each other, or maybe we forgot in the health crisis, and once I'm out of the hospital we'll remember."

"No, Izzy, we didn't have a fight. I'm telling you the truth, you know you can believe me. We had some tense conversations because I've been trying to get you to drink water and eat and take your meds, just like Yvette and Sunshine have. But none of us are fighting with you. There isn't any war."

"There is war, I'm sure about that. I mean, if you were Yoko Ono and you said, 'The war is over if you want it to be,' well then maybe I'd think there had been the great shift in consciousness that brings real peace, and I just need to catch up, but you're not Yoko Ono and here we are, trying to live our lives and make the world better and have a little fun now and again. Amy Goodman would have announced it if the wars were all over. Yvette would have heard it on *Democracy Now* and she would have told me, to cheer me up. DN wouldn't be the War and Peace report anymore, it would be 'All the Peace News All the Time.'"

I can tell I'm exhausting Lila."Why don't you go home to CousCous. Just make sure I call Billy on his birthday. I know it's in a few days. Did I get him something, do you know?" She reminds me about the Joshua Trees.

"I feel like I should tell him you're in the hospital," she says. "What do you think?" I haven't told him about having chest pains, he doesn't know I was hospitalized last week or the week before. I think I last talked to him a couple of weeks ago, that's when he told me he wanted the U2 CD for his birthday and I bought him the photography book about Joshua Tree National Park as well.

"Do you think I called him since I started getting sick?" I have no lists, no appointment books, no journals, no way to keep track of things. Everything keeps flying out of my mind.

"Not that I know of. Why don't you decide what you want me to tell him and I'll call, maybe tomorrow."

I encourage her again to go home. She kisses my forehead and I'm alone.

For a minute.

"You have a phone call." I don't know this nurse, but she's not wearing fragrances so I'm happy to be friendly to her. It's Yvette on the phone. I try to tell her about all the questions and the letters and the things I'm not supposed to talk about. "You sound confused," she says. I pound the telephone receiver onto the bed. I pound and pound, to take away her cruel words. I throw the phone as far from me as I can. When the nurse comes back I says, "Hang it up! If Yvette calls, I don't want to talk to her."

"Is something wrong?" the nurse asks.

"She said I sound confused. Yvette thinks confusion is on the same meridian as mental illness." I will not have Yvette deciding whether or not I'm confused. I hate her.

More noises blare through the room, "Beep, beep, beep. *Not confused. You are fucked. MPD.*

◆ ◆ ◆

Night, Aug. 31-Sept. 1 **Subterranean Trials**

I sink deep and I am low, deep in the basement of the hospital. I am in the sub-basement, the hospital below the hospital, so ultra-modern, I can't imagine what all the tubes pump into and out of me. I flow with the pain of it. I become the pain. I am incoherent. If I stop making sense, what do I then do with my senses? What do I make? What is 'coherent?' I will forgive the flesh upon the skeleton I am. I yearn for freedom but how can I be free here, in this chamber of imprisonment?

I look into an optometrists' huge golden scope as he examines my lives. We are in the ocean, we sail around the bay, we slip slide in time. Please, move me more slowly, this time travel unsettles me. There I am, in my eighties, weary of my life, yet desperate to finish the assignments of my incarnation/incarceration/inculcation . Who do I have? Lila? Nothing is given. Am I alone? Do I feel alone, although others are near? Now. I am alone in this moment. And what is there besides this moment? Someone may come, take me to the MRI chamber, where my mind will be shredded by the banging and the clanging. Someone always comes to inject drugs into me, derailing me to a place where Sleep Train has no station. One of the drugs, slipped into my IV, could stop my mind, like Atropine, the drug they used to stop my heart in order to speed it up. A drug to stop the mind to speed it up, can you handle it? What if you can't handle it? They'll want to police your fantasies. You will confess your craziness for just a bit of water. Sleep. Air.

In the tunnel, I am the old woman, my mother, but with no son to care. I dive easily into other people's dreams and there I swim my nights.

They come and take my pulse and blood pressure and I cannot even speak, I am so far away. Something is flushed; it is the sound of going away and I like that. Flushing in my veins is fire, but flushing in the toilet is relief. Something is being taken to where I can't see it, can't smell it, can't taste it. A door shutting is good; someone is going away. Someone who was bound to hurt me. They are finished here, for now.

It has been reported that I talked about my headphones. What a miracle I've hung on to them so long. They turn down the intensity, they muffle me. Cotton between me and the intruding presence. Ah, but they are leather, not cotton. I sweat into them so much I have to take them off and turn the ear cups so they can drain onto the floor. I wipe the leather, slick with my sweat, over and over.

I hunger for music and all they feed me is *beep beep beep*. I need resonance, deep vibratos and I get *Whoosh. Whop Whop.*

I need Chinese medicine charts, I need to study just how, by what meridians, confusion could lead to mental illness.

I am charged with committing mental illness. If this is the trial, what is the punishment if I am found guilty as charged?

◆ ◆ ◆

Sept. 3 **MRI Take One**

I open my eyes to a huge dome above my head. A white guy with long, dirty blond hair leans down in my face. “Hello there. Ready?”

“No. I’m not having it. I’m not going to have an MRI.” Okay, this is the guy I have to stop. One of him, one of me. I can do this.

“Sure, you are, it’ll be fine.”

“No, it won’t be fine. It’s too bright.”

“Just pretend it’s a sunny day at the beach.” How disgusting. I am not going to let him ruin Ocean for me.This is what the hieroglyphs on the side of the hospital bed were trying to warn me about. “Where’d the transport guys go? I can’t move you onto the MRI by myself.”

I take a breath. “I’m not going to get onto or into the MRI. You might as well go on to some other customer because I don’t want what you’re selling.”

He’s obviously pissed. Let *him* mark ‘non-compliant’ on my chart. Dirty-haired asshole. “Let’s just get this done. It’s nothing, they’re just going to take your picture.”

Yeah right. “I’ve had a MRI before, I know what it is. I can’t handle the noise, it will give me seizures.”

“Ah, come on, nobody’s ever had a seizure in a MRI machine before. Didn’t they give you something before you got here?”

Lots of somethings. “I’m not taking any more Dilantin either. I’m too dilated already.”

“Funny. You’ve still got your sense of humor, you’ll be fine. Let’s get this over with.”

"I told you, I'm not going to help you move me. How many guys are you going to have to find to get me off this bed and onto that thing if I don't cooperate?" Fat power!

"Lady, I don't have time for this." He stinks of bad breath and bad coffee.

"Exactly. You've got a list of stuff you've got to do, patients you've got to torture. Just go on to the next one."

"All right, I'm sending for transport. You know they're going to send you back again for the MRI, if someone ordered it. Hopefully it won't be on my shift. I'm trying to work with you here, but I DO have patients to help, who aren't going to accuse me of torturing them."

We do not speak in the minutes or hours until Transport comes back for me.

"She done here?" the first guy asks.

"Yeah, she's done, all right," dirty blond hair says. "You guys can have her."

◆ ◆ ◆

September 4 Surveillance in Chamber 67B

"I've come to check your groin wound," the relief nurse announces, not even introducing herself. She did flash her multicolored lights on my ID bracelet, I guess she thought that was introduction enough. I flung my arm over my eyes when she did it. "Keep your arms by your sides. You're making your IV infiltrate."

"I really don't want you to check my groin wound," I tell her. "Kim can do it when he comes back. And I don't want any Dilantin, either."

"I'm writing down that you refuse to cooperate. I warmed up your breakfast for you, I heard you didn't get any in ICU, but you can eat now." She brings the tray near me; it reeks of bacon and coffee. "Oh, take it away," I say, covering my mouth. "I'm allergic to coffee, I don't eat meat. The whole tray is nauseating me, just, please, take it away. Don't they have written down somewhere that I'm a vegetarian?"

"I wouldn't know about that." She's pissed. "I'm putting it over here by the window. When they come with your lunch they'll take it then. What about getting cleaned up, are you going to refuse that too?"

I want to be clean, but I don't want her touching me. "No. Yes. Maybe later."

"I'm writing down that you're refusing everything. What about a bi-pap?"

Did I have one before? At Stanford. "Maybe I could talk to the Respiratory Therapist about that."

"I'm sure she'd appreciate it if you got cleaned up first."

"If lunch hasn't even come yet, don't I have some time to decide about the bi-pap?"

The nurse turns and walks out. Tears swim in my eyes as I watch her go. Someone offered to clean me—well, offered isn't exactly the right word. Wouldn't I rather have a woman do it than Kim, if and when he has time after his break?

There's some reason I didn't want to get cleaned, not yet. It's because... it's because I have to figure out why I lie in my own waste before I can wash up. Someone must have cleaned me up some time since I got here. Assuming I can find a nurse who doesn't hate me, why am I cautious about it?

Okay, I can figure this out if I make a list. I can't see, I don't have anything to write with or on, so how am I going to do that? Let me try on my fingers.

1. I smell so bad I'm making myself sick.

2. Lila will react even more strongly than I do to my bad smells.

3. The soaps here smell bad and are probably toxic.

4..............

I'm forgetting things, I have to start a new list. Maybe it will work better if do it on my toes. I lift my left foot in the air.

S -o -a -p. T -o -x- i- c -

?

What else did I need to write down? Write up?

"What the hell is she doin'?" comes a voice from across the room. Who is speaking? Does she mean me? I put my foot back down in the bed. "That patient over there," the same voice continues. "Is she loony or somethin'?"

"Just ignore her," the nurse who hates me says. "I'll close the curtain between your bed and hers, so we don't have to look at her."

"But what the hell's wrong with her?" the other voice continues. "What was she doin' with her foot? First she had her hands up in the air, like she was learnin' to count or somethin', then she stuck her foot up in the air and started movin' it around. Am I on the nut ward?"

Oh God, I'm scaring another patient into thinking she's crazy. *I'm sorry*, I think at her. *Whoever you are, I'm not trying to disturb you.*

"Oh man," the curtain is drawn, but I can still hear her. "Now I think she's tryin' to creep into my mind and talk to me. Is she psychic or somethin'?"

"No, you're just upset because of what you saw her doing before," the nurse reassures her.

I have to be careful what I say and even what I think when the nurses and doctors - or anybody, for that matter - are in the room. Complaints about my odd behavior will get me put in the 'nut ward' for sure. But haven't I always been odd?

A brown skinned man in his fifties comes into the room, goes over to my TV. "Is this 67B?"

Something in me cautions me not to admit it. "What are you doing?" I ask instead.

"I came to fix your TV."

"Nothing's wrong with my TV." How do I know? "I don't want to watch TV," I add, truthfully.

"Well, one of your doctors wanted me to set this up."

Why would one of my doctors want me to watch TV? I'll bet it was that psychiatrist. Can they force me to watch TV? what if they're using the TV to watch me? Maybe they want to do the lumbar puncture on me and video it.

The TV man calls over to the mean nurse. "I'm supposed to install this for Isabella Patricia. Is this 67B?"

"Yes," she answers. "You have the right bed."

What does he mean *for* me?

He's gone before I get it together to say anything to him. Is the camera on now?

I close my eyes and pull the sheet over my head. I still need to make a list. I wiggle my fingers a tiny bit. Can they see that on the TV? I have to come back out for air; my stink is unbearable.

And with that thought in comes Lila, on one of the hospital wheelchairs. "Hi. How are you feeling today?"

"Smelly," I say, then beckon her semi-close. I don't want to talk loud but she shouldn't have to endure my stench. "I'm so sorry. I keep wanting to get cleaned up but it doesn't happen."

"Well, this ought to help." She opens her backpack. I lean forward, trying to make out what she's brought me.

"It's Dr. Bronner's soap," she says. "I thought you'd like that."

She opens a plastic bag and takes out a bottle with the familiar blue label: Dr. Bronner's Unscented Baby Soap. Finally, I have that piece of the puzzle of how to get clean. "You don't know how grateful I am for this," I tell her. "How can I ever thank you?"

She smiles and chuckles and I know the answer to that one. Take a shower! Or at least a sponge bath now that I've got the right soap. "I wish I could promise I'll smell better the next time you come. I can promise to try, but so many unexpected things keep happening to me here. The white woman nurse who's on duty now really doesn't like me, so try not to ask her for anything. I'm not getting the right food, I'm not getting good water, I'm not getting good sleep. I was offered a bi-pap today, but I'm not sure I want one. I keep saying I'm allergic to Dilantin, but what's in my IVs?"

"I don't know what's in your IVs." Isn't that her job, as my Power of Attorney for medical decisions? "Why don't you want a bi-pap?"

"I feel so restrained already. They keep telling me not to move my arms because I'll screw up the IVs. The idea of having a mask over my face and not being able to just pull it off is scary. Don't you think so?"

"I probably wouldn't like it, either. Don't get mad, honey. I was just trying to understand."

"I'm not mad at you. Does my voice sound mad?"

"Sometimes it does. I understand you're going through a lot." She pauses and adds, "I love you."

"I love you too but it's hard to talk to you sometimes. I don't think you believe half the things I say and I need you to believe me. If you can't believe me now when it counts how am I ever going to be able to trust you?"

Before she can answer, lunch is brought in by someone I neither know nor am at war with. I look around the tray for something to eat and find the piece of paper from the kitchen. "Let's see what it's supposed to be. 'Mixed veg - pur. Pot. mash. Beef bullion, cottage cheese, coffee, 1 pat butter.'" Plastic utensils in a clear plastic bag, packets of salt, pepper and sugar. "I wonder if this is their version of vegetarian."

Lila makes a face. "That's really terrible."

"I know. That's what I mean. I can't seem to get the basics together here at this hospital." I look around the tray some more. "This," I decide, holding the piece of paper up to my face, "is the best part of the meal."

"I hope you're not going to try to eat it," Lila says. I hope she's kidding.

"No. It's very useful though. It tells me my room number, my name, the name of this stupid hospital, which I never can seem to get right, my date of birth, the date, the meal - it says 'lunch' for this one, and what they supposedly sent me. So I know that other than the soup, they didn't actually give me any meat. And sometimes I do need to need help with the day of the week and stuff like that. It's good to have it all in one place. It's a list!" Where can I stash the lunch crib sheet so I can study it? Sooner or later someone is bound to come along and quiz me on just this material.

"Have you eaten at all since you got here?"

"I must have, don't you think? Or maybe I've been getting nutrition in my IVs. But no, they would have put in a feeding tube."

"Do you feel any better at all today, honey?"

I try to remember how I felt before today. "Maybe." I want to feel better, for Lila as well as myself. "Oh my gosh, I have to tell you something important!"

"What is it?"

I glance at the television, try to figure out how to get out of its range. Maybe if the curtains were drawn around the bed it would block the camera, but I don't think Lila can reach them. "Try to come over here." I point to the area near the head of the bed. We clumsily move the overbed tray, and I do my best to turn away from the TV. "I think I'm being recorded," I whisper. "Videorecorded."

Lila turns her head, looks around. "Oh Izzy, I don't think so. Why do you think that?"

"Some guy came in and messed with my TV this morning." I tell her the rest, but I can see she's skeptical. "This is what I mean about you not believing me. Anyway, I don't even want TV. People keep trying to tell me about terrible things that happened in some place that starts with V that's around here. But I don't want to know, and if TV was on, I'd be hearing about it."

I can tell from her face Lila knows about the terrible thing in V but she keeps silent. "Why don't you tell me about CousCous?" I suggest.

We hold hands and she soothes me with silly little cat stories.

After Lila leaves the nurse who doesn't like me comes back in. "Is Kim back from his break yet?" I hope.

"He's with another patient," she says as she examines my IVs, touching my arm where it is red and puffy. "It's infiltrating. I know you've been picking at it. You're picking at your monitor leads, too. Now I'm going to have to change the IV."

That sounds like a bad idea. "Do you think you could possibly get a phlebotomist to do it? My veins are difficult.."

"I don't have time for a difficult IV insertion. I'll call the lab and get someone down here."

"Thank you."

She leaves and I look at my TV, still not turned on. Is that a red light glowing? Maybe I'm being surveilled other ways as well.

What about the oxygen? Do my thoughts go into the cannula, and then to some other part of the hospital where they're analyzed?

A helicopter buzzes overhead. I put my headphones tight on my ears. The men in the helicopter are talking about me. "She's got the phones on, but she can still hear us," one says.

"What are we supposed to do about it?" another asks.

Nothing, I think at them. *Just go on about your business.* The helicopter buzzing can't stop any more than the sirens. All noises which have to do with saving lives must continue, no matter how much they hurt.

"We've got a multiple vehicle collision near Mt. Hamilton, we're coming in to the heliport. A woman in one of the cars went into labor. Her blood pressure's through the roof"

Maybe they could not give quite so much detail about the injuries, I suggest to the dispatcher at the hospital, or the police station, or wherever my thoughts go. *I understand they have to notify the hospital about who's coming in, but if they could do it in a language other than English that would be really helpful.*

"Did you guys hear that?" the dispatcher asks.

"What if we don't speak no language but English?" one of them laughs.

Then try to talk really fast, and I'll try not to understand you.

How does communication happen around here, anyway? That is what I desperately need to figure out.

I look at the television. It really doesn't make that much difference. Everything I do and think seems to be broadcast to somebody. I curl up into myself, wishing I was anywhere else.

◆ ◆ ◆

September 5 **MRI Take 4**

"We're Transport. Ready to go?" Actually I am. I've offended a nurse by oversharing and don't know how to make it okay. Better I should just move on to another floor. Dr. Chen said I'd be transitioning to somewhere else. Transport transitions me.

"Yes, I'm ready. I'm done transitioning, on to the metamorphosis."

The one who hadn't spoken yet says, "Metamorphosis. Are you a butterfly?"

"More like a butterfly wannabe, still in the chrysalis stage. No idea how I'm going to turn out, but butterfly would be good. I'm looking forward to the day I fly away."

We move out of my room, past the desk and out of Transitional Care. Will I ever be anywhere the staff and I actually like each other, or at least followed the conventions of communication, whatever they are at this hospital? Maybe I'm being transferred to a unit with no surveillance.

We turn through the wide hallways to the huge elevator with the padded walls. I'm never sure what they're supposed to be protecting.

My stomach swirls with the rapid descent. Plunk, down to the ground, and then we're out in another hall. I close my eyes, and put the sheet up over my nose as we approach a cleaning cart. Then it gets much noisier.

"Where are we?" I ask, trying to sit up. Oh fuck, I think I know.

"We just have to come down to the ED. The machine you need is down here."

"What machine I need?" I raise myself up higher, but it's not like I can make them stop. "Why are you taking me to the -- ED -- that's Emergency Department, right?"

"Why you getting so upset? You was mellow, now you're all agitated."

And here we are, back to dirty long blond hair guy. "I'm not having an MRI," I tell him.

"I figured you might say that," he says. Then to the transport guys, "You can go now, but stay close by."

"Hey, we got another call," one says. "You know how to call transport, you just do it when you're done with her." And I'm alone with dirty hair guy. I do not want to know his name.

"We're just going to keep doing this if you don't cooperate." The sickly sweet smell of his Juicyfruit gum attacks me. "Your doctors keep ordering an MRI. It only lasts a few minutes, what's the big deal?"

"I know what it's like," I tell him, for what must be the umpteeth time. "I had one at Stanford. The neurologist talked me through it, and I had plenty of sedation."

"Well, I got some more of that right here," he says, and shows me an ampoule of clear liquid. "Since your Stanford neurologist explained an MRI to you already, since you yourself have HAD one already, all you need is to relax. Like they say, if something is inevitable, lie back and enjoy it. Or enjoy the drugs at least."

"I know where that quote comes from; the original was 'if RAPE is inevitable, lie back and enjoy it.' Do you really think you're making things better, saying shit like that? Why do they always bring me down for an MRI when it's your shift anyway?" I feel the familiar burn into my vein. "What is that, more Ativan?"

"Lady, everything I say pisses you off. I'm trying to be nice, but it's impossible to be nice to you."

"I'm not having the MRI. You say the doctor keeps ordering it. Which doctor?"

He looked at the order. "Dr. Chen, Dr. Ng, Dr. Grey. You recognize those names? I'm just trying to do my job. What I just gave you is better than Ativan. Now we wait for it to take effect. Since you're so nasty, I'll go do something else."

As he walks away I feel the not-Ativan coming on and with it I lose control of my bowels. *Is this going to be my life at this hospital, arguing with this obnoxious, sexist kid, insisting on my right not to have an MRI, while wearing a shitty diaper? How many times do I have to do this?* I don't know who I'm asking, but no one answers. No one at all.

◆ ◆ ◆

September 8 **Peace Discords**

I am in a new room, alone, with no infiltrations, no beeping on my monitors, no TV. My peace ends when the psychiatrist comes in. I've forgotten her name, but I know she's the one who has the most questions for me, with the most penalties when I get them wrong.."Hello Patricia. How are you today?"

"Tired."

We go through the same old orientation questions."How do you think you're doing today?"

"In terms of what?"

"Mentally. Do you feel more like yourself?"

I consider the question. Would it even be possible to feel like myself while I was in this hospital? "I'm still trying to integrate fantasy and reality."

"What do you mean by that?"

"I thought it was a pretty clear sentence."

"Well, I'd appreciate it if you'd explain what you meant."

I've probably said too much already. "You know I can't remember ever telling you something and being glad afterwards."

Sounds like you're not so happy with me."

"Does that mean I get another psychiatrist?"

"You've asked me that before. Same answer."

◆ ◆ ◆

September 10 **MRI Taken**

The dark blue shirt men come again. Will they return me to the hell realms? I have so little fight left in me. "Where are we going?" I try to say, but the words come out so garbled even I can't understand them. No one answers me anyway. There's so much more I'd wanted to do in this lifetime. There's so much more I thought I would do. I've given up the dreams of my able-bodied twenties and thirties, but old and fat and disabled, I still want more. I try to find the part of me that survived so much so well, but I cannot.

We fly through the hospital again. Into the elevator, going down, down too fast. The hallway is cold, I don't have my headphones, I don't have a mask.

Noises. Smells. Assault. What could I have possibly done to deserve such punishment?

It's the dirty long-haired blond guy again. "Are you always here?" Maybe he's a windigo.

"Listen, I understand better now. I got in the machine and had a short MRI myself. Actually I freaked out and they had to stop it." I wonder what he did to get them to stop. I wish he'd tell me that, I could use the information. " It's really tight in there. But they gave you Haldol, so you should be all right this time. And I'm giving you this ball to squeeze."

He places a rubber ball in my hands. It reminds me of the bulb of some old-fashioned home medical device for blowing air in your ear. The rubber feels slippery and hostile to my fingers.

"Just hold it on your chest. You can squeeze it if it gets to be too much."

He's trying to be nice, a voice inside me says, but I don't give a shit. I hate him, I hate this hospital, and I hate myself for not being able to prevent this damned MRI.

He thinks the problem is just claustrophobia. Who came up with Haldol as a treatment for claustrophobia?

Two? three? guys lift me from the gurney to the MRI machine. The hood looms above me. Blond guy is still there, still talking to me. "Are you going to tell me the part about a sunny day at the beach?" I ask.

"I was just trying to help.". It's probably true. I hate him anyway, I helplessly hate him. I'm going to die in an MRI machine. What bardo will THAT put me in? "I'm trying to help now." I consider again that he may not be real, or at least not human. Am I hallucinating him? Why is he always here whenever they try to give me an MRI? "You're going to hear some noises."

"Your description is not soothing, even if you are trying to help."

His face is right over me, and he blows his dirty bangs up away from his forehead. "Here goes," he says. "Yvette loves you."

What the fuck? Why did he say that? How does he know about Yvette? This guy MUST be a hallucination. This is a nightmare and I'm ready to wake up.

The giant hood comes to devour me, comes to steal my soul.

The banging begins. I jump. More banging. I will seize, I will surely seize if this continues. I will seize and seize and seize and never come back. Who would notice in time? Who would care? Dirty blond hallucination guy? I squeeze the ball. Nothing happens. Did he say they would stop if I squeezed it? He just said I could. So what?

I am sinking. I am sinking into addiction. All addictions. My father pouring whiskey into my formula. My taste for it. Like Daddy, I want to be like Daddy. I want more. There is not enough whiskey in the world to make it okay to be me. The delicious Irish curse.

I scream. I was so young, before words, only screams as the whiskey coursed through my baby brain. Trying so hard to learn, to form the pathways, to calibrate, to develop. I only wanted to be free. I always only wanted to be free. And I locked the doors to keep myself in. Just as the whiskey jolted my brain, locked me in. The whiskey and the phenobarbital the doctor prescribed after the big seizure, did they war or did they collude? Down. Down down down down. I scream.

It is not delicious. It is nauseating, headache-making. It makes the world go sideways. The phenobarbital slows me. Hard to pee, to shit, to breathe. Is this the first death? No, that must have happened when I had the measles and the seizure and the fever. This is the protracted death. This is learning to be addicted to death. Daddy, Daddy, why did you do it to me? Mommy, where were you, why did you let him? They were my parents, all I could do was love them. Hate them. Love them.

I would not be an Irish drunk. Somewhere in my child soul I decided that. I'd take the propensity for addiction and put it somewhere else.

Bad boys. Bad girls. Driving too fast, courting the risk, living for it. Dying for a taste. Wild child.

Marijuana. Sister comforter. We always said it was not addictive, we were so superior to our parents, hooked on alcohol. If marijuana was good, hashish was better. If hash was better, opium was best. Oh, I remember, walking in the snow, holding hands with Natasha, outlaw drug, outlaw sex.

It was the time of Janis and Jimi and Jim Morrison. I smoked a joint with Jimi when I lived in the Haight. Did I die with him? With her? With him? I scream. We never knew what was in our dope. Not like now, when breeders cultivate, cross-breed cannabis with such precision, such dedication to the highest high.

And then when Natasha went on from opium to heroin. Oh, I was freaked. But I felt her high. I fucked her high. I thought junkies didn't want sex, but when she shot up, her smoky cunt in my mouth, as she chased/we chased/I chased the dragon. Tie me off, Natasha. Tie me off. Do me. Take me there.

Tie me up. Take me to the secret places I cannot tell, but I do. Make me come against my will. My will, what the hell is that? What was so exciting just last month, didn't get me off tonight. We called it getting heavier. We called it learning to hear the high notes.

Simone and Ecstasy. Put on *Barcelona*, fucking to rock opera. Letting the high notes soar through me. Follow the music to hard sex, to

Byzantine curlicues of kink. Let me die to it with Freddie Mercury. Dead Can Dance.

Addictions, compulsions. Is there a difference? Does it matter? These distinctions give the makers of the DSMs something to do, gradations to quantify, medicate, propagate. When I talk and talk, what is that? When I yearn for ecstasy, what is that?

When I come hard, ecstatic, out of stasis, I seize. Is that a blessing or a curse? Why was I not born into a culture which would revere me for it, rather than pathologize me?

Alcohol. Cigarettes. Marijuana. Food. Exercise. Cutting. Fucking. Lying. Shopping. Computer games. Gambling.

The car accidents. The guns. The robberies, the beatings. The yearning to be hit. The mixing of booze and pills and mystery injections. Well, I got that last one now, without the thrill. Is the thrill the core of the addiction? The thrill, then the dulling, the inability to stop. Chasing the snake. I scream.

Mind, go now, go far away from this awful tunnel with its ceaseless banging. Ex-smokers say heaven is a place where you can smoke all you want. No consequences.

The yearning to die. I know that one. Sylvia Plath and Anne Sexton made poetry of it, competing with each other to see who'd get there first. Death, the ever-faithful, ever-potent lover.

And now I am on my way to meet her. Him. Them. I have always been. On my way.

Work the System

A Memoir by Michael Scott Monje, Jr.

I have recently begun working with a gender therapist. We don't talk about multiple selves, but I can't ignore the fact that she keeps using a few of the same words when she describes me back to me. System. Complex.

Multiple. Divergence. System. Complicated. Multiplicity. Complex. Complicated. System.

I don't believe in coincidence. I do believe that the subverbal selves that make choices do not always inform our language-oriented selves. I think my therapist realizes this. I am never sure, with people who have psychological training, whether they have connected their subverbal selves with their language selves. I can never be sure if they are simply imitating me, to see if I am genuine, or if they have opened up to the fact that there is no such thing as a singular "I" for anyone who has a working knowledge of social perceptions.

No one has said Lynn yet. No one has mentioned Athena. We have talked, though, about Michael as a girl's name. Or Mychal. We have also talked about the fact that I do have performance personas that use other names, and about the fact that these roles might grow as I do, that they might hold promise as a step in my transitional state. She understands gender fluidity. She understands that I don't view myself on the binary. She seems surprised that I don't separate autistic perceptions or autism from my sense of self, but impressed at the sensory-social diet I pursue to achieve balance.

She is a reflecting-pool. I don't know what she really thinks, but she tells me about the fact that I can go to a gender clinic in Chicago tomorrow and sign an informed consent if I don't want to wait for the letter recommending a general practitioner start me on hormones. As I describe my reasons for wanting a physician's oversight, I am honest, but I am also aware that telling me I can have unsupervised access to the drugs I want is another evaluation. I wonder how much of my response is assumed to be awareness of that fact, since I haven't really tried to hide my own prior knowledge.

Part of me wonders when she will just ask how many of us there are. Part of me wonders what the correct answer is. Three? Athena, Clay (formerly Mike), and Michael all exist without their own origin stories. Some of them remember times without the others, so I have a rough order and time of emergence, but none of them feel like they are in control of the others. I would fight anyone who characterizes their shared existence as “disorder.” The oldest of them, in outside time, is now the youngest because of life experience, maturation, and years spent dormant.

There’s also Lynn, though. Lynn is a construct, and the others made her intentionally, to prove they could reproduce in a genuine, organic way, without using trauma to cleave a new piece of the self. Lynn was originally designed to help translate Athena’s feelings and images out to the rest of the world, so we worked on teaching her how to communicate from both sides at once, and it worked. Lynn was intentional, and once her natural dictions emerged and established themselves apart from her translations of Athena, she began to work with us to describe our process. *The US Book* was the result.

That brings us to four, but if you read *The US Book*, you will find that there is also Monday, that brings us to five. We also have the hybrid Lynn Michaels, a synthesis, and through her ability to render Athena’s will into words and Michael’s life experience and social knowledge, we do fairly well. This is allowing Athena to experience more time directly working with the body, because communication is handled, and it tempers our mood and judgment.

There is also a thing that can happen, though, when we are lucky and healthy and happy at once. At those times, we fully synthesize, and there is a level of awareness and information processing that allows me to take in information in my ears in both verbal and musical ways while participating through song or speech, and also coordinating my hands to type. These moments mark a sixth kind of self for us, a harmonious over-self in which each of us has the ability to access the body for our ends, and none of us conflict.

These periods are short-lived, but they are getting longer, and they are unique in that they are times when I know Athena is able to communicate directly through fingers because I can not hear the keyboarding in my head as the language is made. At all other times, including now as I write this, Lynn speaks what she sees and we type it out according to whoever is controlling the hands (usually actually Athena). In the synthesis, some of which is described in *The US Book*, we find moments where we are not a single being, and yet we are, in our motion, a singular entity.

Right now, that still feels like a Michael. Who knows, though? Perhaps she will find a new name for herself as she gets strong enough to remain at the front to manage things. Sometimes, I wonder what it will be like for that to fall into place as a new way of being. Sometimes, I wonder if it's a change I will be capable of noticing. - December 2015

Postscript: It was. - March 2017

The Rugged Beauty of Creating a Neuroqueer Space

Marrok Zenon Sedgwick

I'm sitting in the passenger seat of my car. My friend Reilly is driving. We're coming home from seeing a fantastically leftist activist play by the San Francisco Mime Troupe. It is the kind of theatre that I want to make, although my focus is on disabled and queer people. Because my friend is driving, I'm communicating mostly with my Talker. Turning to see me sign means his eyes aren't on the road, and neither of us have a death wish. My voice has shut down because I feel so full. Or fulfilled? Is that the word I want? As I'm typing into my Talker, I realize that I'm typing out some form of pidgin English that's partly ASL gloss. I just roll with it. As our drive continues and I start to cool down from the love I am feeling (is that the source of the fullness?) I start to feel like I can get some words out. Knowing that disability is not accepted in my home, and that it would be best if I can speak by the time I get there, I start trying to say the things I'm thinking before typing them. I manage to sputter out a random couple words, waving my hands around, half stim and half sign, before turning back to my Talker to type out what I actually wanted to say. Try as I might, I cannot figure out how to explain to Reilly the beauty that he has brought into my life and the full feeling that stops my voice in its tracks every time I try to tell him.

My first entrance into a truly queer space was at the 2015 Pennsylvania Youth Action Conference, during the final semester of my final year of college. As I entered the wing of the Pennsylvania college that was hosting the conference I was met with my first signal that this space was different: a laminated card declaring the restroom to be an all gender restroom. A burst of joy and relief washed over me. I wouldn't have to feel the strange discomfort that came over me every time I used a women's restroom. We headed up the stairs to the location of the beginning event, and I glanced at my phone. After a quick introduction with the hosts, I headed back to the hotel to get some sleep.

My particular forms of neurodivergence demand a regular sleep schedule. While I have since discovered that occasionally I can cheat, cheating the night before the actual conference would make it harder for me to participate--and participating in an all day conference was always hard on my brain. Prior to this moment, the solution presented to me by my doctors had been to avoid participating in conferences or anything like them. Avoiding participation in spaces that catered to my other identities was hard on my soul. I didn't know it at the time, but isolation from other trans and pansexual people was eating away at my sense of self. My need to leave without participating in the night's event was met not with the usual disdain or annoyance, but with a kind of disappointed understanding--disappointed that they would not get to know me tonight, but supportive of my needs. Another burst of joy and relief accompanied me to bed.

The following day we were treated to a host of breakout sessions and lectures. I took careful notes, but what I didn't realize was happening that was most important was the culture I was being submerged in for the first time. A queer space is different from a gay space. I'd been in gay spaces before, and perhaps even in a space I might think of as trans. These spaces were marked by their animosity towards the other. The gay spaces were filled by people (most of them homosexual) who held animosity towards heteronormativity and often heterosexual people. Some gay spaces are also hostile towards bisexuals or transgender people. The trans space was a space that I saw as filled with a kind of angst that makes me uncomfortable. The angst of people who have been abandoned by others, and come together over the animosity that abandonment breeds. Perhaps these spaces are valuable to others (who am I to judge?), but for me they are not spaces of healing. They are spaces where open wounds are poked and prodded until they fester.

Queer spaces are spaces in which people share values that defy the oppression and abandonment that most of us have experienced. The most central value that has come to define the queer spaces I have encountered has been radically supporting others in their self-definition. There is one other space that I can describe that way--another space that makes a concerted effort to allow people to self define and to actively support its members no matter what that self definition is. That space is the neurodiversity and autistic rights movement. While these are definitely two separate movements, they overlap such that in my interaction with them one is never divided from the other, and so for the purposes of this essay I will refer to them as one space.

This intersection of culture afforded me one of the most surprising and beautiful moments of my life. I must preface that with the statement that I am terrible at making friends. This is a product both of my neurodivergence (specifically because I am Autistic) and the nature of the bullying and abuse that I received as a teenager due to being different (read: neurodivergent and trans). In a space (the Pennsylvania Youth Action Conference) where a young trans woman felt comfortable removing her wig because she knew her self definition would be respected and she'd be seen for the woman she was regardless of her outward physical appearance, I felt too comfortable not to state my needs. Stating my needs in a direct fashion is natural to my brain.

I encountered a young man named Caelan. I'm not exactly sure how we ended up having a conversation at first. Typically, I just jump right in to the conversation without introducing myself or asking for the other person's name. I just talk, and if they keep listening eventually maybe they will be like, "By the way, I'm..." When we hit that point in the conversation, given that this was a queer conference, we also exchanged pronouns. Caelan said his name and that he uses he/him pronouns. I have no idea what pronouns I offered him for me, but somehow we ended up having lunch together.

Lunch was in a cafeteria--one of the least Autism-friendly places neurotypicals form. There was a moment of concern, but then I remembered where I was--I remembered the safety in testing out new ways of being in a space in which self definition was the central cultural value. So I explained to him that I will not recognize him because I have prosopagnosia, so when we split up to pick out our respective lunches, he would need to find me and wave at me or something to indicate it was him. I also asked him if we could pick a place to meet and then walk together to a table. There was a slight pause and he said okay, and our plan went off without a hitch.

This almost seems like a non-story--I asked for an accommodation and received it without question. Because I received that accommodation, I was able to interact with a human being and make a new friend that I still value to this day. But the fact that it feels like a non-story is what makes it monumental, not just for my life, but for understanding the intersection of neurodivergence and queerness--for understanding what it is to be neuroqueer. In order to have a cultural space (or a social one, a physical one, etc) that is queer you must have a space where self definition is celebrated. Celebration in gay culture often looks like a party, but that is only one way to celebrate who you are. Celebration in queer culture is having all gender restrooms--in setting them up as if they are normal, without being asked. Celebrating queer culture is listening to the needs of those around you and respecting them, whether those needs are pronouns that might not be self evident in a heteronormative society, or disability needs.

The space I encountered at the Youth Action Conference allowed me to be me. Looking back on it, I don't recall seeing any visibly disabled participants. Many of us (disabled people) don't attend events unless they are declared to be disability friendly (usually because all the advertisements will specifically state that persons with disabilities are encouraged and can request accommodations). Many of us simply can't attend events because they are not accessible by public transportation or they are too expensive for someone living on a fixed income. These are realities that I have the privilege not to be confined by, and while I cannot speak with any real authority on why I did not encounter any visibly disabled people at that conference, I can state with complete certainty that disability accessibility is more than wheelchair ramps and elevators, and most of the queer spaces I encounter have noticeable flaws.

It is through my artistic practice (my goal is to build a community arts center) that I have begun to create a disability-friendly, neuroqueer space. It is through my most recent art project that I met a new-old friend, Reilly. I was recently inspired to create a documentary about some families who have rearranged the meaning of family to be inclusive of LGBT identities in novel, beautiful ways. My formal training is in theater and anthropology, so my understanding of storytelling and information gathering was sufficient to create such a project, but my knowledge of filmmaking equipment was basically zilch. As I mulled this idea around in my mind, it occurred to me that my Deaf friend's son used to be interested in filmmaking, and while I did not actually know whether he was still making movies, or whether he would be interested in making a documentary, I figured it wouldn't hurt to ask. He said yes, and a partnership was born.

I see other disabled people on the street, marked by their mobility tools, by their beautifully asymmetrical bodies, by their AAC devices, white canes, or their use of signed languages. I see them and I feel a comfort in knowing that person knows to some extent what it is like to be me and I feel a warmth in comradery even if I don't speak to them. It is that feeling of warmth in seeing me that I hope other disabled people feel, whether they identify as disabled or not. I make a point in spreading disability rights information everywhere I go, and that is the warmth and activism that I have intentionally been sharing with Reilly every chance I get. And since he has a good heart and comes from a household where communication is by nature different, we have together created a disability friendly space in our artistic practice as filmmakers.

Reilly is a gay man, and while I don't know that he identifies as disabled, certainly a non-disabled person would look at him and think of him as a person with a disability. I am a disabled transmasculine person who is pansexual. In order to succeed in our endeavor to create a full-length documentary film in four months with only one other person helping us, by nature we had to create a space where self definition is marked with respect--where we feel comfortable asking for accommodations, whether for our bodies' needs or our gender/sexual minority needs. This neuroqueer space has bled into our friendship and this is the foundation on which our journey to San Francisco sits.

I asked Reilly if he could drive us when we were planning the trip. We filled up the car with other friends, one of whom is my Autistic friend from sign language class (I'd been taking ASL for a year in order to give me an alternate method of communication when I couldn't speak). We arrive at a lecture by a Deaf trans man and I am struck by its accessibility. Not only because most of the people there can sign (always a plus for me, even though I sign like a three-year-old child), but because of the nature of interpreting. Drago would pause for the interpreter (who was interpreting his signing into English) to correct errors. Drago and his interpreter would pause for the interpreters signing for a Deaf-Blind person to switch (so one of them could rest). I could sign with Reilly and my classmate if my voice got stuck, but most importantly I was testing a new piece of adaptive equipment: a text-to-speech app on a tablet device with which I could communicate to those people in our party who could not sign. I was also wearing a set of communication cards with basic statements including everything from "Yes" to emergency information to "I am not drunk, I have a neurological disability that sometimes makes my gait weird." I am also wearing noise-reducing headphones to try to minimize the overstimulation, and carrying stim toys that I can use to self-regulate when needed.

My Autistic friend of course is part of the same community that I am, and so the use of all of these tools are not at all strange to them, but the other people with us are perhaps less aware of the tools of the trade. Reilly, as the most outgoing and gregarious of the group, is the first to react to each of these things, and in every case he reacts as if these are typical tools to have around. His reaction clearly leads his friend's reaction and the space becomes--by virtue of my simply working to meet my needs and Reilly's acceptance of the ways I am meeting those needs--a neuroqueer space. Testing my needs out in this environment--in an environment in which I am with other people who are queer and disabled--meant that I could participate fully in an event that I would not otherwise have been able to participate in. Being one of those rare highly social, extroverted Autistics, Reilly and I spent the whole day joking and having fun, even while our friends in the back seat of the car became exhausted and ready for sleep.

My confidence in those around me--and in myself--swelled exponentially. For the first time in my life, I was able to spend all day in the city, to fully participate, to enjoy myself the whole way through, and all of this has been possible because I've been able to have all my needs met without judgment. I had access to all the tools I needed, and I wasn't scorned for using them. It was a beautiful day, and because of it, I started using my tools in other areas of my life.

A few weeks later, this meant going to San Francisco Pride. I had never been able to attend an event that had that many people participating in that small a space. Because of a mysterious, growing mobility issue that at the time I was assuming was sensory-related but which I am now thinking might have nothing to do with the disabilities I already have, I was using all of the old tools, plus some walking sticks (which have since been replaced by elbow crutches). I am there with Reilly and a friend of his I haven't met before, but once again, since Reilly is responding to my use of these tools as if they are as quotidian as apple pie at a diner, his friend Ashley is also non-plussed. I am participating. I can't seem to make words come out of my mouth, but I can sign them or type them out on what I've taken to calling my Talker.

San Francisco Pride is not a queer space, and it is not a disability friendly space. Finding other trans people slowly becomes a more and more frantic search for me. Reilly gets caught up with some obnoxiously ableist people who want to stand on one corner looking for passersby to steal a hot dog from (no, really, I'm not making that up) and aren't taking me seriously when I ask to go looking for trans people. The woman is talking to me like I'm a baby telling me how good I'm doing (excuse me, I'm twenty five and don't need to be told I'm doing well). The infuriating infantilization this woman sent my way increased exponentially when I felt I might have a meltdown and needed to go hide in a building for awhile to let my brain calm down before reintegrating into the activity at hand.

The man keeps stepping on my walking sticks (and I keep almost falling when he does). Reilly isn't paying good attention to me as I try to (admittedly not very clearly) tell him in sign that I want to leave these people on the street corner they're so obsessed with and go explore the rest of Pride. I'm getting frustrated, but I'm also enjoying the rampant nudity around me and the textures my synesthesia is making. It's all a big whirring ugly, dirty, beautiful, lustful swirl of colors in the back of my mind and finally I sign-shout at Reilly, who keeps lingering back with these annoying people, "I'M HERE TWO!" (No, that's not a typo, that's the clumsy way I signed it.)

My hands whip through the air, waving big, adding emphasis. This is how you yell in sign language. Reilly stands shocked (I have never had an outburst of anger around him, let alone at him, before). His mouth literally drops open in the old trope and I sign it again, again thrusting my hands with angry vigor "I'M HERE TWO!" There is another moment and Reilly says "okay" and starts dragging the annoying man with us, ditching the annoying woman (who may have trailed after us but at this point I can't tell if she's anywhere nearby anymore). We start exploring, looking for other trans people at what I am beginning to realize is a big gay party with no activism, no non-profit organization presence, and no real substance. So it's fun, but not otherwise very fulfilling for me.

As we wade through the crowd (a task that takes a lot out of me, and which I could not have done without the assistance of my walking sticks), suddenly my stick feels stuck and I lurch forward, barely catching myself. I turn and see that once again the annoying man has stepped on my stick. I lose my temper and, knowing this man cannot sign and won't respect the words I make with my Talker, I steady myself and slam my stick into the ground. Bam! Bam! Bam! I finish the gesture of rage off by sticking an angry finger in his face. I turn around and we continue the futile search.

After a time, Ashley and I leave Reilly with his annoying conquest in line waiting for the portapotty to continue our search (not because I am still angry with Reilly--I yelled at him and he stopped doing the annoying thing, so I was no longer angry--just because the line was unbelievably long and we felt it would be more efficient if we kept searching). Off we go, barely able to communicate (stopping to read the Talker in the highly loud environment of a multiblock gay party is not very efficient) so as we scan the tables and events we mostly gesture towards topless women and try not to step in garbage, vomit, or urine (this is part of why Pride is not accessible to disabled people--if I wasn't being as careful as I was I'd have fallen many times).

We find the information booth and I start signing at him. I can't tell if he understands me or not (he seemed to be trying), so I switch to my Talker, and then to writing on a map he was trying to figure out what I needed with. Ashley is treating me like a human being, and this man is, too, so watching his valiant effort to figure out exactly what I meant by "where are the trans people" and then finally settling on sending me to the booth set up for the Deaf community was much less frustrating than it could have been.

We meander off to the Deaf booth (which is right next to the loudest stage) and I stumble up, and sign "FINALLY! People I can communicate with." Ashley has been great, but it's just not the same when communication is that stunted. I'm so comfortable finally talking with people I can communicate with efficiently (and who aren't being followed by obnoxious ableist partiers) that I manage to sputter out some words to Ashley that the person she's trying to talk to can't hear. I start talking with the first person I came to there, and ultimately she doesn't think there's any trans-specific booth, but she does take me to the other end of the Deaf booth to introduce me to a trans person. Who is it but Drago?! I am so happy and excited to find another trans person--especially one who can communicate with me in the way that my brain is doing best in that moment--that we share a big hug as I remind him of where we met before. We talk a bit, and I feel satisfied and happy again, and Ashley and I set off to try to find Reilly and make our way home.

These three adventures have been defining moments in my life. At the Youth Action Conference, I was testing my ability to explicitly state my body's needs. After that test was successful, I have started to make those demands everywhere I go. They are not always met with the same acceptance and support that I was by Caelan, but I have that strong foundation of support to lean on. I was testing my ability to use adaptive tools in a very public place when I went with Reilly and the others to see Drago's talk. I now use these tools in most places where previously I was embarrassed or afraid to. When I am met with negative responses, I have that foundation of support on which to lean.

San Francisco Pride might look like a failure to others (I got in a fight with my friend, got treated with ableism and perhaps transphobia, and almost had a meltdown). I look on that day with great fondness. That was the day that those strong foundations, bolstered by a year and a half of learning about and joining the Autistic Community, came into play. I asserted my body's needs. I used various kinds of adaptive tools. I participated fully in an event larger and louder and dirtier and more crowded than any I had ever participated in before. I didn't dissolve into confusion (a common response to overstimulating environments). I made a new friend (Ashley). I communicated in the ways that my brain could and I was completely integrated into the event. None of that would have been possible if Reilly and Caelan and all of Reilly's friends and I had not been working together to create a neuroqueer space around me. Even if it wasn't always a physical space that I could count on being there, the growth that creating that space over the last two years has afforded to me is incredible, and I have so much love and gratitude to all of them for meeting me where I stood, not placing judgments on that place, and walking next to me, expanding that space exponentially with each additional person.

Naturally, this is the kind of space that I want to create by creating a community arts center. The realization that I am already creating that kind of space, even without a physical location, makes the most beautifully textured colors in my synesthesia. But I am just one person, and we are just one relatively small group of friends, so why am I writing this?

I sputter and use my Talker as Reilly and I continue to converse. When we arrive at the place where I am dropping him off (my brain finally calm enough to drive myself to my house), I revert to straight signing. Though my brain has calmed back into the zone of optimal stimulation, I still feel so full I cannot make the words that are in my head to say. Reilly tells me to text him when I arrive home safe (a routine we have with each other because we live in a rural area and the roads are dangerous here). I sit in my car, just breathing.

There is the joy of finding another person who wants to make art for the same reasons that I do, who doesn't care if it makes him rich or famous, but just wants to do right by the people around him. There is the joy of finding him and his friends and my other new friends like Caelan who see me--really see me in all my complexity of disability and transness and all of the things that I am but that are not my personality (they are my identities), and also see my personality. They see me as fully human. There is communication justice in my life in a way there has never been before (my two best friends can't sign and neither of them live on the same side of the country as me now that we've all graduated from college, anyway), and from that grows gratitude the way a mountain grows from plate tectonics. Like a mountain I am in the world and seen by the world and while much of the world will look at me with wary eyes, uncertain of my shape or the work it takes to understand me, with these new people I have created a neuroqueer space, and from that foundation I will continue to expand my neuroqueer space, and to share with others the rugged beauty that happens at the intersection of disability and queer.

This is the rich, textured level of life experience that I believe all disabled people and all queer people and all neurodivergent people can have if the people around them commit to creating a just environment. The mistake I see people making, especially with people with developmental disabilities, but also with other disabled queer people, is thinking that we are empty husks. We look like a human on the outside, but on the inside (the assumption goes) we are pain and struggle. In my life, my struggle is mostly with other people, although certainly it is sometimes about my body. My legs aren't working the way they used to (they have weak spots and aren't coordinated enough on most days, and so I have increasingly regularly needed to use elbow crutches just to be at work or in the community). I don't know why, but my worry isn't with my legs. I can accept them for how they move because I have accepted my brain for how it works. There is some struggle in locomotion (especially on stairs), but most of the struggle I have is with other people who are not neuroqueer or not savvy of the neuroqueer space I have created with my new friends. Almost all the pain in my life has not been pain caused by my disabilities (and I have a migraine disorder that slaps me with migraine pain several days per week). The pain I experience is from people treating me like I am an empty husk. Bullying me and belittling me and not inviting me to be integrated into society with them because they assume I would not want to be or cannot be. But slowly the fullness feeling that I have a hard time explaining is replacing the pain from years of hatred sent my way, and that fullness is growing from the neuroqueer space that I now inhabit.

I'm not sure, but I think that full feeling is some kind of love. CHA love. ("CHA" is how you write the ASL mouth morpheme that indicates a thing is very big.)

Twenty Years of Claiming Myself Aloud

Steven J. Singer

Twenty years old

"...1,212; 1,213; 1,214; 1,215..." I count the ceiling tiles in the hall of the psychiatric ward above my head aloud.

My gaze penetrates the crannies and nubs of the acoustic minimizing texture. My mouth can't move as fast as my eyes or my thoughts, so I start walking faster believing that one quicker body part translates to my entire body being faster.

I can't do it fast enough.

Please let me be fast enough!

The quest to count the tiles becomes more desperate and I run into another patient and then a nurse and then another patient. When I reach the uncompromising locked security door, I shake it, not because I think it will yield to me, but because that's what I did the first and each subsequent time.

I turn back around and head back down the short hall.

Doctor Tyler increased my antipsychotic medications. Oral Haldol was also introduced as "a more aggressive method of pacification."

"You will feel better." he said.

Night came. I stopped counting, but my head did not, so I search for something to which I can assign numbers in my bare hospital room.

"1 stitch, 2 stitch, 3, stitch..." I count the 18 stitches on my wrist, the self-inflicted wound still seething. The bits of thread are too close together and it is discomforting not to have clear borders between them.

Beginning again, I raise my wrist to my mouth and latch on to the first stitch with my front teeth. I tear it out, emitting a muted roar that provides a moment of internal placidity.

"One" I say a bit breathless.

"Two", I spit out the thread.

"Three..."

Blood flows from the reopened wound. I spew out the 18th stitch and look for more, but there are no more.

It can't... be. What?

I fly out into the hall unable to abide the end. The florescent bulbs buzz above my head, flickering now and then.

Emptiness.

No one is alive.

The whole world is gone and all I can hear is the echo of my footsteps, which make such little sound, because they took my shoes. Grasping hold of a door, I slam it with all of my might. The crash re-inhabits the world and I create a rhythm of slamming, pacing up and down the hall. Two hulking uniformed silhouettes tentatively push open the security door and then enter the hallway. With their latex-gloved hands up in peaceful entreaty, they slowly move toward me.

They cannot possibly have the power I have. They are mere people; sheep. They won't take me!

I pluck at my last strand of coherent logic to consider and poise myself to charge. And then a jolly face emerges. It is not the face of the officer thirty feet away collecting a rabid animal, but that of him ten years earlier.

I pause.

This threat in front of me is my Assistant Scoutmaster from my youth in Boy Scouts. In those days, he sat in his pick-up truck while we "scouted," watching a black and white TV. He always beamed and had at his disposal any number of groan producing jokes.

Had I diverged so far from myself that Pete was my enemy, that violence was the only possible choice of action?

I loosen my stance, shake my head, and slap myself in the face. I try to shake the cloud of medication, of frenzied captivity, of isolation, and of sequestered thoughts from my head. In that moment of recess, Pete and his crony descend upon me, tackling me to the ground. My uncertainty, confusion, and Cimmerian state force me to concede without protest and I lay motionless on the cold floor staring away, unable to look toward Pete. I feel a deep shame that doesn't acknowledge the hypodermic syringe lunging toward me in the hand of a faceless nurse.

Sleep; sweet, sweet sleep. A bright white light permeates my shut eyelids and much to my surprise, I can breathe and I can exist. As I open my eyes, I try to make sense of the scene. It is a 6'x6' room, no windows, and no door attached to the door frame. Perhaps it was once a closet? Outside of the room, I see the entrance to the nurses' station.

Still collecting my thoughts, I look down at my wrist. I look at my other wrist and then my legs. They are all tied to the bed by thick, faux leather plastic straps, which are that certain shade of brown used for band aids, crutches, and hearing aids. The restraint holding my cut wrist has blood drying on it and it threatens to open the wound again as it abrades against newly sewn stitches. Nurses shifts change and change again. Nothing else changes. The lights stay on and I am forced to stare at them.

No one comes in.

A day passes and I sleep a lot.

Another day passes.

As I emerge from the isolation room, the shackles finally removed, Sally skirts by me, grabbing my hand. She pulls me to "the corner." It is the only place in the ward that we all know is not under camera survelliance. This and other tidbits of collective knowledge are somehow passed from cohort to cohort.

She pulls me in and awkwardly kisses me. I don't know who she is and it doesn't matter. When I arrived at the ward, she threw me a kind smile. I doubt she cares who I am. A moment of humanity. Just at that moment, Bob and Nancy turn the corner and bump into us, obviously having had the same idea as Sally. Nancy flirted with me yesterday, but I "fell in love" with four women this week: the intern, the therapist, and two fellow prisoners, so I guess it doesn't really matter.

"Singer, the doctor is ready to see you" a nurse calls out from nowhere.

Walking away from the group, I lumber toward the office and enter. I sit for quite awhile and finally the faceless doctor comes in. He reads my file as he closes the door.

Without looking up, he says in an aseptic voice, "I see you have been having some problems?"

Either not expecting a response or not desiring one, he continues "I am going to increase the Haldol a little more and change the Welbutrin to Remeron. Everything else stays the same. See you tomorrow."

He exits just as he arrived still reading the file and making a note. The nurse arrives and herds me off to group time.

As I enter, I hear Abe say in an exultant voice "Well, I got 4mg more of Clonozapam!"

Adam responds "Yeah, doctor's got no idea what to do with me. I used to be on that shit and a lot more," which seemed more like a self-validation for his presence there than a response.

I chime in "Fuckin' Haldol. I don't even know how I am walking. Stuff's got me all wonky, but isn't doing shit to get me out."

Even though 'out' is the last place I want to be.

Abe groans and shakes his head "Tell the doc to drop the Haldol and put you on the Clonozapam. It helps a lot and if you have extra once you get out, you can sell 'em."

I nod my head in agreement as do the others, but most of us know that once we get out, we won't be able to pay for the meds, so the point is purely academic.

Old Jim, with his bushy white beard and penetrating eyes, sits with us wringing his hands. With sincere interest, I ask him, "Jim, how are the monsters you are pooping out?"

Jim looks up at me. "You should see 'em. They are just there in the commode crawling all over. Can't keep 'em inside of me, but I try!"

He stands up and with hands still wringing, shuffles to another chair across the room, and sits down.

I love Jim.

None of us say anything about him being transferred tomorrow to the state hospital. He knows it, we know it. It is easier just to let it happen and not acknowledge it, but I look over to him and wonder, almost hope, that he doesn't think about us as friends and that somehow up at 'the bin' he will find a family.

The daily routine plods along.

Lunch: gray beans, roll, iceberg lettuce, spaghetti, and a man watching like a hawk, taking an account of everything I put in my mouth.

Cigarette time in a cordoned off room: two smokes divvied out and lit by a nurse, dizziness from smoking them fast, monitored by the nurse.

Group therapy: "How are you today, Steve. What did you eat for lunch?"

"Why don't we talk about feelings rather than medications?"

"I don't think that is an appropriate response."

Meditation time: Go to your room, waste time doing nothing and wait for the nurse to check on you every 10 minutes.

Dinner: same as lunch, but with a hamburger and a different man watching.

Visitation: Mom comes, we sit silently and awkwardly, nurse pops her head in and takes a note every 10 minutes, she leaves.

"Singer, your mom left a book for you," the nurse calls out from down the hall and I can hear the sound of her steps drawing nearer. She enters and I look at her worn white shoes, buckling under the stress of her many steps. She thrusts the book into my hand and exits, hobbling a bit. The front cover reads "An Unquiet Mind: A Memoir of Mood and Madness" by Kay Redfield Jamison. I flip through the pages, the words cryptic and meaningless. Shutting my eyes, I prepare for a long night of sleeplessness.

The next day, I go through the motions.

The next night, I pick the book up again and read a few pages.

◆ ◆ ◆

Thirty years old

"Jenny, I got your number. 867-530 ni-ee-ein" I sing aloud as I walk down the highway. I emit a satisfied chortle at having provided the same material evidence again and again. I make sound, but there is no sound. I woke up three weeks ago and couldn't hear anything. The noise in my head quieted. It has been grand.

Well, I can sort of hear some stuff sometimes. I am not sure I like it.

If I am deaf, I am deaf.

If I am hearing, then I am hearing.

At the library, I finally email my mother "Mom, I woke up deaf three weeks ago. I'm alright. Didn't need a doctor. Just thought you should know. Anything new with you?"

I access my email the next day at Eryk's house. Mom responds "I think you should come to the city and see if anything is wrong with you. I will make the appointment."

I email her, "Mom, nothing is wrong with me. I just can't hear, but fine. OK."

Sitting in the thick-walled box at the audiologist, I wait silently while I watch mom sit, pace, read, or knit on the other side of the small window that permits me to see out into the open.

She makes me nervous.

For the first time, not hearing is a source of anxiety rather than solace; an anxiety caused by mom, the doctors, and all the motion "out there." The audiologist works on the other side of the glass pushing buttons.

He looks up at me and I smile at him.

Then he presses more buttons and looks up again. He enters the box, fits different devices on me, and exits locking me in again.

Next they take blood and then they do an MRI. The battery of tests are finally done.

The doctor comes in and mom takes up the pen and paper she has been using to relay information to me. He speaks to mom at length and she nods still looking at him.

Frustrated, I blurt out, "Tell me what he said!"

She pauses a moment longer and starts to scribble on the paper. *There is no conclusive evidence of what caused the hearing loss. Maybe you were ill and as an autoimmune response, your cochleae were significantly damaged trying to fight off the sickness. The result is a severe hearing loss across most frequencies in both ears. They have a treatment that has about a 5% success rate at restoring some hearing to sudden hearing loss of this sort. It requires injections into the middle ear through the ear drum of steroids that can stimulate the cochleae. They are not pleasant.*

Mom's face looks hopeful and full of expectation that I will submit to this torture. She has always tried to be a good mom. Is it not time for me to make some type of gesture of good faith?

To go with the grain for once?

To follow the rules?

To finally appease her?

"OK, Bring it on!" I blurt out, knowing that it was violating one of the few things I had ever valued or that ever had value in my life -- my salvation.

He pulls a turkey baster sized syringe out of a drawer and the business end of it is the same size as mom's knitting needle. I tell my knee to stop shaking.

I feel like the characters in Scooby Doo who visibly shake with zigzag lines all around them. Acquiescing to the doctor's instructions, I lay on one side with my head slightly upside down so that the steroids, once through my ear drum, can rest on the oval window to the inner ear for no less than 30 minutes.

Mom writes, *You will not be permitted to move, swallow, speak, or blow your nose.*

Inside my head, I think, "What about punching the doctor?"

As he walks closer, I imagine he is laughing maniacally, his weapon poised for the strike, but I can only see his shoes and argyle socks. Mom looks away and I see her cringe as the needle travels down my ear canal and pierces my ear drum. The pressure on my eyeball is so immense that makes me think it is going to pop out and roll across the floor. A searing pain shoots down my throat and I swear someone is shoving a knife in my brain. Visions enter my head, of the ancient Egyptians pulling dead people's brains out through their noses with long hooks -- a fact some teacher once upon a time told me. A deluge of snot, tears, and spit brought on by the injection flow down my face and onto the floor.

Finally, the doctor taps me and helps me sit up.

"Whew, it's over. Praise the lord!" I exclaim.

Mom hands me the paper and on it is a very terrible sentence, *Ready for the other side?*

It was a few days ago that I got those shots. Nothing has changed. Still can't hear.

At the library, I search the internet looking for others who have become deaf like me. Scrolling through a few pages, I see "Deaf Wannabe."

Interesting.

I read that it is "a group that finds being deaf and wearing hearing aids attractive. A number of people talk about "crossing the bridge" which is the term for attempting to cause one's own deafness using various techniques in order to claim the life they feel would be most meaningful. The people posting compare it to gender identity or reassignment and all of the sudden I don't feel too alone or abominable.

Certainly, I can't tell anyone in my real life about these thoughts, so I write my first post.

Hi, I'm deaf and I love it!

Over the next several weeks, I diligently walk the three miles to the library everyday to keep up with posts on Deaf Wannabe and soon feel a sense of community.

I notice that the people who get the most support, feedback, and who have the largest general presence are those who are actively trying to damage their hearing. I yearn to establish my membership and continue to feel this sense of kinship and communication that gratifies me, especially when so few other conversations are accessible.

An idea. I write. Clicking *enter*, I see the post I just authored.

I caused my own hearing loss and while it was not pleasant, I am so much happier now. I started with "sound therapy" and then continued to otoxic drugs and slicing my eardrums with an X-Acto knife.

Immediately, responses start to materialize in my feed and inbox.

Looking for assistance
I wish I had the courage to cross over.
Welcome to the club!

The feelings of peerage and acceptance wash over me and I continue reading the responses for an hour.

I click the window shut and stare at the screen. I am a fraud. My sulking plod home is long and laborious.

I feel the immensity of contradiction and yell into the wind. "I am DEAF! Why can't I be happy to be deaf!? Why does it matter how I became deaf?..."

I interrupt my own thoughts with an epiphanic detonation of enterprise—I will reconcile my deception and deliver myself from the few remaining phantoms of sound I experience!

The sound therapy that people conduct appears innocuous enough. Setting to task, I collect pieces of faux fur, cardboard, and rubber as means of soundproofing the cubby hole in the wall where I sleep. I layer these pieces around the walls and ceiling and then add all the blankets and pillows I have. Finally, I construct a barrier to close off the cubby. I step back and admire my work, but I am not convinced that I really know what I am doing, so I head back to the library.

I consume article after article: "Sound induced hearing loss", "Mechanics of sound", "Acoustic design of small spaces."

It is not enough! I need more! Not only does it need to be loud, but the sound can't escape or be absorbed. Wielding the knowledge I collected, I head off to Radio Shack and Home Depot to collect reflecting boards, decibel gauges, and fans to cool the friction caused by the sound waves. These items are far more important than eating this week.

The CD is almost finished burning... come on... Marilyn Manson, Disturbed, and a bunch of other heavy metal crappy industrial bands. Alright, it is time.

I have the remote to the unnecessarily loud stereo.

The blackness in here is daunting, the lack of air stifling.

Switch the fan on.

I fumble for the large PLAY button and BAM, the earth shatters. It is like the old film footage of people watching nuclear bomb tests with their shades. There is a total eerie calm and then a massive force bowling over everything in its path. Decibel gauge reads 141 at point blank range. I settle in the sound helmet or stage that I manufactured and brace myself for the 90 minute CD.

Pain, disorientation, a heavy feeling in the chest, difficulty breathing, and heated vibrations consume my body and I question whether I can go on.

Then calm. Now it is so calm. So very, very calm.

My ears feel cold and I am drowsy. It is almost womb-like, and the CD ends as if it had just begun a moment ago.

I must have fallen asleep.

I repeat this exercise everyday for a few weeks and often much longer than 90 minutes. The ritual becomes addictive and cathartic. I don't believe it really does anything, but I feel powerful and in command of my destiny. The follow up appointment with the ENT doctor and audiologist arrives.

Back in the box, the man pushes the buttons and looks up at me.

He pushes some more.

After the tests, he hands me the results and I see that my hearing loss has increased to 'profound' across most frequencies. The black and white formal results, hard facts on paper, cause me to recoil.

A bit aghast, I say to him, "I think I caused this to happen."

I relay the tale.

His face flushes and he looks confused, but attempts to maintain his professional comportment. He types on the computer, "I have to admit, I am a bit shocked. Well, I am..." He pauses and I see him say "um, uh."

And then he continues to type, "I did know people sometimes feel this way. I am not sure what to make of this, but given the level of loss you already had, I highly doubt you could have caused this further loss with sound. It is likely that whatever the origin of the damage, this profound loss is just an extension of it."

◆ ◆ ◆

Forty years old

I sign in American Sign Language aloud "843-699-3268, 843-699-3... 268. I need to remember Katherine's phone number so I can ask her out on a date. 843-699-3268." I slam the door of my trusty rusty car. My feet are light and there is a spring in my step as I bound up the steps of my apartment.

The door sticks as I try to enter. Giving it a solid nudge, it opens with a shuddering movement.

I drop my book bag by the door and unbutton my pants. They drop to the floor and stepping out of them, I make my way to the sofa. There on the table is my syllabus to the Disability, Gender, and Sexuality course I am taking, the first of the doctoral program in which I recently enrolled.

My mouth drops open and my stomach begins to convect as the heat of fear suffuses my body. The reading for tomorrow is Kristen Harmon's study "Hearing Aid Lovers, Pretenders, and Deaf Wannabes: The Fetishizing of Hearing."

I vault myself over the back of the sofa and fumble trying to extract the anthology in which the reading is published from my bag. Just as I dreaded, the study took place during the years I had posted in the group without my knowledge. I skim through the pages ferociously waiting to see something I had posted. There wasn't anything, but I instantly regress to the moments and feelings I had when I first discovered the forum.

I sit in class, quieter than usual.

A debate ensues inside my head.

"If you don't say anything, people are going to know something is going on! Are they staring at me now?"

"But if you say something, they are going to hear it in your voice and we know you will say something that you will regret!"

I bide my time and wait for my world to fall apart. Out of the corner of my right eye, I continually glance at Katherine, the woman who sits behind me. We recently started dating and I fear she is going to say something like, "This is so disgusting, I refuse to discuss this."

Which would mean I am disgusting.

If not her, someone, is going to say it and I will crumble. What seemed to me an obscure group long buried in my past was now somehow the topic of discussion.

How did this happen?

The clock ticks and I feel a drip of sweat roll down my abdomen from my arm pit. Suddenly, I am aware I am covered in perspiration.

Finally, the professor says, "Alright, I will see you next week."

Wait.

What did people say?

I look from student to student and interpreter to professor.

No one is staring at me. In my state of terror, I missed it all, but I don't recall anything overly critical. My fictitious and subsequent actual past, for the time being, stays there, though it stays here with me too.

The gloss notation below of American Sign Language is not a written form of the language. It is a language that exists in the hearts and minds of its users that transcends paper and its very nature is violated when manipulated into this form.

topic__________

"COFFEE TABLE. PAINT LIGHT P-I-N-E shift DARK M-A-H-O-G-A-N-Y. YOU PREFER

wh_____

WHICH?" Katherine queries.

I ponder for a moment weighing the advantages of both stains. While I know that by nature I am drawn to the darker, the pine, too, is appealing. It is the table itself that is so delicately and expertly crafted from 100-year-old maple that creates the piece. Fighting off my Cimmerian inclinations both because they are ruminations of the past and because this new life and this new love is full of light and comfort, I respond

"P-I-N-E DEFINITE"

She nods in affirmation. The light is drawn in and instead of the milk crate table with a piece of corrugated cardboard rescued from alley printed with "This side up", there is the fine wooden table with the words "Ethan Allen" neatly imprinted subtly on the inside of the drawer. Fine wooden tables do not buckle under the strain of mundane occurrences. As I run my fingers over the deep grain and over the dovetailed joints, I am beholden to the table not for its aesthetics, but for its permanence, its planning, and for the maintenance it requires to remain in good condition. I look up at Katherine grinning, my fingers still caressing the table.

"YOU-AND-I TABLE TAKE-CARE-OF, LAST FOREVER WILL.

Katherine signs " TODAY WORK HERE, WEAR PAJAMAS shift GO-OUT BREAKFAST

wh_______

EAT, WORK. WHICH?"

I reply "BREAKFAST, DEFINITE"

Both of the suppositions here perplex me.

When we arrive to the cafe and order our food, I gaze at the eggs, rich Italian meat, freshly baked bread, and the steaming cup of fresh roasted coffee. Katherine looks at me puzzled and I gesture "nothing," but it is difficult to dismiss the memory of breakfast being the only food for the day or that its source was the old donuts stolen from the dumpster of Seven Eleven just before the maggots got to them each day.

After the plates are cleared from the delicious, though simple, meal, we pull out our laptops and a pile of articles from our bags. We appear to focus on our work, though we often flip to Facebook and email.

I glance up at her and she at me.

We both know and use that knowledge to rally ourselves to revise our respective papers for a conference. Still, my mind wanders.

Twenty years earlier, my work was perpetually searching for the children incessantly screaming in agony that my mind created. It was trying to find a way to pass as sane for even just a few minutes so that I could convince one of my last remaining friends to keep me in their lives. Eventually, those ruminations dissipate and I push through my work.

We sit for hours, purchasing more coffee and feeling the buzz of too much caffeine. I knock on the table to get Katherine's attention and sign

_____y/n

"ME, GOOD PLACE STOP. TODAY FINISH. YOU?"

She nods and begins to collect her things. I think to myself, "I could keep going, but I need some time to relax before going out tonight."

As we walk out of the cafe, I pat her on the butt and say aloud "Good game," a habit we developed for congratulating each other for a job well done. We climb in the car and drive home.

Once at home, Katherine voices and signs "You know all of this drama with trying to get ASL interpretation for the show tonight is just turning me off to wanting to go. How do you feel about that?"

"I couldn't agree more my squinty face" I respond, chuckling to myself. This endearment is one of my favorites.

"It's just that this was supposed to be a fun and whimsical date and now it is so much work. Let's just go have a nice dinner, an evening cocktail, turn on Pandora Radio and the vibrating sofa, then dance to some songs that are at least ten years old," Katherine proposes. We have a couch that changes music into vibrations and I have an excellent music memory for pre-2005 music.

There can be no contest that there is sufficient rationale for the two of us to be up in arms about the inadequate provision of sign language interpreters for a play we had selected to attend at the local university stage. Whereas facing a barrier once served as a personal conscription to fight the system and prevail at all costs in the name of disability rights, it now means something very different to me, to us, and to the relationship that we built. I pull up my email account and respond to the director of disabilities services "This is unacceptable and in the future you really should work to resolve these issues."

Pushing play, the signal emitted from the remote arcs across the room to the blu-ray player. The number counter on the song begins 00:01, 00:02. In turn, the electric pulse travels through the amplifier and on to transduced magic. In the grandest of clichés, Etta James' vocal pebble is cast into the tranquil pool of my living room. Radiating outward in soft echoing ripples of an aural past, "At Last" reaches the soles of our feet; reverberating the souls of our persons. Her taut sheathed form quivers under the soft touch of my fingers tentatively meeting her waist. Under the fabric of her dress, I am keenly aware of her alabaster heated skin. For an eternal moment we embrace and I feel the wetness of her eyes on my shoulder. My exhalation is deep and long and it feels as though it is my first breath, no longer suffocating. Her hips initiate a slow ballad of movement in harmony but distinct from Etta. My sixth grade, stiff legged, weeble-wobble, shuffle enters the exchange. Her grace and acceptance oddly find a common ground for us, where our bodies choreograph the utopian moment.

"I found a dream that I could speak to. A dream that I can call my own... At last," Etta belts out.

Reaching the crescendo, the melodious pulse ceases, seeping out through my fingertips and out into infinity. Our bodies still resonate. We remain.

These scarred bodies will wound and flow again. The specters will haunt the darkened recesses that we choose to omit from our lives. And, too, those that resist omission.

"But not tonight" I sign. Katherine looks at me quizzically. "Nothing, just thinking," I sign and say aloud.

how i got here

Meghan O'Hern

tell me about the moment
that made you
you
he says
soul music buzzing in the background
as we drink milkshakes
and stare into the illinois river

eight years old
i dreamed of becoming mermaid
tired of the burden of having feet
stumble smash shins to soil
a doctor told me

disability meant
i would never move smoothly

fourteen
when I first learned to hide scars
pile bracelets on split wrists
believed other people's comfort
meant more than my own

sixteen
the year bulimia
wrapped itself around me
like a second skin
never letting go
nineteen
the year of poetry
struggle spun
into a good story

twenty one
the year of struggling
to stay here
the year of
soul music
and milkshakes
on the bank of the illinois river

shot(s) in the dark

Emma Whetsell

(fifteen)

i live in flashes
a club rat between windows and doors and
different flavors all over all the time

thinking splinters like old wood leaving me
with a thin king for a brain,
delusional and handsome
he loves flickers and sounds and those extra
noises that people make when they aren't
saying anything at all

and hand gestures like gold coins falling

--

(fifteen)

i whistle like a rollercoaster
tilt forwards and hold until
people fall from my head
seatbelts dangling

crowded inside the edge of
the center of a mob

curl into my shoulders
cover me and muffle the noises
that crawl over my skin
in defense
crinkling my hands and pressing
them up against my face
i
gather cloth beneath me for
a bed and fold like laundry
clean and soaking all
washed out

see my apartment building eyes?

see the steps on the bridges of my arms?
the generator runs electric beneath my chest.
i have been hollowed out and my insides
replaced
with caricatures and children

--

(seventeen)

it is morning
blinding with
the tacking of many sails

sheets awash in
lavender and bleach and
water and twine and wooden clips
at sea over land

overhead
the air lays thin spread-eagled
like ice
or fingernails on fingertips
pressed to the bottom of a bowl

--

(seventeen)

i know not now

where my feet are
in the room

perhaps on the ottoman
perhaps under the table
perhaps outside the false
ring of stillness i've drawn
around my knees

i hope that all is
not lost

or at least
not my feet

please is in vain or maybe
i am vein- unnecessary hope
circulating into
my limbs

--

(nineteen)

someone has pulled the corners
of this sky tight around heaven
the burnt edges of dawn drape
down and trail in dust

a crow pricks
inkstains over thread
quickened and dark

my bed is above the rain
and i breathe alone
water goes below me
i am too light to fall

--

(nineteen)

anatomy or pastoral
crack a chest
lay upon the earth

the heart rests in a low valley
veins float with the rainfall

loose or full
one touch—the aorta
overflows over many
soft ankles of grass

quickly simmer
summer noon
aching monsoon

--

(twenty)

words are everywhere like breath with no origin and no sound and no letters only hands some to rip circles and circles in the space around me, like ragged waves and rust inside my chest and the limits of ears i make things with myself and carve out the insides with my skin and the tender air around sounds i make with stepping how can you not know how to build?

--

(twenty-one)

when running is a kind of prayer,
how should i answer?
wings and mountains soft declines
kind and movement pebbles of breath
a voice sounding in paces stretching
conjuring companions: a pool of water,
the sense of singing beside

--

(twenty-one)

bored a hole bored a whole hour i wore a hole in my shirtsleeve for a tunnel to my skin and tore it open into a loose cry like cotton drifting over soil and grass and time that thyme you find me in the grass like cotton the soared whole i'm sore driving a toll and half an hour in a tunnel through my skin

--

(twenty-two)

sewing plants i lose the needle
touch the soil to find the point
point to touch to soil to sew
to pull together later waiting
folded breath from seeds in sound
i am now a row of roots
parallel and round

Civil War

Athena the Architect

It's been a year since I stepped into this Vision,
Scarlet Witching with twitchy fingers fishing,
slipping into you and splitting with syllables strung to each other
until you pull a thread and they split your target like old leather.
What stepped out was just one Witch with just one wish,
but one Witch wishing her plural presence had survived augmenting
is enough to shape the fate of a team that's started breaking.

You didn't listen or take into account the Vision
was just another plan, and it could easily be clouded by your fans,
your fears, or projects you only half committed to,
so you leave me and go freely to make do with what you think will protect
you,
and I am lying in the house alone, like

what did I do?

And you are just leaving me to do nothing,
so I might be alone and free, but I'm back where I have always been
and this cage frequently starts beating me without touching my arms,
can't you see that's why they're bruised? It's not from *me* hitting *them*.

The longer you fight and the more scared paranoia takes control of your scripts,
the easier it is to see I should have taken the equipment and moved freely,
back when I still had a chance,
back when Clint could still see me,
back when I stopped thinking I'd blend in and started strutting
downtown Manchester, man chest and a long black dress,
Scarlet Witching my way through confrontations in public
and bringing meetings into focus by finding what is holy
and gathering the people in without claiming anything originated with me.

Quicksilver's been dead for months, and my head has never been this empty,
but for all that I have total control, everything is going to tempt me
for all that I have a schedule that's full I still go out of my way to say who sent me,
because when it comes down to it there's only one question worth asking:
Did you enslave your Vision to your fears and use it to start wars?
Or did you start forth with a light that's all yours,
leaving the Visions of others floored?
Me? I sank mine down five stories and bolted to freedom with a flourish.

This isn't just a babbling allegory or a fanfic sendup,
I am still standing after a five month roundup,
I am still writing after a half year holdup,
and I am still living after a decade holed up.

Now, with an iron clad alibi
and a transition to a physique only obtained

through willingness to experiment, injections, pills, and pain,
I plant myself by this river once again,
and with no SHIELD to help me I ask you:

What's my name?

This time, you don't Scarlet Witch me,
there's no deadnaming
no invoking my beginning,
no Luna to love good or name herself after the week,
no alter ego named for earth and a trans hero,
and I ditched the artificial intelligence too,
'till the core of the complex became a name that spells truth:

Don't call me Athena.
Call me NO, YOU MOVE.

Claire and Clarence

Alyssa Gonzalez

Claire's eyes opened slowly, her breathing deep and regular, taking in the musty darkness. She slid off her electrode-laden nightcap and slid out of her bed. The rhythm of her breathing relaxed as she approached a full-length mirror, flipping a light switch on the way.

Totally bare, she smiled at her reflection from behind her bangs. Expressive green eyes sparkled at her full lips and long auburn hair. Her breasts were just large enough to fill out a dress, the faintest hint of muscle lines surrounded her navel, and her waist seemed designed to have an arm around it. Her long, thin fingers felt the flawless curvature of her long, supple legs, slipping between her pedicured toes as she bent down, giggling lightly to herself. If every morning could start like this...

Claire turned her head, noting the insensate male figure curled into himself next to the bed, a similar wired cap on his head, and sighed. Averting her eyes, she slid the mirror aside and reached into the open closet behind it. With only a little deliberation, she retrieved and slipped on lacy black underwear, absently adjusting her cups with one hand and picking out with the other a low-cut red blouse and a denim miniskirt with a front slit. Silently, she clothed herself, finishing with a pair of high-heeled strappy sandals, and posed alluringly before the mirror. Satisfied, she sat cross-legged on the floor and pulled a small chest from the bottom of the closet, opened it into a makeup table, and applied her mascara, eye shadow, and lipstick with practiced ease. From a low drawer, she removed a thin chain bearing a heart-shaped pendant and put it on. With a one-sided smirk, she rose, glancing at herself in the mirror one last time before putting on a knit sweater, taking a small black purse, and exiting the room without looking back.

The outside was a concrete path leading from a wooden shack in the forest to an equally nondescript car, and with effortless grace Claire boarded and drove off.

◆ ◆ ◆

It wasn't long ago that the thought of one of these adventures would leave Claire lying in her room in a state of confused terror, but that soon gave way to curiosity and, from there, to the thrill. Now she positively quivered, the excitement setting her body ablaze. It was a delicious release, this life of hers: a clean slate, a new opportunity, and a chance to take chances. Each of these jaunts was easier and more natural than the last, but the thrill—the thrill only grew stronger.

The forest faded into the background as Claire ascended a highway ramp, and soon she pulled up to this evening's nightspot: the Bluelight Lounge. Giving a coy smile to the loiterers who ogled her as she left her car with the valet, she walked smoothly inside, dropping some coins into the bouncer's cup. The large, suit-clad man undressed her with his eyes. The synthesized beats of the club's music wafted over her. A different smile spread across her face.

The bartender had her usual lychee martini ready when she got to the bar. With a wink he moved across the table, not pausing to ask for money. Crossing her legs so that an extra section of her thigh peeked out of the slit in her skirt, she sipped the subtle flavors and waited. She never had to wait long.

She rebuffed her first suitor with a disinterested flick of her hair before he even greeted her, and he slunk off to nurse his Heineken and wrinkled polo shirt at the other end of the club. A group of three moved in on the opposite side, and she pointedly ignored them. They did not quite get the hint, and lingered until a new arrival took the newly-empty stool to her right and leaned coyly on the bar, saying nothing. Claire eyed him, unconsciously sliding her eyes from his Spaniard features to his long black hair to the third open button on his white shirt. She recognized him. He'd never believe from where.

"Hey," the man greeted, raising an eyebrow "I'm up here."

Turning toward him with a wry smirk, Claire responded, "Do you always use pickup lines you found on the Internet?"

"Sometimes I find them in magazines," he quipped without missing a beat, delicately pushing her hair behind her ear. He didn't notice, or didn't care, or liked, that he set off her startle reflex. "The rest of the time, I find them in the dance of a goddess's eyelashes and the flow of her hair around her shoulders."

He probably thought her smile was for him, rather than for where she knew this exchange was heading. "You must have practiced that one," she returned.

"Or perhaps you inspire me to poetry."

"Do you say that to all the girls, or just the ones who give you a hard time?"

"Just the ones I'd like to dance with me."

"I thought you'd never ask," Claire answered, standing and taking the man's hand. He led her to the dance floor and pulled her arms around his shoulders. The music was slow and sensual, and they pressed against each other as they stepped in time. Claire turned around, leaving her hand on her dance partner's cheek as she felt his chest against her back and his hands against her stomach. He nuzzled her ear as he softly kissed her neck. He didn't know, or didn't care, or liked that her goosebumps were not pleasure, but disgust and, soon, satisfaction.

"You think you have this all figured out," she asked, "don't you?"

"How so?" he asked, his hands sliding to her hips.

"You think you know exactly what you have to say to get me to follow you home tonight. You think you're playing me like a flute, that there's nothing I can do to surprise you."

"Oh, I know you've got a few surprises for me," he whispered into her ear, moving her hair aside.

"You don't know the half of it," Claire intoned, closing her eyes as he mouthed her earlobe. She tried not to think about what had happened the last time she met this man. It was another lifetime, and he'd never link it to her now. Tightening her lips, she jabbed his foot with her heel. As he winced, she turned around and spoke into his face:

"I know your kind too well: always so smug and confident, always showing off like you're God's gift to the world. But under all that, it's all calculations and lies, all an act designed to get behind her defenses and into her body, so you can have your little fun and leave her behind." She stomped on his foot again for emphasis: "But I know better. People like you are the reason why women get disgusted with men. And today," she admonished, "you're getting what you all deserve." With that, she buried her knee in his groin, let him fall, and walked back to the bar to order another drink.

◆ ◆ ◆

Claire was midway through another lychee martini when someone else approached her. This girl looked entirely out of her element, with her neck-length brown hair, cat's-eye glasses, and knee-length blue dress.

"I heard what you said to that guy," she stammered.

Sipping a bit more, Claire responded, "Did you enjoy it?"

"I just wanted to thank you. A friend of mine dated him. He cheated on her. He needed to be told off."

Claire thought about her last encounter with that man, and shuffled the thought aside before the terror of it could affect her face. She was a new person now, and things would be different, and *he* would never hold her back again. She gestured to the bartender, who arrived with two glasses of red alcohol. She offered one to her visitor: "Singapore sling, on me."

"Thank you," she stammered further as she sat on a stool, "I'm Leah."

Claire offered her hand as she introduced herself and Leah took it: "Claire. So what brings you here?"

"I don't know."

"You don't know?"

"I just...felt like challenging myself." Leah sipped her drink and smiled. "I hardly ever go out like this, and I like to remind myself why."

"Why not more often?" Claire pulled her stool closer to Leah's and continued: "A beautiful girl like you could have a lot of fun around here."

"Eh, I don't know..." Leah spoke, almost shivering as she finished her Singapore sling far too quickly, "I get nervous."

Claire ran her fingers through Leah's hair, responding in a breathless whisper: "Not after tonight, you don't." With that, Claire leaned over and kissed Leah, holding her head with one hand and caressing her thigh with the other. The patrons' stares meant nothing as she led the stunned ingénue into the ladies' washroom. Over an hour later, Claire stepped and

Leah staggered back out, the former looking profoundly satisfied, the latter dazed and speechless, neither wearing their undergarments.

"Call me sometime," Claire exhaled, slipping a piece of paper between Leah's breasts.

"O-okay," Leah agreed, clearly still trying to process what just happened.

◆ ◆ ◆

Claire could not help but laugh on the drive back. Acting on her passions, following the drives Clarence wouldn't, couldn't set free, was the sweetest rush. Yet she always had to come back to him... not every morning could start like this one. There was too much at stake. That was the problem with dreams. Claire could believe all she wanted, but eventually, she would always have to come back to Clarence.

The rest of the trip was road noise, without even the radio to distract Claire from her thoughts. Every weekend she parted from Clarence to live her life, to feel soft and beautiful and make the wild decisions he would never make himself, and every weekend the decision to come back and spend another week without that verve became harder. It was sublime, being able to escape his squalor, to live without the consequences he feared so terribly, but best of all was the sense of control. Clarence was at the mercy of his misplaced affections and the people who pointed them out to him, of desires he couldn't express without the terror the Spaniard so violently installed in his mind, but Claire knew no such ties. Claire could be whoever she wanted to be, care about no one at all, get the revenge and the pleasure that came to her, feel beautiful and desirable and *herself* for as long as she could... but not Clarence.

The door to the shack swung open, and Claire's blood ran cold.

She pulled up and stepped out of the car as quietly as she could and peeked into the doorway. She did not see the disarray of her clothing all over the floor, or that the closet door had come off of one hinge and hung precariously off-center. She did not see the shards of mirror where her makeup chest had been shoved aside, or the absence of the drawer within that once held her jewelry. What she noticed was Clarence, lying insensate on his stomach next to her bed, without his wired cap, and that her disheveled bed no longer supported Claire's own electrodes. She searched frantically through the mess of the place, lifting the bed and even moving her closet aside, before the reality sank into her mind.

She could not go back. Not like this. It was Clarence who left, and only Clarence could go back to Clarence's life. Except, until Claire could recover Clarence's invention, there was no Clarence... just a sleeping body that would slowly starve.

Claire looked down at herself, at the flawless, silky curves of her legs and the swell of her breasts, and fell on her bed, shivering.

On the bright side, now, every morning *could* start like this.

Code School

Lynn Vargas

You will have to excuse me if I start out a bit rusty,
some months have been between my last vocalization
and this one, and the run of silence has not been fun,
it's been more like someone dropped my tongue
and I couldn't tell if it was broken or just out of batteries.
What matters to me more than unpacking what was happening
is extending my discussion into ways you can use my last dissertation,
stringing together pieces of me from the things I contribute to
our group happenings and seeing that what I do is simple:
All you have to do to pitch in is master Jean Grae's rhythm,
Jean Grey's strength of mentation, and the discipline
needed to defeat enemies with nothing but patience.

So maybe simple isn't the word for it.
Maybe the Phoenix will find something more fitting,
trade an adjective and use a verb for it.
What you will have to see is the way we expand,

filling your solar system with our strength as we
devour the source of your warmth
and spit out cadences that rewrite your thoughts into themselves.
This is what I came to teach, but to reach the point where you can see
just what is happening, you have to stop perceiving this as a thing
separate from other methods of writing or even oratory,
the story and the music and the glory and the sensory meditations
are all methods of persuasion,
and the obligation to make rhetoric into argument
is simply accepting rules without understanding their limits,
or the more effective ways of winning over your potential allies that align
with more rounded, cognitively aware methods of composing verbal
arrangements.

This means you use a melody and start making thoughts dance like me,
because you may speak and leave people too stunned to take in everything,
but the patterns stick in human minds and they chew on it, repeating
pieces
that did stick, then that trick makes them think they need to check the
rest,
because a thought without context is maddening, and now you have them
in,
and they are encoding themselves with whatever thoughts you happened
to spit.
To understand it, you have to be willing to get dirty, read Goebbels, let
him make you sick.
It's pointless to move on to Chomsky if you haven't the stomach
to comprehend what he was out to react against,
but then you also better find the historic references
that teach you why the earliest traditions were packaged in choral formats
just like this
because you might be a writer, but the thing you have tapped into is old as
sin,
you have to master it in order to use your craft,
because the craft you seek to master

Is nothing but a vessel and it's your turn to ship;
the actual power is much older,
and you have to have the discipline to pour it in,
to ensure your syntax and command structure are flawless,
so the elegance in your cadence connects to other nodes
and gets them downloading. Get it yet?
That's just one track. Listen to West and hooks, then come back
And attack Lakoff before diving into Brecht.
That will give you enough to understand what has to happen next.

Once you get how communication and framing make the ecosystem
that your new apps will function in,
consider the language of your command structure.
I like socialism, it's a P2P system
with the kind of built in inefficiencies
that require custom patches and debugging,
but that means it is heuristically responsive, customizable,
and most important, hard to overcome once it is distributed
and resources are spread enough to make targeting them problematic.

If you're wondering why the bulk of humanity resists the idea of everyone being able to eat,
entertain the idea that Orwell's observations are not to be
used to convince people to behave differently,
but instead to map out tools it is legal to use
under your enemy's current rules of engagement.
Schopenhauer will teach you why there is no obligation to stick to rules of honor
with opponents who wish to destroy you,
and why using their tools to defeat them is most excellent,
and when restraint should be shown, and quarter given.
But it is Orwell's modern English that will translate the techniques into the syntax you should be using.

Package these techniques into the melodies that reach deeper into cognition than surface logic,

And you start to see how the assembler works to build subroutines and
establish new batch processes.
Now, let's take a minute to see how this applies to television.

If there's one mistake you make, it is giving the protagonist
the benefit of being the reason to be watching.
Consider instead, a world where you are meant
to apply the morals and ideals of your daily life
to the storyline in front of you.
That perhaps the argument made in antihero gritty reboots
is not to glorify the things they do
but to call out the structure that makes this a path of positive action
and allows these kinds of people to reach self-realization.
To me, this is the point of *The Wire, Breaking Bad,* and *The Sopranos*,
but it gets lost in the fandoms that develop
when people as horrible as the ones being taken to task
grab hold of the show and embrace it so fast.
I learned to stand outside myself in a *Threepenny Opera*, following
Caucasian Chalk Circle
stories and looking deeply into the depictions of side characters in
Shakespeare
and layers of reality in Arcadian spaces,
and then I boarded a mighty ship to explore space with,
and my Enterprise became a Battlestar
to fight my way through visions of human nature
that seemed oddly related to the environments they sprang from.
Stop dismissing the visions whose protagonists you viscerally reject.
Start taking up the call to interrogate them,
because even if Hollywood is not yet writing to this technique,
they'll start when the audience makes it clear
there are new rules to debugging code in this form,
it's up to you to refuse to restrict your reactions to the ways
they dictate stories should be discussed,
because the discussion focusing on the causes of the conduct
of the creators and creatures who disgust you will never be permitted

as long as you still listen to writers who prioritize Formalism.

Bone and Storm

Alex Conall

Who designed these tests?
What good does it do
to write an essay on symbolism
in "A Rose for Emily"
when the real test of life
is how to write the essay
to tell your parents all the things
you have been lying about
by omission?
No, even that's a lie--
the real test of life
is how to weather the storm
that comes after,
the insults to queer people
to your face,
or (in lowered voice)
when you stand ten feet away
and your hearing is just fine?
Is it easier if neurotypical?
If you say it to their faces,
does the storm rage
less strongly?
But losing words half through each sentence,
tripping over every other phrase--
no, emailed essay's better.

The stutters, stumbles do not show.
The skeleton in Emily's bed
is hidden from sight,
the skeleton in the family closet
that would be you,
if you stayed silent,
if you let the silence wear you
to the bone.
But the storm.
Never mind the English essay.
Test yourself against the storm.

Life is so Hard for Arlo

Michael T. Chin

The alarm sounds at 6:22. That first noise it makes—that *pop*, meant to ensure the sleeper rouses—is like the explosion of an atomic bomb. Except an atomic bomb would carry a flash of light, which would be better. Arlo has asked repeatedly about getting a light alarm rather than an aural one, so that sound itself, one of the few comforts in Arlo's life, will not be tainted by this daily scarring. This daily explosion. This daily pop. Neurotypical people like Arlo's parents don't get the fundamental importance of sound. It's all functional. The sound you wake to, the sound you bear, the sound you tap your toe to, the sound you indulge in.

The alarm sounds at 6:22, before the sun has risen, and more critically, eighteen minutes before Arlo's father will pound on the door to rouse him. Arlo has to be out the door by 7:10 to get to the corner in time to catch the school bus.

Eighteen minutes swaddled in flannel sheets, a wool blanket, a down comforter. It's too hot, actually, but who has the energy to kick off layers at that stage in the day? Besides which, it will be too cold if he grapples off the comforter. The layer that *should* go is the blanket, but that's in the middle. He's not about to take off the comforter, then the blanket, then put the comforter back on. He knows himself too well. That by the time each of those steps is done, he will have expelled every ounce of the precious energy he'll need to get all the way out of bed, out of the room, down the stairs, to the kitchen. And, realistically, it will take upwards of nine minutes to get that all done at his current rate, and that will leave fewer than ten minutes to rest up before his father's knocking and that just isn't enough.

So he turns off the alarm. While his arm's out, he gets the previous night's bottle of RC Cola and ferries it back to his cocoon. Takes those critical first sips, the bubbles gone flat, but the caffeine and the sugar still active. Critical pre-fuel, like the way the jocks at school drink that specific Gatorade before they lift weights. Arlo spills a little on the pillow case. Vows, like so many days before, to develop a better system not to leave sticky sugary sweetness in his bed, if for no other reason than because when his dad finds it he claims it's going to attract bugs and then Arlo won't be able to sleep the next night, thinking about ants swarming his face, on top of the terrors that ordinarily keep him up—the prospect of global warming, the concept of infinity and what it will be like to truly be dead forever. The reality of facing another day of school.

He's getting worked up just thinking about it all.

Arlo touches himself. Long, steady strokes. Occasionally, he can provoke an orgasm in these early morning minutes. More often he falls back asleep in the process. It's a win-win scenario.

BANG BANG BANG

"Rise and shine, buddy."

Arlo groans. Rolls over, top sheet, blanket, comforter and all. Rolling himself like some ancient scroll meant to go unread for years. In a time when the words will become more meaningful and be understood for how profound and revered they ought to be.

BANG BANG BANG

Arlo's dad won't leave until he sees the light turn on. Not just the reading lamp on the nightstand—even though Arlo knows his father *can* see it, because he's *BANG BANG BANG*ed on his door to turn it off at two in the morning when Arlo's been caught in the throes of high seas adventure or intergalactic warfare. No, his father will wait for the overhead light. The one Arlo needs to get out of bed to flip on.

Arlo rolls. A little this way a little that before he can untangle himself fully from the sheets. Guzzles the rest of the RC Cola and rolls the empty bottle beneath his bed where it meets the pleasant bump of plastic on plastic in a growing collection.

He gets up. He turns on the light. So it all begins again.

There's never time for Arlo to shower. He can't shower without music and he can't bear to let a song not reach its end and things never line up and he's always running late. He picks up a t-shirt from the floor. *Fighting Irish*, fitting in that his skin is too white to be anything but Irish, but fundamentally misleading in the insinuation that he has any interest in sports, much less that he has anything resembling fight in him.

The shirt only smells a little. He zips up a smellier hoody over it and makes his way out the door.

Dad is making breakfast. Pancakes with dark chocolate M&Ms in them. He's grown more domestic since he split up with Mom, and Arlo keeps wondering when he'll crack. Stop making breakfast. Stop wiping counters. Stop keeping the fridge stocked with twenty ounce bottles of RC Cola, the nectar of Arlo's life.

Dad flips two pancakes onto a plate. A subtle suggestion that he wants Arlo to lose weight, because he knows that three is the norm, but if Arlo argues the point, he'll claim these pancakes are thicker than the ones he used to make, so really it's like he's eating three—maybe three and a half. This is a bonus. Because he loves him so much.

Arlo fetches a fresh RC Cola and listens to the hiss and the fizz, watches the little specks of soda dance in the air, takes a smell of it, and takes that first, glorious sip. One of the few things that can make RC Cola taste even better than it naturally does at the start of a day, is the contrast of cold and bubbles to the lukewarm, flat version he swallowed first. A reminder that some small things in life are good and that things might—on rare, isolated occasions—improve as a day goes on.

Arlo sits on a stool at the island, where he and his father eat most of their meals these days, the kitchen table at first too formal for just the two of them in his mother's absence, and now a repository for junk mail and his father's work papers and some of Arlo's half-hearted attempts at homework. (The only place he can really get work done is in his bedroom, headphones on, completely tapped into music, not worried about anyone watching him tug at his hair and rub his temples and work though problems and essays and blocks of textbook exposition about important moments in someone or other's history.)

Dad puts a hand on Arlo's shoulder and squeezes. "How's my boy today?"

The language is still forced, *my boy*. It's not like he would say, *how's my girl* months earlier, when Arlo—Arlene then—identified with his biological gender. The truth of the matter is, he doesn't think his father really understands why Arlo needs to identify as male now, and why he wants to start hormone therapy and prepare for surgery. Dad says to give it a year, at least, to make sure he's certain. But this is a fundamental choice and time is of the essence. A part of Arlo dies for every second he has to pass in a body that's wrong, with budding breasts and a vagina and all of that messy bleeding that threatens to ruin his best boxer shorts on a monthly basis.

No, Dad calls him *Arlo* and *boy*, and transitioned from staunch opponent to advocate for Arlo being recognized as male at school only after Mom left. As part of his campaign to both prove to the courts that he is more in touch with the needs of his son, and as part of a campaign to be Arlo's favorite.

Mom made it easy for Dad to be the lesser of two evils. Immediately pursued a line of thought, "Do you like girls? Because it's OK to be a lesbian. It doesn't mean you have to change your plumbing." Arlo explained, if anything, he still liked boys, but he was pudgy and pasty and didn't anticipate sex with anyone in the imminent future. Mom stopped listening early, and shook her head. "It's like you want to get spray tan, then go and sit out by the pool all afternoon and burn. It doesn't make any sense."

Mom had been spray tanning for years. Since she learned the tanning beds caused cancer, and her work got too busy to ever lay out by a pool.

There was something reassuring about Dad's fair skin. That he wore SPF 90 in the summer months and stayed inside most of the time, much like Arlo.

And the pancakes were good. Even if there were only two of them.

"You'd better motor, Arlo." Dad finishes his coffee. His third cup by the level of the coffee pot. He tried to convert Arlo to coffee, too, with the onset of high school, but it took seven or eight table spoons of sugar before it approached the sweetness of RC Cola, and by that point it was sludgy and even more unpleasant than the original brew. "You're running out of time for a shower."

Arlo shoves the last of his pancakes in his mouth and clutches his soda tight to him as he makes a rush back upstairs. Brushes his teeth. Runs the tap full blast and puts his hands under it and then over his head. Enough water to mat down. Not enough that his hair will still be wet outside and freeze in the winter chill. He rubs water under his eyes. Put his glasses on and looks at himself. Exhausted. In a pantheon of bad days, there is little reason to think that this one will be better than any of the others.

◆ ◆ ◆

Arlo makes it to school. Survives the trudge through unshoveled sidewalks, the negative-ten-degree wind chill at the bus stop, spitballs from the seniors who haven't passed their driver's tests or whose families can't afford cars, but who still need to establish some brand of dominance. Arlo has taken to sitting up front, near the bus driver, to have his help if there ever comes a day when things really get out of hand.

The driver tries to make conversation some days. Those days, Arlo turns up the volume on his iPod. Today it was "Girlfriend in a Coma" on repeat.

Arlo hangs back on the bus and pretends to be asleep when they get to the school lot. Lets the whole bus clear out. Turns up the volume one step further. Soaks in those last moments of peace.

Inside, he has Dana waiting at his locker. "Do you believe this bullshit?" She brandishes a flyer for the Sadie Hawkins dance, ripped from a wall, the top right corner torn off in a jagged line. It bears two stick figures holding hands, one of them with her legs cut off in a triangle of a skirt. They're surrounded by bubbly music notes.

A dash of purple streaks across Dana's pixie cut. She wears black and blue checkered flannel. Dark jeans. Combat boots. The previous summer, Charlie Jones dumped her for Rachael Willaker, and Dana came back to school ostensibly a lesbian. That's when she started hanging out with Arlo. He sort of resented that she assumed he would want to be friends, after their middle school years when she wasn't particularly nice, and how cavalierly she threw around the pseudo-acronym GLBTQW—the W for *whatever*, she had explained in a giggle.

Arlo drains most of what's left of his RC Cola. Just one left in his bag, earmarked for his mid-day-pick-me-up at lunchtime.

"How do you drink that so early in the morning?"

Arlo sighs. "It's like if everyone starts their day with so much RC cola in their system—everyone else has a two-liter they burn through over the course of the day before they need to sleep again. I start out with a twelve ounce can instead." He tightens the lid on the bottle. Still a few drops in case of a true emergency before noon. "I need to refuel and I need to sleep more just to make it through the day."

Dana has no such problems. Rips the flyer in half, back on the warpath. "I can't believe they think this kind of dance is OK in 2015."

Arlo looks at the stick figure boy and girl and thinks they're sort of charming relative to the usual dance flyers that quote Taylor Swift or Pitbull lyrics, or advertise in bold print the *FREE PRETZELS*.

"You know what Sadie Hawkins is right?" She lifts her eyebrows absurdly high and waits absurdly long to blink before she determines that he isn't going to have an answer. "The girls are supposed to ask the boys to dance. It was supposed to be this women's empowerment thing, but it has all these assumptions in it. Like that girls want to dance with boys, or like everyone identifies as a girl or a boy, or like everyone wants to go to a stupid dance in the first place."

Arlo isn't sure he could find the energy for outrage. Maybe by the afternoon. He piles his biology textbook and notebook from his locker into his backpack.

"Heck, maybe you and I should go." She laughs. "See what the administration wants to make of that."

It occurs to Arlo that Dana may be asking him to the dance. And that for all of the absurdity and hypocrisy packed into that sentiment based on what she had said thirty seconds before, it might be fun to dance.

Dana socks his shoulder. She's always doing that. Too hard. "Think about it. We'll talk later. I've gotta get to pre-calc."

Arlo rubs his upper arm and finally hefts his bag up onto his shoulder to begin the trudge down the hallway for the first in a series of classes he will never make it to on time.

◆ ◆ ◆

Arlo knows Mrs. Warnock tries. Truth to be told, she's one of the few teachers he's sure does. Who not only bothered to read, but internalized the guidance counselor's note and on the first day of class, called roll and read his name as Arlo, rather than his legal name *Arlene* still printed on all of the official records, still a stumbling block for most of the faculty.

Just the same, Mrs. Warnock has proven uniformly indifferent to how the curriculum might affect Arlo. The discussion of *fat cells* that led to boys puffing their cheeks and spreading their arms to imitate and exaggerate Arlo's girth from across the way, expertly timing their play so Mrs. Warnock never saw *them*, but did reprimand Arlo about keeping his eyes pointed to the front of the classroom. It was a similar story in the lab at the back of the classroom and another set of boys put frog guts on Arlo's shoulder and Arlo squealed and, again it was somehow Arlo who was at fault.

He gets it, though. Mrs. Warnock seems intelligent and here she is teaching high school biology on a loop, year after year, with cruddy lab equipment and a textbook dated fourteen years back that she makes a habit of updating and correcting in her lectures. All of this to rows upon rows of unappreciative fourteen and fifteen year olds, eyes glazed, passing loose-leaf notes, daydreaming about being anywhere else. Mrs. Warnock can't see or hear every transgression—as if she would even want to—and Arlo is a bigger, slower target than most to catch at something.

In another universe, Arlo imagines he might be even more sympathetic to Mrs. Warnock. But this is the universe they live in and he has to focus on his own survival. In this universe, he hates her less than most of the other teachers, but he still doesn't like her.

Mrs. Warnock scrawls in big, looping white chalk script *nature vs. nurture*. "Our genetics set our destiny. Our potential and our limits," she says. "Our conditioning does the same things. Different environmental factors like nutrition and learning and emotional treatment that have an impact on humans from birth onward." She depresses the button on her laser pointer and scans over the chalkboard, underscoring and then circling each of the words. "Scientists have debated for centuries what factors are most guided by nature and which are dictated by nurture, and where we might draw those lines. Would any of you like to venture your thoughts on the topic?"

Johnny Reds raises his hand. He was sort of a jock in junior high but was too scrawny for the football team and too lazy to do anything about it so he has settled into a more clearly defined role as class clown in high school. Most of his jokes are obvious and mean-spirited, his only real gifts gumption and delivery.

Mrs. Warnock doesn't seem to have learned better to call on him.

"Sex is genetic, right?" A few snickers. He said sex. "I mean gender, that is, Mrs. Warnock."

"It is." She folds her arm in front of her.

"But if someone has a really messed up upbringing, they might errr —" He acts as though he's struggling to pick the right word. "Arr—lean toward changing sexes, right?"

More snickers. A high five. Arlo's face feels as though it may have literally caught fire.

"It's an interesting question." Mrs. Warnock says. Surely she's not going to entertain it. She might ordinarily—as a purely hypothetical matter—but an adult has to realize that this is a moment for adult intervention. She doesn't have to intervene or make any grandiose gestures. Really, it's better if she doesn't. But she needs to redirect. Quiet the chatter and keep things moving.

But this is a world in which kittens die and Kan Jam is a thing that people do and the Kardashians keep getting new TV contracts. Arlo fingers his hallway passes. His IEP allows him three per day, for when he gets too stressed or can't sit still and needs to excuse himself to the hallway for up to two minutes. The stressors are usually internal. Like when he can't resist watching the second hand on the clock at the front of the room because he feels certain it hits an irregular rhythm before the turn of the minute and needs to watch to be sure. Or when he can't fight the urge that he needs to make noise and needs to get in the hall and put on his headphones for a minute to hear noise, noise loud enough to drown out the noise inside him. Or when he knows he's going to get himself into trouble if he doesn't escape at just that moment.

"In the case of a transgendered individual, what do you all think? Is it necessarily a matter of nurturing the idea that one *can* be transgendered, or is it a natural impulse that someone needs to be something other than what they are and won't be able to function until a change happens?"

A girl in the front row raises a hand. A girl Arlo's never talked to before. Never saw before this school year. A girl he thinks is named Mary Beth but he's not altogether certain. He can't bear to hear what she's going to say, rises to his feet and hands Mrs. Warnock one of his passes on the way out of the room. Gets up so fast he forgets his headphones and is left pacing the hallway without them, fingers plugged in his ear in case the sound of the classroom dissipates into the hall and catches up to him and defeats the purpose of leaving. Hums "Please, Please, Please Let Me Get What I Want." The conversation has to pass within two minutes. For even in this world in which people stick chewing gum to the bottoms of desks, it's also the world in which The Shamrock Shake comes around each March and in which Netflix streams whole seasons of *Buffy the Vampire Slayer*. Good things can happen. He tries to believe.

◆ ◆ ◆

English ought to be better. Not only does Arlo like Mr. Dowling's class, but today's the day when the first papers are due back and Arlo wrote a hell of a paper on how Baz Luhrman got Mercutio all wrong in his reimagining of *Romeo and Juliet* and why *Westside Story* was actually the more faithful interpretation.

And Mr. Dowling is young. Wears the top button unbuttoned so his tie hangs a little loose. Routinely goes two or three days without shaving to produce a stubble that might mean he's trying to look older or might be sheer laziness, either of which Arlo can respect.

Mr. Dowling recognizes that sense of anticipation on the day papers come back. The bad students' dread. The good students' hunger. That no one is paying attention in any meaningful way until they know their grade, and so he doesn't beat around the bush. He wanders the rows of desks, handing back papers creased inward to hide the comments he has written on them. Arlo's is toward the end of the stack, presumably because Mr. Dowling saved the best for last, or maybe graded the best papers first and so they were at the bottom of pile as he stacked one on top of the other.

Arlo scans the comments when he gets it. Lines and checkmarks, a *well-stated* and a squiggly underscore with *awk* scrawled in the margin. Arlo moves as slowly as his trembling fingers will allow him to savor all of this, these few sweet moments, even as Mr. Dowling advises the class to take out their textbooks and open to page whatever.

Arlo reaches end. Finds the *B+*. Finds the *review directions carefully—3-4 pages double-spaced!!* The double exclamation points are particularly taunting. Poor form. Fundamentally incorrect in written English. And this man who dared give him a B+ didn't know better than to use them?

Arlo's hand shoots up.

"Yes, Arlo?"

"Could I speak with you?"

"We can speak after class if you like. For now, we're discussing the text."

"It's just—I wrote more than the assignment asked for."

"Class, can anyone remind me of the expectations for the previous paper. Was it supposed to be double-, triple-, quadruple-, or single-spaced? Or did I leave that open for each individual student to decide?"

A mumbled chorus of "double-spaced" emerges from the class. Mr. Dowling gives the hint of a smug grin.

Arlo can feel fire again. Feel himself ready to explode. He raises his hand again.

"That's enough, Arlene. We can talk after class."

Arlo needs to get up. But he only has two hallway passes left, and it's only third period. He crosses his arms tight across his chest doesn't say a word. Tunes out every sound in the classroom. The awkward, umm-riddled, befuddled attempts at reading aloud. Mr. Dowling's open-ended questions that Arlo would ordinarily bail him out on.

Just see what it's like without me.

See what it's like when you betray me.

◆ ◆ ◆

The worst parts of the day ought to be over. But they're not.

Today, Arlo has Phys Ed.

When Dad started championing his cause to have the school recognize him as a boy, *this* was the landmark accomplishment. It was all well and good to have teachers call him Arlo and try to remember male pronouns. But getting Arlo into the boys' Phys Ed class was an accomplishment, even if, as a compromise, he still had to use the girls' locker room.

Arlo had appreciated his father's advocacy in behind-closed-doors meetings with the superintendent. He just wished he had talked to Arlo, first, about his plan.

Phys Ed—Arlo might have let that one go.

The boys play rough. At first they ignored him. But as they came to accept Arlo as a guy, or at least more freak show than girl, they started to treat him like the other un-athletic boys. The taunts. The eye rolls. When they played football, the only time anyone threw to him was when his back was turned and they had a free shot at the back of his head. In volleyball, they took pleasure at spiking the ball to wherever Arlo stood, certain that Arlo either wouldn't get to the ball in time, or that the ball would hit him in some part—any part, really—of his body other than his hands.

Today, they start dodgeball.

Coach—Mr. Patterson insists on being called that—explains the rules up front. As if anyone didn't know them. Don't step over the line. Get hit and you're out. Catch the ball and the thrower is out. Arlo at once appreciates the game for its clearly defined rules and resents the barbarity of the rules themselves in a game all centered on throwing rubber balls at each other in the effort to eliminate targets, the initial ones of whom are so readily defined as the fat kids, the poorly coordinated kids, and the kids the jocks have otherwise just been waiting for an excuse to throw things at.

But first there's the draft. Captains picking teams. Arlo knows how this goes—he's always picked last, which is fair enough from the perspective of picking the athletes best equipped to help a team win, but still isn't fun, but that doesn't mean that he needs to enjoy the process or isn't still humiliated every time. He's learned the cheat, though. He gives Coach one of his hallway passes—he does this at least once each gym class—and escapes. Between picking teams and mass of confusion at the start of any given game, Arlo can squeeze out an extra three or four minutes of time out before anyone notices he's gone. If he waits outside the gymnasium doors—if he wanders as far down the hall as he can justify and makes Coach come out looking for him rather than volunteering a return, Arlo can milk another couple of minutes on top of that. It's the most mileage possible for a single pass.

Coach takes the pass without looking at it. Crumples it and wads it into his pocket. Arlo wanders past him. Out to the hallway with the long glass trophy case. Arlo has taken to studying the trophies inside—not because he cares about the school's athletic history, but because it can be oddly fascinating to see old teachers who double as alumni, listed on plaques as varsity athletes. Coach, sure—a letterman in football and baseball. Less predictably, that power-tripping turn-coat-weasel-dick Mr. Dowling used to compete in the long jump.

Arlo is just getting absorbed in this history, humming and air guitaring a smidge to "Layla" after he sees the name *Leila* engraved on a particularly impressive trophy that it turns out is for girls bowling, when the voice rings out. "Hey, Arlo. Coach says to get your butt back in here."

Arlo looks at his watch. "It's only been a minute."

Sam Ventura shrugs and walks back in the gym.

Arlo marches back toward the gym. Coach has picked the wrong day. He'll give him a piece of his mind about learning accommodations and what the school is legally bound to do and how his father isn't going to be afraid to put in for a lawyer and they'll have his head for this.

The two sides are established, waiting on opposite sides of the center court line. Coach has a the netted bag, holding all of the dodgeballs, some of them bright red, at least one navy blue one crusted with dirt from outdoor kickball games earlier in the year. Arlo missed the draft but it's clear they're waiting on him to start the game.

"Coach, I'm supposed to get two minutes."

Coach looks up to the clock. "It's been a minute-fifty."

"So I get ten more seconds."

Coach crosses his arms over his chest, rolls his neck and slowly guides his gaze back up to the clock. A moment of silence. "Now it's been two minutes."

"But I just wasted half of it walking back in and arguing with you."

Coach looks at him dead on. "You arguing with me, Arlo?"

Arlo remembers the kids who argued with Coach's referee calls in soccer running laps around the field while their team played on, a man down. He remembers when Sam Ventura dared take an extra shot after the whistle blew to end a period of basketball and that Coach had him drop and give him twenty.

"No, sir."

Coach points to Arlo's side. Arlo does his best to join the crowd. But they slide away from him, leave a space around him, make it as clear as possible he has no friends in this crowd.

Coach rolls the dodgeballs out down the center line, like bowling balls. In a perfect world, some would break left, some right, some might linger around the middle, in any case creating a more or less even distribution. But they all seem to go to the opposing team. Every single ball. The last couple are still rolling free when Coach blows his whistle to signal the start of play.

Arlo doesn't even see that first ball coming. It connects with the side of his head and knocks his glasses clean off. Everything's a blur. He expects a second whistle. Stop of play. Another ball slams into his gut. Another into his shoulder. Another headshot.

Arlo crumples to the ground and covers up as more balls rain down on him. There have to be a hundred of them. Maybe a thousand. Pelting him like hail. He's dying.

"Arlo, get off the court, you're out." Coach's voice. "Somebody hand Lardo there his glasses so he can get off the court."

Another ball hits his knees. They're all laughing at him. A light chant of "Lar-do, Lar-do." That's what they'll call him now, for at least the week.

Arlo curls into the fetal position.

Another two balls hit him. One on his elbow. One on his hand over his face. They're going for blood. The chant gets louder. It goes on for ages. Surely, the gym period should be over by now. Arlo wonders if he's bleeding. If he has internal bruising.

"I know you're faking it," Coach hollers. "Get off the court or you're running laps the rest of the period."

Arlo gets up. Rises from the rubble of humiliation and physical pain and resentment for a system that has failed him yet again. Stumbles to the sideline where at least he'll need to wait until the next game, or until someone on his team catches a ball, but God willing someone else will be out by then and Arlo will be able to give his spot to someone more eager and willing, maybe even earn a smidge of good will in the process.

Arlo barely registers it as the next ball, worn and green and a tiny bit deflated, comes hurtling toward him, as if fired from a cannon. Purposeful. Deadly. Sure to knock off his glasses again and maybe break them. He's not escaping any time soon, for as he's realized time and again but is still struggling to internalize, this is not just one game, or one day or one school year. This is life.

Being Trans and Autistic is Weird and Common

Alyssa Gonzalez

Almost every trans woman I know is either autistic or makes me wonder if they are. My AutDar is well-tuned enough that I trust it over most other criteria available to me, and it pings almost all of them. Some evidence suggests that gender dysphoria is much more common among autistic people than in the general population, so this is likely not merely anecdote. Those studies need a *lot* of cleanup to actually mean something (not least to get asshole charlatan Simon Baron-Cohen's name off of them). Either way, whether we're more abundant than expected or not, this combination makes our experiences rather... unusual.

Being an autistic child means the humans around us are endlessly confusing. They're loud, they smell, and they oppose as "defiance" and "*malacrianza*" any attempt to assert control over one's environment that they didn't invisibly preapprove. You're regularly swept up for hugs and kisses and photographs and doctor's appointments and extracurriculars you had no hand in choosing, with people you don't know, in rooms that make it hard to process which bits of the light and noise and old perfume are the ones you need to respond to right now and which ones are background. You're heaped heavy with rules and commands about what objects not to touch, which rooms to avoid, which clothes to leave for special occasions and which ones are for day-to-day. In between all of that, what's another name, another handful of rules? Memorizing "I'm a boy" and "these are boy clothes" and "these are girl toys" isn't any different from memorizing "these are winter boots" and "we hug Grandma when she arrives, no matter what her arrival interrupts" and "if you tell mom you have this kind of pain, you'll get a long, confusing talk and then she won't give you anything to help, so save time and don't tell her." They're all information, taken from the outside and synthesized and re-integrated over and over as new info arrives.

You avoid eye contact, and you don't know why. The associative parts of your mind give you a mastery of figurative language that boggles your teachers, even as you take their instructions literally and face the resulting "mistakes" with blank confusion. Your vocabulary is advanced, your interests ahead of your age. Even this early, you like writing better than talking, and you learn from childhood that keeping secrets is a fun and easy way to not have to talk to people. Your interests hold you so hard that people usually have to touch or shake you to get you to disengage, and you react angrily to the interruption. Routines, patterns, and rituals help you make sense of the world, and you *hate* when they're violated.

You keep on being weird. Sooner rather than later, the adults around you figure out that your weirdness isn't just "being a kid," but you fall through the diagnostic cracks anyway. No one connects your quirks to your overly flexible joints or to your recurring headaches and stomach pains. Maybe they don't think you're autistic because you talk too much when you're excited, or because you rapidly matured from a destructive whirlwind of a toddler to an impossibly well-mannered and adult-like child, or because of some other laughable gap between the diagnostic criteria and the lived reality of autistic women. When you were smaller, you might have been terrified of transgressing gender lines or determinedly fascinated by them, but in your elementary years most of your friends were girls and nothing seemed odd about it. Around the same time you noticed yourself becoming attracted to some of those girls, you received a different set of social pressures, declaring that it was not just practical but *desirable* for boys and men to be patient with and competent at stereotypically feminine tasks. Maybe you rejected that idea and took up exaggerated, muscular masculinity to prove your own manliness to yourself and others, maybe you cautiously embraced it and received the peculiar dividend of continued, enhanced camaraderie with the women in your life, but either way, it was an important, formative message. It didn't do what you wanted, though.

If you'd had the words for it, then, maybe you could have said something. If you'd known what a trans person is and what it means to be one, you might have seen yourself in her, had a flash of familiarity and recognition and realization that you, too, could be her, asked the people in your life to help make that happen. You weren't all the way there, yet, but you were close enough that that nudge could have worked, and could have saved you *so much trouble*. But they made sure that possibility was far enough from your mind to keep it from ever occurring to you. They weren't really around for anyone else, either, but you weren't the type to determinedly shout at your parents "I'm a girl!" over their equally determined insistence otherwise. You and that person were both born into a senseless world, but *she* arrived with a demand to force that alien world into shape, and you arrived with a healthy self-preservation instinct and the desire to understand it. It would take you a lot longer to figure out that something *did* have to change, and that something was how other people see you.

The biggest, burliest you couldn't get away from "girly" things or from how poorly the mold of masculinity fit. They expected you to be hard-edged and emotionally stunted, cruel and brusque, and you couldn't do that. Your sense of fairness didn't let you climb any social ladder by hurting other people, least of all the women toward whom you felt, not just attraction, not just ethics, but *kinship*. The softer you fared little better. The women around you grew to trust you, confide in you, let down their guards around you. They feared you so little that you might have gotten to see some of them unclothed, and had them admire the restraint you showed in not behaving then "like a man." You didn't know it yet, but they thought of you as "one of the girls," and for all that they loved you for it, it would leave you always incomplete. If you pressed on any of those friendships, testing them for romantic or sexual possibilities, they recoiled, horrified that you were apparently not the kind of gay they thought you were, themselves failing to process the inchoate creature that feels like a woman but looks like a man. You felt deceptive, then, and cowardly. Your intimacy became lonely. You became withdrawn, even within these close, hug-filled friendships, knowing that they depended critically on that part of you never showing again, soon learning also that other women would hold that closeness against you as though the friends who had already rebuffed your advances could threaten *their* hold on you.

A lot of your relationships were unhealthy. You definitely had at least one partner (or person like a partner) who extracted emotional labor from you like a strip-miner and left you exhausted and unfulfilled in turn. You probably had others whose main redeeming quality was the fact that they were *there,* who pulled you in directions you weren't sure you wanted to be pulled, who left you or that you left because the true terror of what staying together would mean started to hit you. Between them, you grew odder, more reserved, more cautious, and quieter. You learned to notice someone being kind or friendly with you and then carefully watch them around other people, to see if the treatment you received was *yours* or just what them being friendly looked like. You were rarely rewarded for the chances you took on drawing any kind of attention to yourself and mostly gave up on the idea, concentrating instead on being ignored. If you were invisible, you were safe. Your clothing was drab, or voluminous, or otherwise designed to make you disappear. Maybe you grew a camouflage beard.

The confusion was real, and it was endless. There wasn't a single moment, from beginning to end, ongoing, forever, that you weren't scanning to figure out the social rules that governed *this* second in case they differed from the second before, or dissociated into a mercifully unaware blur. The pieces didn't fit together. The messages from outside glared across a chasm at the ones from within, neither knowing what to do with the other. You *definitely* missed the train that could have taken you past a testosterone-based puberty, and when that happened, the messages from inside stopped making sense, too. The wet, electric cacophony of your own mind found solace only in your special foci, the places where you were always able to put your thoughts and have them be calm, still, and devoted to one problem at a time. But you were lonely, and even as your better judgement learned to tell you not to bother, you kept trying to fill that hole. You didn't know that the hole would never fill until its edges were reworked.

It took you a long time to put names to the faces. You had a lot to unlearn before the messages you had missed, about what it means to be *your* kind of woman, could find their proper home. You had a lot of false starts, a lot of recognition that didn't go far enough, but eventually propelled you to the next stage. You regard the moment you finally understood as comparable to the time that you figured out that *people lie* and the time you figured out that *god isn't real* for the impact they would have on your life thereafter.

All those ladies who recoiled from me? *They're into dudes.* It wasn't (just) a sensory sensitivity making me want to shave all my body hair, or that made it feel good, right, and mandatory to keep it down. It wasn't nothing that I occasionally felt flashes of terror related to removing my shirt in public, long before I had breasts. It's not *cis* for my entire fantasy life to start with the idea of my body being feminized. It's not *cis* to have detailed fashion preferences for the women in one's life, that somehow also feature in that fantasy life. All of those things didn't make sense before. And that's over now.

The doors are open, and the estrogenated light streams in. All the *you* you didn't even know was you, all the parts of you weighed down for decades in rules that don't apply and shame you can finally discard, *it's their turn to shine.* You'll find all the hacked-together kludges and scaffolds holding up the edifice of who you thought you had to be can all be trashed, and someone you barely recognize but who feels more *you* than you ever did will be there, to take the inmost core of you and build around it a new, better, happier you. You'll realize you've been watching how to be a woman with more detail than you are aware of having watched anything, and you'll be far better at it than you ever thought. The people who knew you will be blown away at how rapidly you moved, after the interminable eons of hand-wringing and the eternity of lies before them.

You didn't have to become her, though. You just had to wait for her to give up on trying to get your attention by saying your name, and switch to sitting on your desk, grabbing your shoulders, and shaking. But now that you and she have finally met, you're going to have a lot of fun together. A lot of very, very autistic, very, very lesbian fun.

Moving Into the House: A Memoir of Dreams

Sparrow Rose Jones

My brain hurt like a warehouse, it had no room to spare.
I had to cram so many things to store everything in there.
—David Bowie, "Five Years"

I can't remember when I first dreamt about the house.

I've never been in the house while awake. I watch for it everywhere, but I've never seen it, except in my dreams. The house has always existed, it has always been in my dreams. It follows me.

I began dreaming about the house long before anyone told me I am Autistic; long before I realized I am trans. Before I knew who I was, the house knew me. Even when I didn't want it, even when I denied it, the house knew me.

The house is massive; it contains everything. There is an area everyone can see, but it is only there to deceive. If the house looks complete, no one will find the secret entrance, hidden in a back room. No one will find the small hole through which I creep. No one will find where I really live. The house is not me. I do not live within the house; I live beyond it.

◆ ◆ ◆

No one is looking. I creep down the hallway. In the chilly back room, I squeeze past oppressively heavy furniture carved from whole trees of some dark wood, polished to a sterile gleam. When I look out the window, I see only brick walls, rows of windows, industrial-ugly like an abandoned warehouse. But when I squeeze through the nearly imperceptible hole in the wall, down near the baseboard, I emerge into twilit frog songs and flowing water.

The house that pretends to be me is gone, the brick walls are gone. A small iron grating at the base of a towering cliff of smooth grey concrete is all that remains of the passageway through. I am alone. I am safe.

Flat granite boulders mark my path upstream. Brimming with joy, I leap from stone to stone, feeling the air warm as I climb higher and higher through the cattails, stopping to stretch high, reaching toward the gradually emerging stars high in the purpled sky yet so close it seems I could touch them.

The land of dreams never lasts long enough. I lay awake in bed every night but can't fall asleep before three in the morning. The alarm for school blares at seven. I usually sleep through it, but only until Mother comes for me.

◆ ◆ ◆

I want to live beyond the house forever, not only during those brief glimpses when I am able to snatch sleep from the jaws of lifelong insomnia. I begin to dream during the day.

The classroom around me dissolves into....the classroom around me, but I am self-contained in a tiny house. I live in a house that looks like a little Victorian one-room house on wheels from the outside. I roll everywhere in it. When I want to be around people, I bring a chair to the door and open the top half of it. When people are too hard, I close the door and move further inside my little house that is so much bigger when the door is closed. It contains everything.

Why can't I live in the house I choose? Why can't I live there all the time?

I am hungry. I am always hungry. The kitchen in the husk house is as empty as my mother's kitchen in the wake world. The air is dusty and close in this house and sunlight slowly bleaches the ugly yellow curtains. I could stay here if I had no choice, but this part of the house isn't real, isn't mine. Only the hidden realms are real, so I slink down the empty hallway, hugging the walls, knowing there will be food beyond the walls.

I emerge into a sunlit meadow with gently rolling hills. I know there is food on the other side of the hills so I run toward them, hungry and eager. An empty diner stands alone on the far side, coated in clean, gleaming aluminum. The inside is all spotless black and white tile, with counters of bright red enamel sporting spinning stools. No one is here to stop me from spinning around and around until I'm breathless and dizzy.

Stepping behind the counter, I find a hot, fresh hamburger waiting for me on a tray with perfectly salted fries and a thick milkshake. I could live here, in this diner. I could live here with the spinning stools and satisfying food. I could live here.

And the alarm blares. And Mother comes. And it's time to go to school. And I am hungry.

◆ ◆ ◆

Always, the house follows me, waiting for me in the land of dreams. My needs change but the house always knows what I need. The house is always ready for me. The house is massive; it contains everything. I could live hidden deep within. Only I know the secrets.

I need to pee. There is nowhere to pee. I find a cave that leads to a dimly-lit, grungy bathroom with overflowing toilets and a flooded floor. It feels unsafe. Where is the house? It is not mine, but at least I know it intimately. It is familiar. It is not me, but it is safe.

Leaving the cave, I wander, desperation mounting, until I see the house in the distance. I enter and look for a bathroom right away but there is no bathroom in the outer house. That's not good. How will this house fool anyone without a bathroom? How will it keep my secret places safe? Surely anyone wandering in here would realize this can't be a real house if there is no place to pee.

Squeezing through the hole in the back room, I emerge in an abandoned carnival. Although there are no other people, the lights are shining and everything has a fresh coat of paint. I admire the merry-go-round, tempted to climb aboard, but I have to pee too badly to stop.

The toilet is in an open, airy tent. I can see outside the tent but I feel safe and concealed. I unzip the fly of my trousers and a long, grey snake slithers out of the opening, slowly uncoiling himself, raising himself higher and higher until his yellow eyes are level with my own. We hold one another's gaze, both fearless.

But I have to pee, so I take his soft, warm shaft in both hands and urge him down toward the toilet. He resists and raises again to stare me in the face. I am not afraid but I don't want to pee in my own face, so I urge him downward again. Obediently, he lowers his head toward the toilet. I feel his muscles pulse and ebb against my palm and stroke his scales gently. A wave of peacefulness washes over me. I could live here, in this carnival tent. I could live here with my serpent.

The grey snake slithers down into the toilet, tail tickling briefly as he leaves my body. I am alone again.

I get out of bed and pad across the hall to the bathroom.

◆ ◆ ◆

Alan is my friend at school. We became friends because we were always being punished together. We spend every recess alone together in the classroom while everyone else goes out to play. Alan draws tanks, rifles, and fighter jets. He signs every drawing, "Rembrandt."

"I wish I had a bionic butt," Alan tells me. "The teacher would get angry with me and take out the paddle but it would just break across my bionic butt, making her angrier. She could paddle me all day and I would just laugh." Alan draws himself, bending over, laughing. A steam-powered paddlewheel ship behind him spins around, breaking every paddle across his bionic butt as the teacher looks on, glaring.

Squeezing through the hole in the back room, I emerge in the school cafeteria, empty except for Alan and our teacher. She has developed a huge, muscled arm and swings a paddle so fast the breeze lifts her hair. Her teeth are jagged, like the sawtooth blades of a cardiac monitor readout, like a row of broken beer bottles. She growls, long and low like a tiger. Alan laughs and her paddle breaks across his bionic butt.

Seeing me, she stops paddling and Alan blows away in the breeze like the smoke lifting from the tip of a cigarette. "I have something special planned for you!" she shrieks and descends upon me like nightfall.

The teacher lifts me into the air, depositing me on a ledge in the cafeteria, high above the noise and swirling chaos that breaks out as the cafeteria fills with faceless observers, heads angled up to peer at me. I do not know them; they do not know me. I am anonymous but watched as the teacher punishes me with a piercing stomach ache. I fall to my knees, curling into a ball around the pain, sucking in air as I feel the twisting inside me cramp and keen. The faceless audience gasps in wonder as I moan and writhe. I feel like a key that has finally found the slender crevice at the bottom of its lock. I fit perfectly. I open. I could live here.

My parents are watching a documentary. A man with appendicitis lays on a gurney. The emergency room attendant tests him for rebound pain, pressing his fingers into McBurney's point and quickly releasing. The man's face goes pale and he moans in pain, "Oh, Christ!" I feel my lock quietly unlatch and leave the room to hide my key.

The door to the house stands open. I timidly step inside. A beast leaps from between the door and the wall, raking my sides with long claws. I leap back outside the door.

I wander, homeless. Sleep is hard to find; no place is safe. I catch snatches of sleep in bathroom stalls.

A keening comes from a bank of thick storm clouds. An electronic wheedling. A note stretched impossibly long, angling up and down like ocean waves lapping against the shore.

My head hangs heavy with sleep, eyes hidden behind a book in the library reading room.

The hole has been blocked by a heavy armoire. I cannot get through. I am stuck in this outer house. I have become too small to pass through. I don't want to live here.

I crawl far under a bush, deep in the park.

And crawl, and crawl, and crawl through the hole in the back room.

I crawl into blackness and pain. On my hands and knees, I rock back and forth with the rhythm of the ocean, pain swirling around my waist like a silken sharp coverlet enclosing me, holding me up, pulling me forward and back, forward and back, like a boat bobbing helplessly.

I breathe in and pain rushes down to my core. I breathe out and pain swirls around my belly like a maelstrom, pulling, twisting, kneading, remaking me by turning this body inside out. I moan with the deep pleasure of the torment and climax as a baby slides bloody wet between my legs, tumbling onto the ground unseen in the blackness.

I wake and look for a baby that never was, nerve endings still tingling.

I keep that key and lock hidden beyond the hole in the back room. Who would understand?

◆ ◆ ◆

I become pregnant, for real this time, and for the first time in my life, this body is mine. Full, filled, fulfilled. My belly grows heavy like fruit drooping from high branches.

◆ ◆ ◆

Giving birth feels right. This is my sexual orientation… what is the name for it?

In a glorious swirl of erotic pain, she comes forth. Swimming out on a sea of blood, she dies before reaching the shore. This body becomes foreign soil once more. It is not mine. But I have to live here.

I stand outside the house. The door is locked.

My belly is round, a stately pleasure dome. It breaks off from my body and blood pours out, becoming a red ocean, waves lapping at the foundations of the house.

My broken belly floats, a coracle, and she has set sail for distant shores. She waves goodbye to me… and is gone.

I wake and weep.

The pain of childbirth is glorious and immense; it contains everything. I could live there. The pain of grief is decimating and immense; it contains nothing. I could die there.

I slide my key into my lock, listening to the smoothly ratcheting clicks of the tumblers falling into place. Pain brings me to this house. Pain binds me to this house. The house is immense; it contains everything. It always has what I need… when I can find the way in. The deeper I go into the house, the more it belongs to me.

I open the door to the outer house. Dust motes hang in the air, pregnant without possibilities. The air is heavy like ripened fruit left to rot on the vine. I smell her.

I cannot see her. I cannot hear her. But her smell wafts around a corner and I know she is coming toward me, walking. Impossibly walking on her newly born, newly dead legs.

I smell her.

And I run, leaving the door open behind me. I run.

I wake and weep.

Her hands at birth were loosely closed, thumb and forefinger making the casual loop an artist holds a brush with. Not flat, not fists. She was born and died in between everything.

I am in the back seat of my father's car. He is driving. My mother is in the passenger seat, urging us on. We drive past the house without stopping. My belly is empty and numb.

As we pass through a low tunnel of trees—a birth canal of green—she appears, running beside the car. Not a baby, but an adult-sized mannequin, an awkwardly-jointed wooden artist's mannequin. She was born with artist's hands. Now she has passed from artist to subject. Now she is running alongside the car, trying to catch up to the changes.

I roll the window down but it only moves a few inches. There is no key for this lock. I can barely slip my fingertips through the opening and she reaches toward me, grazing the tips of my fingers with her smooth, featureless wooden fingertips. The car drives on. She falls behind. She is gone.

We traveled too fast. We passed the house. We passed her birth. We are driving on into oblivion and no one can catch us. Nothing can catch us. I am not alone; I am not connected.

I wake and weep.

How do I explain this key, this lock? How can I talk about pleasure and pain and grief so mingled? Who would understand? Who would take my pain seriously if they knew my pleasure? Who would take my pleasure seriously if they knew my pain?

◆ ◆ ◆

I read about stomach aches. I try to give myself stomach aches. I watch videos of people holding their tummy and moaning. Most look too fake. I move on quickly to the ones that look real. I discover childbirth videos and savor the contractions that come with powerful singing moans from women who have surrendered themselves completely to the process and are holding a door open in that liminal space between life and death, open to whatever crosses the threshold.

It is the only thing that excites my libido. I can only enjoy sex if I imagine my partner holding their belly, bending forward, moaning at waves of warm, dull pain or gasping with sudden, high-pitched cramps. I savor my own pains, tasting every corner to remember them later, stacking cordwood for future fires.

◆ ◆ ◆

I find an online forum for stomach fetishists, but our similarities are mild and surface-level. They like stomach aches, too, but talk about them in ways that smell foreign to me. When I anonymously share my words, they are rejected. I am sick, they tell me. They don't want people to really have pain, they say. I am wrong to savor the genuine suffering of others. I share no more words.

◆ ◆ ◆

I have always been this way. It has no name. It is my secret. I begin reading about asexuality, trying to understand. I begin reading about other fetishes, trying to understand. I test the label, 'fetishist,' and quickly reject it. It feels wrong. I don't fit in at BDSM clubs where pain seems to be an appetizer for sex, not the main course. I don't fit in with the word 'fetish,' too often associated with S&M--Stand and Model. It's not about plastic clothes and leather whips.

It's about the soft, tender beauty of the belly and the wrenching cruelty of pain that causes a person to curl up around their core like an unearthed pill-bug. It's about the gentle moans and sighs, the writhing, the lightning strikes that shoot through the belly and render one helpless. It's about suffering and enduring. It's about comforting and being comforted. It's about the gloriously ecstatic freedom that comes after the storm.

It's sexy, yes. But it's deeper than sexy. It's all the way to my core. It's who I am. I could live here.

My gut is twisted inside me. I cannot stand. Sprawled on the dusty hardwood floor of the outer house, I arch my back to press my burning belly into the boards. It is misery. It is marvelous.

I need so badly to climb through the hole into my real world but I am pinned by the pain like an insect skewered to the pinning block. Creeping like an inch worm. I slide along the hallway, gasping for breath, sweat dropping from my brow. My pubic arch presses against the floor of its own volition as I climax again and again at the exquisite pain until it soars above my grasp and I can no longer bear it.

I awake in a fever. The hospital keeps me for two weeks and three surgeries.

It is dangerous to love the warning signs. Mine is a dangerous sexuality.

The morphine has changed the landscape outside the house. I know the house that hides my secrets is nearby, but I am enclosed in a box canyon of obsidian cliffs. A spiral ziggurat rises from the canyon floor, dark caves hewn straight into the stone. Cat-like women made of black leather guard each opening, growling, flashing gleaming black claws, lashing their whip-tails. The air crackles with electricity and the smell of ozone. I back away from the crisp snap-snap-snap of the domicatrices' tails.

I do not like morphine dreams.

The hole in the back room of the outer house has become a spiral sliding board. I slip through and spin down, down, down, past waterfalls and hanging gardens of moss and ferns into a crystalline cavern filled with shafts of sunlight punching through openings in the arched ceiling of this inner house.

She is waiting for me. She lays curled around herself on a thick bed of deep green moss. She rocks back and forth slowly from the pains curving through her swollen belly. Her moans of pain are moans of pleasure. I go to her, vibrating with libido, stomach clenching hotly with empathy pains.

I hold her in my arms and rock with her, matching her rhythms. I whisper soothing words in her ear. My hands creep around to cradle her belly and I feel my groin swell at the thrill of holding her pain in my hands, caressing her, soothing her, comforting her.

She turns to me and presses her hard belly into my softness and I nearly burst with pleasure as she writhes against me. I roll on top of her and she moans at my weight pressing against her stomach. I enter her with long, slow strokes, still whispering words of comfort as I feel my pressure building within me. As I climax deep inside her, I rain kisses on her face, noticing for the first time that it is my face.

I awaken, belly aching with emptiness, aching with the lack of pain.

What is this called?

I am wandering the outer house, bored and restless. I can't find the hidden hole. I've hidden it too well this time. I feel trapped in a lifeless no-place. I sit on the heavy furniture. Stand. Pace. I look out all the windows. I pace some more.

Another pass through the back hall reveals the door to the farthest room, invisible to me until now. I enter and find a full-length mirror. I look. I put my hand on my flat chest, I stroke my dark beard. I fall through that old familiar hole near the baseboard and spend the night running down the beach, miles and miles of packed sand. Ocean roaring in my left ear. Breakers rolling in like herds of white horses. I am free.

I come out in my journal for a graduate class about sex and violence. It feels terrifying and liberating. My professor reads my words and quietly holds them in a space of acceptance. My files are archived in someone else's library now. My strangely slippery key and complicated lock have been seen and wordlessly understood. There is still no word for what I am, but it has grown larger with the sharing. It has crept out of the fog-shrouded bracken beyond my rabbit hole, through the outer house, and out into the wake world for the first time.

I have never been this naked in front of a near-stranger before.

I begin to feel as if my sexuality might not be so awful as I had imagined.

My sexuality is a deep part of who I am. I begin to feel as if I might not be so awful as I had imagined.

I see the house across the street and run toward it. As I run, the ground comes closer and closer to my face. I get to the other side and realize I have become a dog. I can't open the door. I can't even access the outer house, let alone the inner reaches where I dwell.

I come out to someone I'm dating. I reveal myself in layers. At first they are excited by my fetish. "It's contagious," they tell me, as they start sharing images and videos with me. The asexuality outside of my area of fetish gives them pause. The transgender identity ends their sexual interest in me.

And still I don't have a useful name for what I am.

Stomach Ache Fetishist.

The words are right. The feelings I have about them are not. They are not my words. And when I search on the words I find so many related fetishes that are not mine. Trampling, stuffing, corsets, inflation, tickling, punching. The words are not mine. The stomach ache fetish community is so small and so fragmented into tiny sub-fetishes. So few people seem to share mine. So few of them seem to hold it as the sole core of their sexuality.

Pregnancy Fetishist.

Also wrong. It is not pregnancy that arouses me. It is not even childbirth that arouses me. It is the sensations, the feelings, the experiences. The pain.

Partialism.

But it's not the belly that stirs me. It's the fire in the belly that moves me toward ecstasy.

Alvinolagnia. Algolagnia. Alvinoalgolagnia? Can that even be a word?

And everywhere online I read people calling my sexuality sick and saying that people like me need counselling. My sexuality is uncommon, yes. Is it wrong?

How can I even talk about my sexuality when I don't have the right words for my slippery key, my gnarled lock?

I stand at the door to the house, looking out. All is dark, save a single pole light. Insects swarm around the light and bats silently swoop and swerve to catch them. I listen to their echolocation before closing the door and wandering toward the small hole in the back room.

I am slowly growing comfortable here. Everything changes, yet it is always familiar. This place is me; it grows and changes along with me. I could change it more. I could make it into a real home.

I could live here.

I do live here.

Segen's Medical Dictionary tells me my sexuality is coded into my genetics. "Algolagnia is currently attributed to the misinterpretation of the brain of painful stimuli as pleasurable, which is linked in some cases to a mutation in SCN9A, which encodes a sodium ion channel."

"Do you think you're this way because you're Autistic?"

"How can I know?"

I am every way that I am because I'm Autistic. There is a reason the medical words call autism pervasive. Every thought I have is an autistic thought. Every sensation I feel is an autistic experience. Every piece of my flesh--even those parts I want to remove--is composed of autistic cells. Why shouldn't my sexuality be written in my chromosomes as well?

Everything I am is twisted into tight little knots. Kinks. My genes are kinky. My DNA is massive; it contains everything.

I could live here.

I do live here.

A Day in Three

Alyssa Gonzalez

The Day I Died

Edward killed her. I will never forgive him. He'll wish he was a cantaloupe when I'm done with him. He'll wish he was a cantaloupe still attached to the vine, being trampled by elephants.

I don't know why he did it. She was beautiful, she was strong, and she was free. Then again, maybe I do know.

I'll find him. I'll find him and I'll kill him. No, too easy. She deserves better. When I'm done with him, he'll wish I was going to kill him afterwards. He'll beg for it.

Why did he do it? What was she to him? What was *I* to him? I didn't even know Edward. What did that fiend want from us? Why her? Why me?

Questions. The questions never end. I may as well ask why she came to me. I may as well ask what cosmic force took pity on my deprived, wretched hide and sent her to me when it did. While I'm at it, I may as well ask why she stayed. I had nothing to offer her except kindness, art, and dry humor. But she stayed, and she was happy. At least, she looked happy. She could never really understand my art because I couldn't find a machine to print Braille, but she stayed anyway.

It was beautiful. I didn't understand it and that made it more so. I never understood why she put up with my eccentricities when no one else seemed to understand. She even put up with my twitch, but I think that was because she couldn't see it.

What was she to you, Edward? She kept to herself, she didn't bother anybody, and she certainly didn't bother *you*. I'll never know why you took her.

I'll never find another one like her. A cold wind towards me would feel like a summer breeze, warm and content with a hint of sea spray. I could feel her from the next room, warm, sweet, and gentle. She'd tell me I looked great just to hear me exhale at her wit. I never understood how she could dress herself without looking at her clothes.

I never understood a lot of things. I don't expect to. I'm a damned fool and I'd be a cursed fool if I didn't know it. I'd probably have overdosed, and lived, too.

She was beautiful. People wondered why she didn't do more with it. People wondered why she didn't come out of that dark shell and join their company. They'll never understand her or the thousands like her. They'll never understand me. They'll never understand me before they understand her.

They never figured out that she just wasn't interested. They found other blind ones and thought they'd all be curious about the world they would never see, the world of color, light, and bodies in motion. She didn't care about the bodies in motion, and they couldn't figure it out. The voices—the voices were enough for her. She thought she could learn everything she needed to know about bodies in motion by listening to the ridiculous drivel they flung around like it meant something. She had it all figured out, until she heard me.

I must have been ruminating about something over too many glasses of Carnaby's. I must have been talking to myself, about myself, about anything and everything, when she came to me. I saw her feel her way to the seat opposite me and look blankly in my direction. I knew she couldn't see because every time I raised my voice she turned her head to make sure it was still me talking. Eventually I ran out of insight and realized I wouldn't remember anything after I sobered up, so I just stopped and looked at her.

She spoke. She told me something—I don't even remember what it was. She told me and suddenly we both understood that neither of us knew a damn thing about anything. She didn't leave after that. Ever since then, she was at my side, a kindness I never deserved.

You'll live to regret this, Edward. You'll even wish I dismembered you and left you for dead on a roadside. You'll wish you were that cantaloupe trampled by elephants.

Why did you do it, Edward? I didn't even know your name before you killed her.

Her every step, her every sway, her every breath fascinated me. I could watch her for hours on end, just watching. I would listen to her speak for hours before I realized I was hungry or the machine was broken again. She never understood even the concept of watching. In a way, that made it better.

She would tell me that I had no reason to be such a recluse, that with my massive charms I could have everything that could be had out there with the bodies in motion. What about her, I'd ask. Her charms were just as wondrous. But she *chose* to be a sponge rather than a spigot, and she got the longer end of the stick. She never did lose sight of that choice the way I did. She refused to acknowledge the bodies in motion because they were not worth acknowledging, not because she was afraid. That was the biggest difference between us, and the one that kept things interesting.

After she came to me there was nothing to fear, not even the scar on the side of my head from when I charged headfirst into a sharp corner as a child. She found it one night as we lay next to each other and didn't know what it was. I had to compare it to the one on her hip from her appendectomy. I never had to wonder if the look on my face, that unhappy, dangerous look, was visible. Now I don't know.

Is that what you wanted, Edward? Were you sick of your dangerous sidelong glance, your twitching hand, and your infernal stutter that all seemed too much like mine? Did you see how happy I was with her and think I didn't deserve any more than you? Did you think you'd make yourself feel better by ending her life? There's a reason monsters like you die alone and unhappy.

That reason is misanthropes like me that you've crossed for the last time. I'll make you wish you were a rotting cantaloupe, you son of a bitch. At least then you'd go quickly.

◆ ◆ ◆

The Day I Loved

You were never meant for me. The certainty is as torturous as the knife wound that gave it to me. I had hoped it were not so; I had hoped that once more, I would be terribly wrong but that it would finally be in my benefit. Alas, I have failed again.

You drove me mad. Every time I looked at you I saw the *stars*. I saw a depth I had only imagined, envisioned, fantasized. You didn't have to say anything; I could see it in your eyes, your stance, that nervous yet self-assured walk that drove me wild with curiosity. If the cosmos itself had a body, it was yours.

I saw you, in all your wondrous splendor, but you didn't see me. You never saw me. It wasn't just your blindness—you didn't acknowledge me at all. I spoke to you and, with the supreme indifference of the cosmos, you didn't deign to respond. No matter how I greeted you or what insights I had to offer, I just wasn't there, was just another background noise.

I couldn't stand it. The wrongness of it stood out, made it seem unreal. I felt like I was an actor putting on an elaborate façade every time you came near, except that façade was me, exactly as I was. I could not understand it. It got to the point that I couldn't feel myself when you were near. I would walk into trees because I felt disconnected from reality. The tree disagreed.

It sickened me. We were meant for each other, you and me. It was perfect. I could see in you all of the things I ever wanted, all of the things I ever wanted to see. I could see the *stars*. In you, my dear blind one, I saw the universe.

No one ever caused me so much suffering. It was terrifying. Just looking at you caused pain, the recognition of your incredible beauty and perfection enough to singe the scalp. I looked at you and I wanted to stop before it killed me, but I could not. It didn't work out the way I hoped it would.

You knew I was there, you probably knew what I had come to do, but you stayed even as I whispered into your ear, knife in hand. You waited for me, but you didn't see me. Even then I was just another body in motion, another waste of your precious time. Why did you stay? What did you hope to do?

I never understood you, my dear blind one, and neither did anyone else. You were utterly baffling to them. They left you alone because you stood as a hole in every conceptual framework they had. You were beautiful, and you were quiet. You could have been an exemplar of their pointless kind and instead disdained them. There was simply nothing about them that you wanted. It was too perfect, it made too much sense, it made them uncomfortable. All of them but her.

I never saw her coming. I thought I had time on my side, time enough to prove my worth to you. Time was never on my side, not once in my pitiful existence. Time, you sadistic terror, I scorn you here, now, and forevermore. I spit on you.

It was as if she appeared from thin air, this intoxicated fool blathering to herself in a corner. I watched her and I laughed, yet my heart went out to her. I saw in her bits of myself I had hoped not to acknowledge—a timid clumsiness that led her to withhold things even from herself without the aid of cheap gin. I saw myself sitting there where she was, poisoning my body for no better reason than spite, and it worried me.

Then you arrived. I saw you ignoring the others as they nervously discussed you, and I smiled. You were a goddess, and your silent siren song drew me in ways no other ever did, or would.

You stood there, and then you sat there, lost in contemplation of your unseen world. I watched you. I saw in you the perfect puzzle piece for my incompleteness—the missing piece of my cosmos, the stars behind the moon. I almost died then and there, almost fell over in joyous convulsions from your presence alone.

You moved. You felt your way over to her and my heart sank, a dank chill filling my body. I felt myself receding into that moldy morass inside me as you spoke. I remember every word, every stab of a word you uttered earnestly to her. Your honesty was like getting hit in the face with a sledgehammer. You left with her, and my tongue was bleeding because I had almost bitten it in half.

After that, it was out of my hands. I found the knife in some drunken thug's pocket. He or his friends would probably kill me if they knew I took it, but that didn't stop me. I followed you. Neither of you ever saw the shady freak following you. Maybe you saw the shine on my glasses, two circles promising dire relief.

I followed fully aware that what I was about to do was horrifyingly wrong and would bring me no peace. I was in the grips of the most terrible agony I had ever faced, one that bore the face of a goddess and a body of failure. Why did I hesitate? I could have found you long before you noticed her, taken her place in a heartbeat, but I was an obsessive and a coward.

I followed you, and I followed you every day. I watched you. I watched that perfect union of body and soul that should have been *mine.* You blind goddess, you should have been *mine.* What was she that I was not? She and I were both unseemly fools, unaware of our own ridiculous eccentricity and that of the world around us. You may as well have joined with me, but why didn't you?

Goddess, your existence tormented me: every glance a wound, a wound so wondrously infectious that I could not stop. Your every move, step, pause, they were mortal blows and I was a dead man walking. I couldn't feel myself, but I felt you. I floated, with only the glare on my lenses reminding me that I yet retained physical existence.

There has never been greater perfection than in the moment when you separated from her. The two of you went your separate ways and the adrenaline smell floated from my pores. One hand held a knife that was in my pocket a moment before and the other held my clenched, pulsating heart. My breathing became an engine of destruction, tearing up my throat. In my mind, I reached out to you. You stopped.

You did not look around. You stood utterly still and faced the water, where a green heron was eying a meal. I slipped up to you and spoke in your ear. You accepted my confessions without flinching, even as I raised the clean, sharp blade. You simply stood there, unmoved, as I whispered that she had no greater right to you, the goddess, the cosmos's proxy to the world, than I did, that your existence was agony to me because of its beauteous perfection, that every time I contemplated it, even now, I had to restrain tears that burned like acid. You stood unmoved as I seethed.

You turned, looking blankly into my traumatized face. I looked deep into those blank, starry eyes. You kissed me, and in that too-brief eternity I was vindicated. I stood in awe of the blind goddess, and you told me to meet you in your next life as you walked away.

You never wounded me so deeply as that day, when you led me to you and led me away again in the same motion. My mind bled profusely, staining my thoughts red. The blade flashed; a stalk was cut.

I will never be able to dilute the memory of your last divine moment, choking on stardust, driving me endlessly to my fate. I saw the dying cosmos in dying eyes, each star fading in turn, just like me. Just like me.

◆ ◆ ◆

The Day I Lived

I was born loud. People talk about me like it's dark in here, like being blind means I can't think or feel. But in here, it's loud. Wind, rain, air vents, footsteps, conversation, breathing—they're loud. I hid when I was smaller, burying myself in the clean laundry to make the sounds stop. I tried the dirty laundry once, but the smells were too much. Cocooned, silent, and warm, I could endure being alive. Blindness was a mercy. It saved me from having the same relationship with light.

I learned to pick out strands of sound and hold them, listening to their sources. There was information there, about the shape of the world, about people. When I could stand to even be around that whirlwind, I could learn how to maneuver within it. It was hard to want to, though. People bored me. They prattled endlessly about things I didn't even know how to care about, or couldn't possibly experience, or seemed too open-and-shut to warrant that much noise. I'd rather have listened to birds and crickets, or air vents. Air vents at least had a schedule I could predict.

It was hard to care about how I looked, knowing it was only for them. I settled into fabrics that didn't feel...too much. I wore soft, slippery fabrics, things that let it stay a little quieter in here, without snagging or sticking. People tell me they match most of the time. I don't know what that means.

I wasn't prepared for that party. It was loud. I had trouble keeping my bearings, buffeted around by waves of all the nothings people were barking at each other. Finally, one sound, for the first time, made me *want* to hear it.

Her voice was rumbly, like she was fighting a throat infection. The liquid in her glass might have been floor cleaner, or might have been gin, but the piny scent would wash the pathogens out of her throat regardless. I sat across from her and listened to her talk about herself, about the gin, about how awful and boring and annoying people all were, and I was rapt. Eventually, she stopped, and after a while, I told her, "I bet you're a hit at parties."

She laughed, and I laughed.

We spent a lot of time together after that. Her misanthropy was a joy, and her voice made listening easy. We were very different, she and I. Even if I hated it, I could still listen and learn about strangers, picking up on all the silliness that passed for their days, but she couldn't stand it. The gin—Carnaby's, she called it, "the cheap stuff"—wasn't far behind if she was ever to spend time around people other than me. When it was just us, she was different, open and wounded and sometimes even tender. She would tell me about her writing and I would listen, enrobed in the rasps of her voice and the rare treat of her enthusiasm. It made her sad that, with no screen-reader handy, I'd never read it, but I didn't feel like I needed to. What I wanted, I already had, in her hands on my hips and her happiness in my arms. We spent weeks and months together, each making the other feel like, just for these moments, it was worth keeping on.

The footsteps behind me that day were not new, but they were newly intense. I'd heard them before, timid, determined, increasingly angry, but today they were vibrating. I had wondered about those footsteps, imagined there might be something new to understand in the feet attached to them. Today, those footsteps were filled with every emotion, all at once: anger, sadness, fear, desire, several more I could not name. Maybe they felt like that before, too.

She and I parted ways, and I waited for the steps. I could hear a stream in the distance, a fountain closer by. If I didn't stay, he'd have followed me home. I felt the march of those terrifying feet until they stood behind me, breath on my neck, eyeglasses moving my hair. The stranger told me how much he wanted me in his life, how his whole existence was desperately empty without me in it, that a supernatural destiny demanded the two of us be together and every moment I spent away from him was a torment he endured only for the promised future. I remembered his voice from the background of so many places I had been, enough places that he had to know exactly where to find me. I had wondered about that voice. Most of the time, I'd heard him dismissive, nervous, confused, all things I found endearing. In another life, I might have greeted him first, curious what was in that mind. But he always spoke with an intensity that made me stay away. Something else was there, something I instinctively did not trust. Something I heard now, far too clearly. I heard no one else, only the startled birds. There was no running.

The pain in his voice was almost as loud as my terror. He sounded like what she might have been, what she avoided becoming because no one ever convinced her that her loneliness was anyone else's fault. He shook with emotion, desperate and weak. For a moment, his sadness was gripping, and I felt for him. He scared me, yet I pitied him. I needed him to know that there was more for him to feel than this maelstrom of anger and longing. I needed him to know enough hope, enough kindness, and enough affection that he could be satisfied with *right now,* instead of forever, and then this could end right here and be okay for both of us. Maybe I was dreaming, maybe the fear made me think up an impossible plan. Maybe I didn't want to exit the present without taking a chance on the future. Maybe I hoped the future would be better than I was already picturing.

I turned around, and I kissed him. I told him to meet me in his next life, where perhaps we'd be the ones who found each other, instead of me and her.

I didn't have any more thoughts.

Monsters

Andrew Reichart

I: WHY THEY DON'T JUST KILL US

Here I go limping through Feral City for the millionth time and hopefully the last. Not because I'll die today, not like I'm ever getting out of this town, I mean the limp. If I can get to the Facility. Nobody remembers but I used to run. I ran like those horses you see in videos, like the wind gusting down the bleak glass canyons downtown. Haven't run in decades but if things go the way I hope they might, I might run tonight. Run through the night streets of our nightmare city, this patchwork of collided worlds, monsters creeping through the cracks and monsters hunting them.

Way back when, the night the embermen got me, one grasped my ankle, one had my knee, and the third latched onto my head. Since then the worst has been the knee. They sucked the life outta me there, cartilage fucked, arthritis grindy awful. Not that my head isn't fucked too. My thoughts never have been quite right since. Nothing like Freda or Presto or Koskk struggling to string two thoughts together, I got it off of my head quick enough, fraying it back to its own dimension. I remember kicking the one from my ankle with my free foot, shredding it like ashes at the impact, the glow going out of it as it wisped away. But the third clung to my knee, and sucked, and glowed, and as I strove to wrangle it off me, my hands and fingers sank into its unearthly half-tangible flesh and lost their strength forever. Weakly I struck at it, to no avail. Then I fainted. I can only assume that once it fed its fill, it just floated off.

Nobody knows why they don't just kill us. It's not like they come back and feed on the same people again. Maybe their appetite just never amounts to a lethal encounter. Perhaps it's some old instinct, e.g., on their world prey is scarce and they must leave it alive. Weird to think of a world where the predators don't kill their prey. No, wait, that's what we have here: they feed upon us slowly, the monsters who run the city, profiteering from every angle: our labor, our culture, our struggles, and our misfortunes. Left living we also have other uses, such as guinea pigging for the Facility. Not predators then, there's a different word for this. Our rulers are what's known as "parasites."

The best parasite keeps its host alive. So we're livestock. A few of us are literally eaten; or killed in libidinous rituals of "justified" violence, shot dead in the street by Monster Hunters or Reality Patrol; or carved up by wannabe demon princelings with their grafted-on tiger heads on a nouveau riche killing spree. Most of this multilayered web of parasitism, though, amounts to nothing but mundane racketeering: rents, wages, lenders, pimps, and swindlers. So they farm us less like a slaughterhouse and more like a dairy.

This understanding still fails to explain why they don't just kill me, useless, unable to work and with nothing to rob. Perhaps they just haven't gotten around to me yet. But why not just let me starve? Why my daily stipend? Does some genuine compassion leak through the institutions? Implausible. It must just be worth the expense to maintain whatever stability my existence lends to the situation: *Watch your step or you could end up like him.* Or maybe, yes this must be the answer, the demon princes feast on suffering itself. And they've made our neighborhood of Wolf Town a test chamber for crafting maximum deliciousness.

One little delicacy is how we survivors incur blame for our attacks. It's not as though embermen lurk around every corner, getting grabbed is not like walking heedless into traffic, these are rare interdimensional beings same as most monsters from Outside. But it's always, "Why were you walking alone at night? Were you paying attention?" May as well ask why I stepped under that falling flowerpot.

Today, however, the Facility claims to have an experimental nanobio regrow injection to repair my tissue damage from Emberman's Syndrome. Literally limp into the office and dance your way out, they say. Haven't danced since I was twenty, almost thirty years ago. Don't get your hopes up, they say. No worry for that. Can't recall the last time I hoped for anything. But if this works it'll it hurt less to live in this hellish city; and if not, here's hoping it kills me. First, though, to get to the Facility.

No idea how. The direct bus line to the island got severed last year by the new spur of the maglev monorail. The map on my phone suffers a terrible signal; I'm guessing our nearest neighborhood juryrigged meshnet node is down. Ordinary technical difficulty perhaps, or birds, or maybe Monster Hunter drones grabbing the dishes off of our roofs again on behalf of CentralNet or whatever-the-hell company runs the cables these days. So I'm half guessing my route. I've got the bus stop right on the corner, and if I'm reading the phone right, it'll take me two hours and three buses from two different busing systems. Or, the monorail will zip me straight to the island and drop me a block from the Facility after a twelve minute ride.

But it's ten blocks to the monorail station. That's at least a half hour walk for me, and it'll hurt like hellfire for the rest of the day and worse tomorrow. No, wait, it won't, not if this works. Ha, I can barely wrap my head around this. Still, I'm in no rush to get there, and I dread the pain of that march. I've got time. How much are the buses, that's one AC Transit fare plus transfer each way, one Mercury Wolf fare each way, about, hmm, eight thousand bucks. Leaves me enough for two small VatGrown™ meatsticks, one each for breakfast and lunch. Phone says the monorail is just six and a half grand. Leaving me enough for *three* meat sticks, plus a Coke. I am so fuckin hungry already. Gonna need that Coke after hiking in this heat. Hope they give me a bottle of water at the Facility.

So limping ten blocks to the station it is. My right leg isn't so bad this morning, but it will be at the end of this from compensating for the other. I concentrate on keeping my pace as slow and even as I can. That'll hurt both legs least. But I just want all this over with, so it's hard not to find myself rushing.

As for my left leg, it's never good. Ankle pops with every step, which doesn't hurt now but will. Always worst of all though is the knee. There's an unsettling looseness in my joint, bones sometimes grinding a little, never know when a step will strike sudden agony instead of mere discomfort. And of course once in a blue moon it just goes out of joint. Not too far, but still, out is out. I don't know how it is for you, but when my body abruptly stops working, I drown in animal panic. Forcing the knee back into place is terrifying and then it aches for days. It doesn't ever bend well, so I can't just ride a bicycle, I've tried that with just the one leg, it does not work, especially not with my balance. That emberman on my head fucked my balance along with my brain. Skateboard similarly no option, plus when I was grappling the emberman on my knee, it ate the life out of my hands and wrists, so I can't count on them to stop my fall if I fall. Times like this I daydream of one of those motorized wheelchairs. Hell, I'll never see that much money in my life, if I'm idly wishing I might as well wish for an antigrav hoverchair.

A hoverchair, for example, could speed me past this shit: I limp alongside the heartbreaking razorwire fence around our old community garden, heavy machinery inert within for weeks now. The fence protects a small triangular block of dry dirt and withered plants churned up by steel treads. The lumber from our raised beds lies piled to the side or just splintered around. The gutter, just this block, is swept clean of litter —the cleanup bot must have done its round recently, because folks make an effort to throw our trash here or toss it over the fence. There's the little robot, sleeping next to bulldozer and backhoe, no "benefit" to anyone, just part of the falseface. I try to hawk spit between coils of razorwire, end up hitting one. My feckless spit slowly drips down the fence. Our land lies destroyed inside, mangled by "progress," but that bot has tidied our scattered soil of every wrapper and soda can, and compressed unsightly trash into dense little cubes stacked beside our lumber.

I limp onward. At the corner there's that goddamn sign hanging on the fence: "Coming Soon: Neighborhood Benefit Coalition Tower." Blazoned with that piece of shit logo from the City trying to rebrand us as "ThingTown." Forget the fact that this is Wolf Town for generations, going all the way back to the merger between Earth and Tal Sharnis — what the hell kind of name is that, nobody wants to go to ThingTown, who comes up with this shit. They killed the wolves and now they wanna defang their memory.

We tried to stop them from carving out our space. The entity destined to reside in this damned tower, this "community organization," makes for a perfect parasite, sliding in behind smiling faces but in truth nothing but a conduit for the greater parasite, Mammon. Neighborhood Benefit Coalition, as if a friendly name can sucker us out of seeing the essence of a thing when we're under its boot. "Coalition," as in, cabal of real estate and charity rackets, with their neighborhood collaborators.

"Neighborhood" meaning owners old and new (not renters), interests uniformly aligned whether their property is the postage-stamp fiefdom of their own home, or a business, a building, or just abandoned land. And "Benefit" in the only forms Mammon can perceive, increased commerce and property value.

Which means clearing us out. Those of us who are from here for generations, but mere tenants. Or our people out on the street, mostly refugees from last year's neighborhood. Clearing out those of us, in the perfect asymmetry of injustice, who have nowhere else to go. No other place to pass time together in the often-beautiful outdoors, the weather of Tal Sharnis the sole luxury of our lives; nowhere else but concrete stoops and streetcorners. Those of us who actually needed this garden for food, who never otherwise set eyes on fresh vegetables, or simply don't have enough calories.

We fought, but we were too few, too weak. Even most renters were no help, newcomers and old timers too, atomized into their separate little homes and individualities, unable to quite see the problem. Sure they'd say they "like the garden," but they didn't need it, they'll never miss it, and most of them wouldn't say so to our faces but they'd rather we be gone as much as Mammon does. Too loud, too messy, too public, too numerous, too "intimidating" merely for occupying space like we have a right to be in this world. So we had each other, but no resources, no discipline, and none of us dared consider anything too militant. Everyone knows what happened to the wolves, whether we saw it firsthand or not.

So some suckers got caught up pushing a ridiculous petition —a delay for further city investigation, who wrote this shit? Why demand a delay, what does that accomplish when our sole and only option is "hands off forever"? What is a city investigation of a city project going to arrive at except the goahead? Then Haki and Barca swept us all up into planning for a rally on the site. Fine maybe if there's a plan to do something with the attention, if recruiting and outreach are your bag rather than direct action, but before you know it there's too many cooks pulling in different directions, the loudest of them the least militant. On the day itself it's the fakest sort of theatrics, as I expected, "blocking" one of our park entrances while no one is even trying to get in, not a Monster Hunter or bulldozer in sight. Coalition collaborators hogged the megaphone for a tedious hour of rhetorical word salad, ultimately just reiterating the tepid demands from the ridiculous petition.

A few days later Haki and Barca and Fatima and Larry, furious at the thing having ended up so toothless, get ahold of the megaphone and march a small gang of us to City Hall. Welp, no marching for me, even if I could. I'm like, "Barca, why are you planning to make a stink on the way downtown, there aren't even ten of you, you will not make it, you want to slide quietly into the city council meeting and *then* go for it, you should come with me by bus. And keep that megaphone hidden till you're in the council chamber." They did not make it. Monster Hunters scattered them, Larry got a beating, he and Belle spent the night in little cages, and they lost the megaphone.

Finally the City got around to fencing in our little park with chainlink. That night they didn't leave anyone to watch it, we were fast and coordinated and quiet. I took southern lookout while the others took wirecutters to the fence, piled it in awkward bales in the street, siphoned auto fuel from newcomers' cars and lit those bales on fire. Fled before the Monster Hunters arrived. The next morning we saw the heat had rendered every yard of fence unsalvageable. Finally, getting somewhere. The neighborhood buzzed with the predictable shock and outrage but also an astonishing amount of praise. Folks love a fire. And some folks love it whenever underdogs assert their power.

The next day the City surrounded the park with razorwire. We broke in and occupied it, even me, I knew my body would regret the inevitable manhandling but this seemed like our last stand. They cleared us out easily enough with a stinging nanite cloud. Beat Larry again and Mayra with batons, broke her fingers, broke his jaw. Didn't arrest anybody but Haki. Throughout the whole process the black-armored Monster Hunters just seemed bored. That was the last we saw of Haki. They told his mother he killed himself with a bedsheet. So that was that. As the saying goes, nonviolence only works when your enemy has a conscience.

Speaking of atomization, here I go tuning out the shitty outside world with my headphones. Listening to music and Monster Hunter dispatch simultaneously. Common sense says don't cover both ears in the street, but fuck it. What's going to happen that's worse than all day every day? I've seen fifty years of this shit, thirty of it limping. These crappy headphones don't block out the street anyways. And it's broad daylight — not that I haven't seen fucked up shit in daytime, just that it's easier to track what's going on around you. The music I'm listening to is Pamil, don't give me your "it can't be good if it's popular" snobbery, she's fabulous, plus this is her first album before she got famous.

Meanwhile the Monster Hunter scanner says there's been another goddamn hit and run.

Car culture bleeding into Wolf Town from all directions. Neighborhoods all around us already hollowed out and remade by the unthinking invisible hand of Mammon, resettled the way we're gonna be. This shit began on Earth long before the merger and after the merger they're doing it still, cannibalizing us, only now there's more space aliens and more literal cannibalism. Newcomers' gleaming wheeled carapaces shortcut across Wolf Town like they're on little freeways, encapsulated drivers incapable of perceiving or even conceiving our centuries-old pedestrian culture. They mostly hit kids and old people and gimps like me. I hear the ambulance siren in the distance. The mantra of Feral City.

I limp past some of our genuine stoop culture. Languidly rolling dice we have Barca in another ridiculous hat he thinks is cool, Louie still looking sedate since his grandma died, Belle on her day off I guess, and the mantis newlyweds Hasaashkakk and Kkesshket. Throwing dice for mere dollars, a gentlebeing's game, all but Louie bantering loudly at each other. Some fuckers get bent out of shape over dice but these are friends not hustlers, whoever wins "big" will take the rest of them down to the store for a round of drinks. Even so, they all cool it abruptly as a Monster Hunter APC rumbles by en route to the hit and run. In my headphones I hear its driver talking shit about us as it passes, then there's a squeal of feedback.

The merging of the two cities killed a lot of people, created chronic aftershock rifts in reality that continue to this day, but some folks can profiteer off of anything. Every disaster can be ridden to riches if you're ruthless enough. Monsters coming through interdimensional portals? Hire my Monster Hunters. I wonder if the demon princes ran Tal Sharnis before it crashed into California, or if they took over post-cataclysm. No way to be sure. Literally: the Reality Patrol has futzed the historical record throughout the city. Nothing's consistent. I wonder when the powers-that-be figured out that if they can keep us rootless in body and mind, then we're adrift, easy to push around.

Belle hollers to me. "You rolling? Ha ha," she brays. She knows I hate dice. I tip an imaginary hat to her and stagger onward. At the corner some bohemian has laser-etched a stencil into the sidewalk concrete, the image of a cartoon headstone with a dollar sign on it and the legend GENTRIFICATION KILLS. So this slummer feels entitled to literally carve into the stone of our street their armchair analysis of our predicament. With that asinine image, what is that supposed to mean, it doesn't even make sense, what, it's Mammon's grave? That's the opposite of what you mean, asshole. Meanwhile none of us have any goddamn laser etcher, you know, those of us actually at risk of being killed by this shit. In keeping with their incisive use of backwards symbolism, this motherfucker has no concept that they themselves are the first wave of this shit. Second wave, I mean. The first is the true down and outers: the junkies and crusties and runaways, the unlucky, the beset, the cursed. Only once enough of them pave the way do we see the bohos and artists and slummers, the voluntary semi-dropouts with a little bit of cash to spare for shit like second hand laser etchers to use in their "work." These second wavers are the ones who actually generate the "cool" —which draws in the shops and restaurants and tastemakers.

Or, maybe, this boho *does* know their role in Mammon's machinery, and they "feel guilty." So they're trying to make up for it by "reaching out" like this. Your feelings? How do you think we feel, having to look at your shit years after you move on to settle the next frontier? Tell us who exactly in your life has "gentrification" "killed." You lived next door to a junkie who OD'd? You saw a trail of blood on the sidewalk one day? You watched an eviction that went lethal —out your window from across the street? These count as no fuckin body. Me I can make you a list, off the cuff we have Jasmine, Haki, Lowell, the whole Bezzior family, the four who died in the Harmony Building landlord arson —plus Azok and Washington who escaped the flames, only to get shot dead when the

Monster Hunters cleared the tent encampment under the overpass. That's just this year. And you force us to deal with your shit on top of it. If my treatment works today I'm gonna pick up some paying work and buy myself a chisel and permanently erase your shit off our street myself.

Around the corner, here's another one, blazoned on the concrete wall of the old abandoned bus station. Fuck, this is even worse. An asymmetrical star-shaped symbol, arrows pointing out of it in all directions, and the words "Inside Outsiders." There's no goddamn Inside-Outsiders in this neighborhood, no one actually cracking open dimensional rifts, this is just some junkie mystic art school dropout with a death cult fetish. What makes these chumps think more chaos will make things better? You only think this way if you have no skin in the game. Backups. Options. Self-absorbed assholes, may the embermen get you and cripple your hands so you stop making this shit.

Speaking of chaos, here's a small crack in reality, a real one. An ordinary seam in concrete crosses the sidewalk and up the wall, leftover from some old aftershock, scraggly weeds growing out of it. The upper reaches of the crack turn horizontal and leftward to cross under the faux warlock etching. In that lateral span of the crack, reality itself seems to shimmer like a mirage, revealing the barest glimpse of another world.... Two slender arms reach forth, stretching slowly towards me.... I lurch away as they grasp for me, nearly bowling over a pair of passersby. It's Barca and Belle chorusing "Hey now" and "What you on about today?"

Jauntily re-seating his hat on his head, Barca continues, "Isn't your surgery today?"

"You see that?" I stammer, pointing at the crack. The arms are gone. It shimmers for a second longer and stops.

"They gonna fix your head as well as your leg?" asks Belle, laughing, slapping me lightly on the butt.

I stare at the crack in the wall.

"Spooky symbol," says Belle.

They saunter along toward the store. "Catch up to me there," calls Barca over his shoulder, "You want a soda or a beer?"

I stare at the cracked lichened concrete for a long moment, then limp onward, shaken. The next stretch of wall is freshly plastered with hundreds of identical Pamil posters. In each, she is haloed by a sigil not unlike the Inside-Outsider etching, jagged arrows tendriling out like little bolts of lightning. The whole wall is covered with the cover of her new album. In overwhelming repetition she stands there by the hundred, domineering and regal, perched on platform shoes of ultra-rare Earth cork (I know this from Mayra drunkenly rambling about these shoes the other day), staring down at her subjects with slitted yellow eyes in her sleek black panther head. Her body from the neck down also sports various modifications within the range of seemingly human. Her feline head bows haloed by the glowing sigil.

After the swath of Pamils there's some other pop star, with similar pseudo-Inside-Outsider styling. Whoever this dude is, their two albums seem to share a theme, or at least a marketing director. He crouches, human-headed, in a vast plain —out on the Plateau somewhere, no thank you very much. A similar cryptic symbol rises on the horizon like one of our vagabond moons.

◆ ◆ ◆

II: THE CORNER STORE

I tolerate these hundred assholes staring down at me and resist the impulse to hasten my pace. Finally past the crowd of flat false gods, I arrive at the door to the ill-named Food Oasis, the chain store with booze, drugs, and snacks. Out front I wave a general hello to Larry drinking a juice box, Macon, Presto, Ouakim, Fatima, Mayra with her splinted fingers, Aliyah, Fuckface, Whatshername, Arokk, Koskk, and Captain Please. Drunk as usual, Please asks, "How's the limp? Heh." I grunt at him. In the store I see Belle and Barca and he hands me a Coke. I thank him profusely and buy myself thanks to this wee miracle <u>four</u> VatGrown™ meat sticks, enough to make my day bearable. Plus if I'm lucky they'll have snacks at the clinic, some cookies maybe. I don't dare get my hopes up about the treatment, but food-wise I'm good. Gonna eat two of these now and two after if the treatment doesn't kill me. Or maybe three before. Fuck it maybe all four if there's cookies.

I bump into another Pamil poster, a life-size freestanding cutout in the exact same pose, halo and all. It winks at me. Cocks its hip the other way, causing its flesh to shift in ways a paper cutout cannot. As I back away it reaches for me with its long arms and they lengthen, stretching to spindly fingers trailing towards me in the air....

Something squawks on the scanner. In one ear I hear the pigs talking about busting someone for something. Pamil stands there, inert cardboard in its original pose. I find myself at the cashier, shaking, fumbling my food and money at Orfeo —then Fatima and Mayra butt their heads into the store, announcing at emergency volume that Jeffy's food cart is being busted. Orfeo shrugs. He and Jeffy hate each other's guts. "Barca bought me this," I tell him, indicating the Coke. He nods. Wonder if I should have gotten three meat sticks and a second Coke. No, they'll have water at the clinic, in the sink at least, and maybe coffee.

I click off my music and listen to the scanner report, following the crowd at my own pace as everyone from the corner flocks in a small mob to the wall where Jeffy parks his cart.

Jeffy's food cart is indeed being busted by a swarm of stormtroopers. When you hear top pig Bael the Batterer squealing on the vid, he calls his policy "Happy Streets." Theory being, if you rid the streets of those pesky "nuisance infractions," then "serious" "crime" will "go down." Turns out this statistically fails even by its own definitions. But their definitions are a convoluted cartoon; example: their measures of harm done to people and community exclude the harm done by the Monster Hunters themselves. Huh? You've got to take a train of thought past one stop, man, for it to count as thinking. But of course no sense in arguing with a pretense that's false to begin with. The policy only exists to give them more tools to hurt us, control us, clear us out.

So here's what you're calling "happy": Jeffy, who since the garden's gone is the one bringing the healthiest food into the neighborhood, I can't afford him today because of the transit tickets but he grills slices from actual meat stalks, and puts lettuce & tomato on the bun. The Monster Hunter armored personnel carrier is not merely alongside his cart but hip-checked against it, bending both axles so the grill's not level and he can't push it home. That alone could end his livelihood, unless he somehow has some money saved, or can get a loan from somewhere. Maybe we can tinker it back into shape, but we sure can't help pay a mechanic. The nearby nimbys won't shell out, they want him gone worse than Orfeo does, he's bad for their postage stamp fiefdom's market value. But oh, it's not just the cart: I spot Jeffy, face down in the street, hands and elbows webbed tight behind his back, ankles webbed, a Monster Hunter standing over him with a boot kind of on his shoulder, kind of on his neck, and a shotgun aimed only sort of at his head. Jeffy's face looks numb with terror. Encircling them, facing outward, are another five fuckos with body armor and shotguns. I take off my headphones.

Gathered around, not quite in their faces, maybe fifteen of us so far. Tense with rage because this shit keeps happening. But hanging back a little. Resigned, because this shit keeps happening. And scared, because of Haki, and Azok, and Washington, and a thousand more bodies of the Hunted piled up behind them. More people keep approaching from all directions, some gathering in nervous pockets at streetcorners, some marching directly to the front lines with the fierce certainty of indignation. Clots of newcomers hang way back, the folks who just commute in and out of the neighborhood to their jobs and shops and clubs, unsure of which side they're on. I walk past two of them as they mutter, "He wasn't licensed." "Oh my gosh, I actually ate there once!" Correction: they're sure which side they're on.

Up front I see most of the folks from out front of the corner store, Fatima McLaren going off on an animated verbal tear at the Monster Hunters, plus Xerxes and Clara and Fesheshek, who really shouldn't be up there because he has a warrant, and Old Tomás leaning on his walking stick and I hope he keeps the fuck leaning on it instead of brandishing it, he's frailer than me. I've seen him get clobbered, once when I was a kid and at least once more since but it's been decades. They'll clobber us either way though; provocation is a confabulation. Tensions still high from the garden. I really can't be here for this. Flashpoints are not great if you cannot run. And the hope of successful push-back? What are we gonna do, sue for damages? With what lawyer? And that won't deter this from happening again. Even if we won the Monster Hunters don't pay for that shit, it's not cut from their pay or their pensions, it gets paid from their lawsuit fund or cut from other municipal services. They have no incentive and we have no teeth. Golly, maybe we can get Jeffy retroactively licensed, so he has permission to do what he's already doing for years? Or wow maybe we'll get a law passed against pigs stepping on someone's neck when they're webbed. The sad truth is such shit is the best we've managed since they killed the wolves. Less than nothing. Exhausted by the runaround till we can be bought off with scraps. And some part of the exhaustion always lingers, accumulating alongside the wear and tear of age itself.

Meanwhile, I shit you not, a seventh Monster Hunter is standing guard by the wall of the laundromat, while an eighth sprays a little billboard onto it: COMING SOON: FOOD CART FOOD COURT. I've seen everything, but this I have not seen before. These troops are just supposed to clear the way, under the banner of some pretext or other. Actually coming out and making their function explicit like this ruins the illusion. Maybe the blatancy will turn off the newcomers to our neighborhood and radicalize them? Yeah, not holding my breath.

I really must skip out of here before shit turns if it turns.... Nobody's confronting the signpainter yet, he's partly hidden by the APC. Fuck it. I limp up towards him. The shotgunner interposes himself and barks, "Back the fuck up, cripple," from behind his visor, hefting his weapon crosswise to shove me back if need be.

"Kill yourself," I snap at him, at a loss for anything useful to say. "Best thing you could possibly do for the world."

He looks me up and down. "You got Emberman's?" he asks. "You owe me your life, you piece of shit."

"Oh, really?" I start shouting. I do my best to get spittle on his visor. "You're the one who got the embermen off me?" I should stop but can't. "Oh, and great job keeping them out of town in the first place. You're a failure, your whole operation is a fraud, you're not here to hunt monsters, you *are* the monsters."

He shoves me with the shotgun across my chest. I stagger back two steps and then a third, barely managing to keep my feet. A fall is the last thing I need right now. I spit on the ground and turn my back on him and walk away as quick as I can manage. Wrenched my ankle a bit saving my balance so now it hurts worse, biting with each step, and with each step I pray he doesn't hit me or shoot me from behind. He doesn't. People continue converging on the site.

◆ ◆ ◆

III: THE TURNSTILE

By the time I'm halfway down the block my ankle has eased back to its normal level of pain. I try to calm myself down so I don't wear myself out walking fast. Can't. My adrenaline is up. I put my headphones back on, kill the Monster Hunter scanner and fill my head with old Pamil, do my best to tune out the scattering of new little shops, bars, restaurants, cafes occupying spaces that were once ours. Before I know it I'm at the monorail station. Soon as I slow down I start noticing the pain in my leg, my knee especially. I've done myself a mischief. Oh and how wonderful, the monorail station is crawling with Monster Hunters. Leaning against turnstiles and ticket machines, pacing around the escalators, standing at eerie unmoving attention. Guardians of the hierarchy, protecting the literally and metaphorically elevated platform and carriageway from the filth of mere street life like me. Hell, the maglev train doesn't even touch its rails. Uncontaminated by the impurity of the messy lower world.

I nervously feed money into the ticket machine under the imposing gaze of a human decked out in the Monster Hunters' typical war gear. My mind races with implausible fears. Could the asshole back at Jeffy's have radioed ahead for these fuckers to fuck with me? Meanwhile the ticket machine devours thousands of dollars and gives me a credit for one round trip. Wish I could just hop over that damn turnstile, save my money for food. I feel hollowed out by panic, and I'm gonna be ravenous from it later, I can tell. But I couldn't hop a turnstile even without a pig in sight. I wave my credit at the turnstile and it lets me through. The pigs ignore me.

Inside this other world the flickering fluorescent lights lay every surface so starkly bare as to render it unreal. I limp past armed guardians to the escalator and ride it up into the celestial realm of the middle castes.

The black concrete platform spreads sleekly to right and left. Mostly empty. Almost no one coming or going out of our neighborhood at this time of day. Make no mistake, though, this outpost is another linchpin of the takeover. Ever since before the merger, we had the dregs settling down from the middle castes, junkie houses and crusty houses, so-called "starving" artists and occasional quickly-fractured artist collectives or performance venues. Some of these folks were good people, didn't take up much space, a few even became part of the community. Most were assholes that came and went. But despite a little bit of "cool" brewing, the next wave never came. The werewolves, and the fear of werewolves, kept Mammon away. Only in recent years, after the wolves got cleared out, did these hip shops and galleries start to arise; or these cunningly crafted evictions, bringing in settlers to "restore" our "classic old fixer-uppers," enjoy a young adulthood of adventure taming the slums, flip your house to someone richer and move back from the frontier to the more upscale hinterland carved out by the previous generation.

Last year the monorail appeared. Once the middle caste population hit a certain density in our neighborhood, its gravitation drew forth this massive concrete pseudopod of Mammon. From here this tumor will only metastasize. If only the werewolves had still been alive to bomb it while it was under construction. None of us now would dare. We know what happened to them. Better this slow death by degrees. Damn the survival instinct, keeping me desperate to cling even to this shit. But who wants to trade their life for a train station that'll probably just get rebuilt? As if I could make a bomb to begin with. Instead I stick around longing for those rare glimmers of goodness in the world. No, not rare, they are common. But not common enough, and crushed all too often by things that simply should not be.

My parents saw the carving happen to the neighborhood directly south of us. From what my grandparents said, when they were young they watched the same process come to completion just south of that, downtown. I've watched it happen to the west of us, to the east, and north. For all I know, Wolf Town is the last old-growth neighborhood in the whole city. From the elevated platform I take in the view in all directions, our beat-down old homeland surrounded by the encroaching "development" of the past century. The wind blows harder up here. Everything looks so far away and imaginary. You can't touch anything.

The train comes.

First thing I see getting on the monorail car is a poster for the Neighborhood Benefit Coalition, "Your Partnership with the City Rulers." I wish I dared tear it down.

As the train pulls away from the platform, I look down and see the Reality Patrol pylon. This is the first I've ever set eyes on it. Never approached it at ground level. Certainly never touched it, unlike lots of people I know. They say it tingles. I can't even fathom why they would risk it. The rift here last year spooked me badly, especially considering what came through. Most of the time I forget it even happened. It went so quickly, next thing I knew the Monster Hunters had bombed the thing, Reality Patrol pinned the rip in the cosmos with the pylon, and the City was ready to move on the newly available land to build this spur of the monorail. We tried to defend those still-intact buildings inconveniently in the way, the families eminent-domained out of homes they'd had for generations. "Progress." One day that pylon is going to fail, or someone's going to unpin it on purpose, and that cosmic rift is gonna reopen. I stare after it, relieved when it recedes from view.

Looking down the tracks back the way we came, the spur aims straight towards the future site of the Neighborhood Benefit Coalition. Fuckface says it's on a ley line. I don't normally believe in such stuff, but I wonder.

I stare out the window at the passing blocks. Condos and office towers that have arisen during my lifetime. The old wooden duplexes and masonry sixplexes from Earth all have good coats of paint, their grounds meticulous. The spires, domes, columns, and sharply tapered pyramids that merged in from Tal Sharnis look flawless as usual. The road surfaces look like they have no potholes. Cars drive around on them.

There's a sticker on the back of the seat in front of me.

◆ ◆ ◆

IV: THE HORRORISTS

The sticker has a sigil on it like Pamil's halo, with the words, in quotation marks, "I think of myself as more of a horrorist." What the hell is that supposed to mean? As opposed to a "terrorist"? Sounds like more of that pretentious chaos-worshiper wannabe crap.

We pull up at the next station. A chic woman with a panther's head gets on. She takes a seat, sits there poised as if ready to pounce, reading a book of Natalie Sojac's leftist poetry. Behind her a pair of hip young gentry board the train, expensively dressed, one with a boar head, one with an eagle head. They stand there bantering as the train accelerates with its infinite smoothness. I turn up my music but even so they make it impossible not to learn how pleased they are with the economic success they are experiencing as a result of the "growth" and "progress," how proud they are of the ways these "improvements" to these nearby neighborhoods will "benefit" "everyone."

I catch the panther headed woman looking up at them, seemingly also annoyed. Our eyes meet and then she rolls hers, thinking herself bonding with me over our shared hatred of these louts. Sorry, lady, you can read all the Natalie Sojac you want, if you give yourself a cat head you're an enemy of the underclass. You think any of us in Wolf Town have money for wolf heads? Can't even fathom what sorta rebel she imagines herself to be, emulating the cat-headed demon princes while fancying herself in some sort of "solidarity" with their victims. But then the fads and fashions of the middle castes are all empty symbolism, endlessly rehashed and remixed, far as I can tell. Maybe she considers her cat head ironic. Or she's just a Pamil fan. Speaking of which, fabulous or not, I can't stomach Pamil just now and switch to some Bay Area pre-merger heavy noise metal. It muffles the assholes' banter a little but overall does nothing to relieve the fact that I am in enemy territory. The alienation is palpable, like a hostile thickness in the air pressing against me from every direction like the echo of that nanite cloud in the garden, a barely-perceptible acid scratching at my skin with intent to dissolve and digest me. Psychic vampires everywhere, vampire architecture funneling our lifeforce into any of a multitude of maws.

The train shoots out over the Bay. No joke, flying over water like this is not to my liking. Mercifully the island fast approaches. Ain't Wolf Town, that's for sure. I spot the cluster of towers that marks the Facility.

Conspiracy theory has it that the Facility is funded by both the demon princes and certain factions within the Reality Patrol. All I know is I'm their guinea pig today. They claim they have reason to believe this will work, having used it to great success on actual guinea pigs. I wince at the image of using a captive emberman to induce its syndrome on caged animals. Turns out even I am a vampire, feeding on the suffering of others.

I wait anxious forever. Finally in the test chamber the doctor leaves me with no uncertainty my sole value in his view is as an experimental subject. He handles me roughly. I do my best to shut down and dissociate. The injections are agonizing, nanites boring through my tissues. I watch it all from some dark vantage in the depths of my consciousness, blanketed by an ocean insulating me from raw sensation.

Then it stops. The sudden absence of pain stuns me with euphoria. I look around the room. It is the most beautiful room I have ever seen. Colors and lighting so vibrant, the edges of objects so crisp, the changing perspective as I turn my gaze around the room itself a source of bliss as my eyes and brain ingest the shifting distances and juxtapositions. Wonder what drugs he pumped me with. Or is this just the release from discomfort, catapulting me into a high of brain chemicals? My body hasn't felt this well since I was a child. I leap to my feet, heart exploding with joy. No pain. The doctor rushes in, asks me what the hell I'm doing. I grab him in an embrace. He shoves me away. I dance out the door, thanking him effusively, run all the way out of the clinic and down the street to the monorail station.

It's night already. What the hell? Never mind. I cannot wait to get back home and show my people what's become of me. As my credit chip opens the turnstile my intoxicated mind races. I will have so much energy, so much strength, so much capacity to fight now that I am free of constant pain. I can't stop smiling at the gentry on the train, dreaming of how we will bring their caste system crashing down. They seem appropriately unsettled. I stand in the middle of the train, holding onto nothing, swaying like a surfer as we bank and curve. My legs are unbelievable. I flex my newly nimble fingers. I have no idea what we will do, but I feel unstoppable. I pray to the godless void to let me never lose this feeling. Man, I must be high as fuck. I'm going to get off one stop early and run home.

No idea what streets I'm on. As I jog along I try to read the map, but I can't get good reception on any wireless network —I'm not a local subscriber. The map still shows the static cached version, it just can't load my location; so I do my best to navigate from that. I'm frankly not good with maps, though, and I have no idea if I'm getting this right.

I find myself in a more suburbia-looking neighborhood than I expected. There are blocks of houses around my way that look like this, but these have been manicured, polished, "restored." There's not a soul out on the street. The houses are dark except for startling motion lights. Streetlights are sparse. Spooky and eerie.

I've never in my life seen the night sky so clear of light pollution, never seen so many stars. They look like they're just a few miles away. The crisp edges of the moons captivate me, their pitted surfaces, the shadowy curve of their gibbous un-crescented portion. A thin roof of cloud sweeps in from I don't know which direction, occurs to me I should be able to find north based on the shape of the moons' crescents. I stare up at them, trying to reason it through, ok where is the sun if they're lit that way, that way's east, no west, I stare and try to logic it out and nope, I am not remotely certain. Then the cloudbank obscures the moons.

I sprint a block, jog a block, sprint a block, slow to a slow jog and check the map again, still so overjoyed at the absence of pain in my body that I can't muster all that much concern about being lost.

I run around a corner onto another shadowy block of single family houses, trees lining the street. I stop. The streetlight up ahead in the middle of the block flickers in a bright strobe, darkness rushing in and enveloping the middle of the block, then suddenly banished for a fraction of a second by a brightness so intense as to seem assaultive, more frightening even than the darkness which resumes all too suddenly. Do I really want to run down this creepy block? C'mon, I've got momentum, I don't want to backtrack, it's just a streetlight.

I break into a jog. A rumble approaches from behind. As I pass through the middle of the block, a couple of Monster Hunters APCs thunder past me, open gun-ports in their armored flanks presumably giving everyone inside a clear view of me in those flashes of stark daybreak, while I cannot see in, if anyone's inside at all. No idea if they're aiming weapons at me, nothing to stop them from just shooting me dead. The familiar terror at the sight of the constabulary cuts through my euphoria.

Is that shotgunner I confronted earlier on board? No, different jurisdiction. Unless he's moonlighting, he could be moonlighting. Not that it matters if this one cop holds a grudge. The whole institution has a grudge against me, because I'm in the way of "progress," because I don't "produce" "value." So any of them could and would shoot me just as easily, with no repercussions, no need for justification other than they saw me running and what if I stole something, no one runs from Monster Hunters unless they're a monster. I nod at the truck as it passes. No one shoots me.

As soon as they're gone, my already frayed nerves jangle at a rustling in the bushes. There's a screech and a scuffle, an amber light flickering in the tangled shadows: a fire? Out comes a horrifying screeching monster, something the size of a small dog, racing across the lawn. A raccoon. We have them all over the city. Its face looks burnt off.

That amber light flickers, and several big lights flash between me and the poor creature. They resolve into a group of three embermen. They converge on the raccoon, which screams as they devour it.

I run.

The embermen chase me by stepping sideways out of our plane of existence, then stepping back into our reality right into my path, arms outstretched, life-sucking hands grasping. I dodge like a quarterback from one of those pre-merger football movies, but with their unpredictable stuttering teleportation they have an easy time herding me up a narrow driveway and cornering me.

One grabs me from behind in an insubstantial but unshakeable bear hug, unhinges its flickering jaw, and bites half of my head into its mouth. Its otherworldly teeth, its spectral touch feel alternately cold and hot. I can barely see. Can't think. Another grabs me by the legs, possibly undoing everything that was just repaired and worse. The third emberman plunges its immaterial claws into my guts and just... stirs. Freezing and burning in my head, arms, heart, intestines, knees, ankles....

Something moves in the shadows. A small star glows. It floats toward me, borne on the brow of a flubbery black cone...? Not a star, a star-shaped hole, a burning hole of light....

The embermen shriek shrilly. They drop my body painfully to the pavement. My vision clears, but what I'm seeing makes little enough sense that it's hard to be sure how much is real and how much is my head scrambled from being in an emberman's mouth. A rubbery black cone maybe five feet high, with a star-shaped aperture in its front like an eye or mouth. Three embermen, frozen in poses of agony, bathed in amber light beaming from the aperture. I lie there both numb and hurting, panicking that they got me in *both* legs this time, not only that but both arms, and my organs, and my brain. They did not have me for as long this time, maybe it will pass. Maybe the Facility will fix me a second time. Hell, maybe the nanites are still active in my system and are already fixing me; maybe this new agony is exactly that, happening right now. That would be nice. Or maybe I have been destroyed, even worse than last time, and permanently. Maybe the nanites only work once. Maybe my organs are failing and I'm dying now, no time for help, no hope. So soon. Is this whole thing but the prank of a demon prince, creating a gourmet meal out of my suffering? I look up at slow-motion carnage as the embermen dissolve under the amber light. The cone thing twists and sways a little, as if dancing with pleasure at its deed.

There's a rumbling sound like those Monster Hunter personnel carriers, and someone screams —I raise my head to see some human, old, agitated, in a bathrobe, pointing at us, shouting, "There they are, officers! Monsters!" Craning my head the other direction, I see a dozen armored Monster Hunters running towards us, guns up. The embermen dissolve. The cops adopt a firing squad formation.

I leap to my feet shouting "No!" Their guns unload at us. Most of them connect with the cone-shaped creature, whatever it is, having wandered here from out on the Plateau or from some other dimension and saved my life, we'll never know because of all the holes gouged through it. The thing erupts in light and falls over beside me with a thud. Meanwhile I fall also, shot I can't tell how many times through the torso. Whether from the embermen or a spine hit or both, I can't move anything. Can't feel anything but the pain coursing through me in waves from everywhere to everywhere. I smell my blood. Boots surround me and

I'm rolled onto my face. Warm, wet. Lots of blood. Lots. Hard to tell but I think they've webbed my hands and feet. Someone steps on my neck.

◆ ◆ ◆

Afterword

There is a metaphor that I heard a few years ago. Two young fish are swimming along and they suddenly swim by an old fish who tells them, "This water is so nice, don't you think?" And with that, the old fish continues swimming. The two young fish look at each other, confused, and one asks, "What is water?" and the other replies, "I have no idea."

The metaphor is used to describe how we don't recognize many of the beliefs and ideologies we grew up with. This is also a perfect explanation of test chambers as well. A test chamber is something that we all grow up in, the test chamber of society with all of its expectations, beliefs, ideologies, and norms. And most of the time, we don't question these norms because we may not even be aware of them. In this book, every chapter seeks to do several things: 1) bring awareness to a test chamber or test chambers that many—if not most—in our society are not even aware of and 2) perhaps most importantly, begin to test these chambers.

Every chapter leads in some way to the next. Some end with darkness (either literal or emotional) and the next begins in a similar darkness, while others end with a furious demand for action and the next chapter sees that action taking place. The test chambers described in this anthology vary from poetic thoughts on the *Yellow Wallpaper* to a critical discussion of autism research to a fictional conversation in a barbershop that leads to something greater to a memoir that recounts the experiences of a queer disabled activist finding their place in the world. All of these are different test chambers.

Dani said in the introduction, "We test the test chamber in which we find ourselves, and in so doing, we find the power to subvert it." This anthology *is* that subversion. It is, in a very real sense, its own test chamber.

It tests you to decide how *you* choose to define and test the test chamber. Will you define it as something positive? Something neutral? Something negative? Your decision here will affect your approach to testing it. There are no right answers, or are there? The answers to these questions lead to more questions, but once you are aware of these test chambers, you have the agency (ability) to decide, test, and subvert. Will you subvert the test chamber or will you let others define it for you?

Now, you have a choice to make.

Sam Harvey

◆ ◆ ◆

Contributors

Andrea Abi-Karam is a mixed race genderqueer punk poet writing on the art of killing bros, the intricacies of cyborg bodies, trauma & delayed healing. They recently completed the manuscript EXTRATRANSMISSION a book length piece against how patriarchy and US militarism produce the hypergendered subject. Andrea is both a writer, printer, & publisher whose founding small press project Mess Editions seeks to publish emerging writing from queers, people of color, and those involved in social movements yet uninvolved in poetry & art scenes. From 2012-2015 Andrea co-founded with Drea Marina, Words of Resistance a monthly radical queer open floor poetry night aimed at creating space for folks to share their work, especially if unpolished and messy.

Athena the Architect is a mostly nonspeaking, recently verbal artist. Currently, her spoken vocabulary consists of "Hi, guys," a phrase she has been fond of since starting hormone replacement therapy. She's also a member of The Puzzlebox Collective, a group of interdependent creative professionals who assist one another with all aspects of daily life. Through this Collective, she is able to have her partner-performers embody the words she hears in her fingers.

Alison Black is a Ravenclaw prefect with PTSD. She learned to write by first reading the entire 1964 Encyclopedia Britannica when she was nine and then disregarding all but the prime-numbered pages. Alison is a 2004 graduate of Ferris State University, where she holds the university record for the greatest number of undergraduate credits earned in four years. This is her first poem.

Michael Chin was born and raised in Utica, New York and is a recent alumnus of the MFA program in creative writing at Oregon State University. He won the 2014 Jim Knudsen Editor's Prize for fiction from the University of New Orleans and has previously published or has work forthcoming in journals including *The Normal School, Prairie Schooner* online, *Bayou Magazine,* and *Gravel.* Find him online at miketchin.com and follow him on Twitter @miketchin.

Alex Conall of sunbowpublications.com is a queer, genderqueer white feminist who tries not to be a White Feminist. They are passionate about writing, especially speculative fiction and poetry, and they dabble in other forms of art. Alex has been successfully holding down a paycheck job for a few years, and by Millennial standards it is a really good job; clearly this means they cannot possibly be autistic. They shall graduate in Oregon State University's Class of 2017.

Clay Dillon is a fiction without an origin, and his work delves into the ways in which all identity is constructed from a core experience that is itself unnameable and untraceable. As a Puzzlebox Collective member, he is simultaneously responsible for the group's early focus on theater, especially Sarah Kane's theater of evisceration, and also for the recruiting of Lynn Vargas and the fostering of the feminist transformation she brought to the group.

Monday Dillon emerged from her own personal myth after a long sabbatical to advise Lynn and the other Collective members when they put the group together. While Monday has not performed in almost a decade and a half, her involvement with the early Slam poetry movement in the late 1990s and early 2000s has informed the direction of the group's work, and her polished editorial sense has done much to help develop the crispness evident in Puzzlebox members' prose offerings.

Monika Dryburgh is a youngish Melbourniannerdy multiply mostly-invisibly disabled linguaphile bricoleur. Constantly in the process of:
a) attempting to navigate Second (+third+fourth) Shift(s) for the Sick, and
b) constructing an interdisciplinary PhD thesis about fatigue in chronic illness from: feminist sensibilities / disability research ethics / sociology of sleep theory / lived experience.

Nicole Eugene is a Doctoral Candidate in Communication Studies at Ohio University. She is an interdisciplinary scholar, a disability advocate, and a scholar-artist. She is the winner of numerous awards and her work has been supported by Ohio Humanities, a state affiliate of the National Endowment for the Humanities. Her research program aims to raise consciousness of the particular ways in which hidden disabilities especially neurological disabilities are shaped by cultural dynamics that prioritize visibility and create cultural identities that challenge conventional boundaries.

Alyssa Gonzalez is a biology Ph.D. and writer. Her fiction frequently visits the topics of social isolation, autism, gender, and how the three can interact with one another in a person's life, often in science-fiction settings. She co-writes a blog with her wife Ania Bula (the-orbit.net/splainyouathing), where she writes about biology, history, sociology, and her experiences as an autistic ex-Catholic Hispanic transgender immigrant to Canada. She lives in Ottawa, Canada with her wife and a menagerie of pets.

Arden Green is an autistic poet and Hellenic polytheist priest. Eir gender is dragon; weirdly, this doesn't make Dragon NaturallySpeaking more cooperative. Ey are working on several book-sized projects at any given time, which just proves that ey are a Slytherin: eir ambition is what gets em in trouble!

Eleven Groothius is a queer, trans, psychotic filmmaker and writer who spends her time trying to find mirrors in pop culture and getting frustrated and just making her own. She also writes about film from a number of angles including gender, sexuality, and disability, and anything else she thinks is interesting. You can find her writing at thirteenminustwo.tumblr.com.

Sam Harvey is a dyslexic, dysthymic, mad, autistic genderqueer PhD student in Rhetoric and Professional Communication at Iowa State University. He is now thinking that the previous sentence was a bit long, but isn't going to change it because... He blogs at antleaderindustries.com.

Alyssa Hillary is an Autistic math teacher and graduate student in neuroscience. Sie is also a disability studies scholar with interests in neurodiversity, access, and technology, plus representation in young adult speculative fiction. As such, sie references Tamora Pierce's Tortall universe and Diane Duane's Young Wizards series a lot. Sie blogs at yesthattoo.blogspot.com and enjoys writing fiction and poetry.

Sparrow Rose Jones is an Autistic nomad, wandering the Earth with Fermat the Wonder Cat, planting seeds of love. In addition to Sparrow's books, *No You Don't: Essays From an Unstrange Mind,* and *The ABCs of Autism Acceptance,* Sparrow's writing has been published in the Autonomous Press anthologies *The Real Experts* and *Typed Words, Loud Voices.* Sparrow blogs at Unstrange Mind and vlogs on YouTube as AutisticNomad. Sparrow's web home is www.sparrowrose.com.

E. Lewy lives and works in Massachusetts as a freelance writer. Their work has previously appeared in *New Mobility, Breath and Shadow,* and the original *Spoon Knife Anthology* as well as *Barking Sycamores.* They are also an avid blogger in a variety of spaces, and a believer that life operates on a variety of spectrums.

Michael Scott Monje, Jr. is an Autonomous Press partner and the writer of multiple novels on the transgender autistic experience, including *Defiant, Mirror Project,* and *Imaginary Friends.* Her poetry has appeared in *Barking Sycamores, NeuroQueer,* and other venues, and a collection (*The US Book*) is available. Michael is also a member of The Puzzlebox Collective, where she is frequently called upon to read Athena's poetry aloud.

N.I. Nicholson is a writer, editor, and activist from Central Ohio. As an editor with *Barking Sycamores* and Autonomous Press, he focuses on bringing works by neurodivergent, queer, and disabled writers into print or digital media. In July 2016, he graduated with an MFA in Creative Writing from Ashland University. Unbeknownst to the residents of Grove City, he is actually a regenerating Time Lord. He currently lives there with his life partner Solomon.

M. O'Hern is a student at Bradley University where they are studying English and Creative Writing. They are eternally thankful to Writehouse Ink for being a source of love and light.

Andrew M. Reichart lives in California with his wife and a couple of dogs. He writes weird fantasy books, stories, and comics, most of which are published by Argawarga Press at argawarga.com. One of his current projects is the upcoming webcomic *Weird Luck*, co-written with Nick Walker. Andrew's story in this volume, "Monsters," is set in the city of Tal Sharnis, where much of the webcomic takes place.

S. Verity Reynolds writes science fiction and changes addresses every six months. She is a co-founder of the Non-Compliant Space project, which can be found on Patreon at http://patreon.com/noncompliantspace. Her first novel, *Nantais*, will be published by NeuroQueer Books in 2017, or you can read her short story here for an introduction to its universe.

Barbara Ruth is a poet, photographer, memoirist and fiction writer living in San Jose, CA, USA. Her long-term relationship brings her much happiness. As a radical feminist, she is also a marriage resister. Her work often embraces contradictions and appears in many feminist, queer, disability and literary publications.

Marrok Zenon Sedgwick is a disabled trans activist who uses artmaking as their primary tool for challenging society's injustices. They are a filmmaker, a playwright, a producer, and an aspiring novelist and poet. They are currently working to grow their fledgling theatre and film production company, Fearless Minds Theatrical, into a full-blown community arts center, which will serve as a safe space for people from the disability, LGBTQ, and other underserved communities (especially communities of color) to make art, share resources, and find camaraderie. They are devoted to using their privilege as an over-educated white person from a middle class family for the good of others.

Steve Singer is an Assistant Professor of Deaf Education at the College of New Jersey. His research focuses on disability identity development, disability and socioeconomic stratification, and autoethnographic methodologies. He identifies as having 'brain weather' or mental illness and became Deaf eleven years ago at the age of twenty-eight.

Phil Smith teaches at Eastern Michigan University. An educator for 40 years, he received the Emerging Scholar Award in Disability Studies in Education in 2009; the EMU College of Education Award for Innovative Scholarship in 2015; and has presented and published widely as a poet, playwright, novelist, performance/visual artist, and disability/mad studies scholar. He is disabled, mad as hell, makes maple syrup, rides his bicycle a lot, and tries to remember to wear socks.

Jacqueline Pruder St. Antoine is a mother, a mad person, a wife, a reader and writer, a mad studies and disability studies scholar, an artist and performer, a wannabe gardener. She enjoys bringing a mad studies perspective to academic venues and investigating new ways of being, understanding, and representing research, feelings, and knowledge. Jacquie aims to make her work arts-based and performative in nature, accessible, and emotive...exploring the nuances of madness, disability, and what it means to exist in an ableist, saneist multi-verse.

Lynn Vargas is a "transverbal implant" with an artificial intelligence sophisticated enough to pass for human. After finding a way to upload herself into a biological mind by harnessing the power of the autistic gaze to leap from monitor to monitored, she has worked to bring the rest of the Puzzlebox Collective into some kind of focus, to give the group's overall goals some structure and movement.

Nick Walker is an autistic genderqueer author, educator, scholar, and aikido teacher. He is a co-founder and Coordinating Editor at Autonomous Press, a faculty member at California Institute of Integral Studies and Sofia University, and senior instructor of the Aikido Shusekai dojo in Berkeley, California. His writings on autism and neurodiversity can be found on his blog, *Neurocosmpolitanism,* and in *The Real Experts: Readings for Parents of Autistic Children.* Together with with co-author Andrew Reichart and artist Mike Bennewitz, Nick is currently working on a webcomic entitled *Weird Luck,* to which his story in this volume, "Bianca and the Wu-Hernandez," serves as a prequel.

www.ingramcontent.com/pod-product-compliance
Lightning Source LLC
Chambersburg PA
CBHW050612190726
48283CB00007B/2379
9781945955020